GLOBALISATION AND HEALTH SECTOR IN INDIA

GLOBALISATION AND HEALTH SECTOR IN INDIA

BISWAJIT CHATTERJEE
Professor of Economics
Dean, Faculty of Arts
Jadavpur University

Published under
GLOBAL TRADE PROGRAMME
Jadavpur University

DEEP & DEEP PUBLICATIONS PVT. LTD.
F-159, Rajouri Garden, New Delhi - 110 027

GLOBALISATION AND HEALTH SECTOR IN INDIA

ISBN 978-81-8450-178-0

Printed in India at MAYUR ENTERPRISES
WZ Plot No. 3, Gujjar Market, Tihar Village, New Delhi - 110 018.

Published by DEEP & DEEP PUBLICATIONS PVT. LTD.,
F-159, Rajouri Garden, New Delhi - 110 027 • Phone : 25435369, 25440916
E-mail : ddpubs@gmail.com • ddpbooks@yahoo.co.in
Showroom :
2/13, Ansari Road, Daryaganj, New Delhi - 110 002 • Telefax : 23245122

Contents

Preface vii

1. INTRODUCTION **1**

2. GLOBALISATION, GATS AND HEALTH SECTOR **11**

I. Globalisation 11

II. GATS 20

III. GATS and Health Services 23

IV. Implications of Trade in Health Services 36

V. Conclusions 43

3. HEALTH AND DEVELOPMENT— SURVEY OF LITERATURE **45**

I. Health and Development 45

II. Review of Literature 58

III. Studies on India 82

IV. Conclusion 110

4. HEALTH SECTOR IN INDIA—AN INTERSTATE ANALYSIS **112**

I. Introduction 112

II. Health in Post-Independence Era 114

III. Family Welfare Programme in India and its Relation to Total Fertility Rate 137

IV. Anaemia Among Women and Children in India 142

V. HIV in India—A Fast Spreading Epidemic 151

VI. Effect of Cancer in India 156

VII. Heart Diseases and Coronary Attack 161

VIII. Health Care Expenditure in India 163

5. EFFICIENCY OF HEALTH OUTCOMES IN RURAL INDIA : INTERSTATE VARIATIONS **174**

I. Health Status in India 175

II. Efficiency in Health Outcomes—An Interstate Analysis 180

6. POVERTY, UNDER-NUTRITION AND MORBIDITY IN INDIA **192**

I. Health, Poverty and Human Deprivation 192

II. Undernutrition 198

III. Undernourishment and Government Interventions 219

IV. Infant and Child Mortality in India—Case Study of Three States 222

V. Burden of Diseases in Rural India 247

7. CONCLUDING OBSERVATIONS **262**

Bibliography 268

Index 282

Preface

Following GATS Agreement, trade in health services has become one of the important components of global trade in services. Considered as non-tradeables earlier, some of these services like health and education are now increasingly traded globally, and this is one tangible effect of the globalisation process. India being one of the founder members of the WTO, is also an early signatory to the Articles of Agreement under the GATS, and after some years of grace period, has to open up its health sector to the forces of international trade. What constitutes the direction of effects of globalisation of health services in India is an important issue of policy research on international trade, and the present study is an attempt to undertake this research. This study was undertaken under the Global Trade Programme of Jadavpur University with the support of University with Potential for Excellence Scheme of UGC. Spread over seven chapters, the present study reviews the GATS provisions regarding the globalisation of health services and the implications for developing countries, and provides a critical review of the literature on health and economic development and cross-country evidences on health care services and health sector outcomes, including India. It also provides an account of the Health sector in India and in major states, the link between income, health outcome indicators and distribution of health facilities across states and socio-economic groups, and examines analytically the efficiency of health outcomes in different states of India and discusses the link between health, poverty and undernutrition in India, that provides implications for policy choice. The impact of globalisation on the health sector of the Indian economy are examined in the final chapter of the study.

While I thank the UGC's UPE scheme for Jadavpur University for the generous financial support to this study, different research scholars associated with the different phases of the study—Sarmistha Pal, Dolly Naskar, Sangeeta Kundu and Nabanita Chatterjee, deserve special mentions for their sincere help and meticulous support towards the completion of the study. I also thank Professor Asok Nath Basu, and Professor Shyamal Kanti Sanyal, former Vice-Chancellors of Jadavpur University, Professor P.N. Ghosh and Professor Siddhartha Datta, the present Vice-Chancellor and Pro-Vice-Chancellor of Jadavpur University respectively, for their continuous encouragement and support. Shri Rajat Bandyopadhyay, Registrar, and Shri Gour Krishna Pattanayak, Finance Officer of Jadavpur University, have always been supportive of my academic endeavours. Needless to say, the infrastructure supports of the Planning and Development Unit and of the Economics Department of Jadavpur University have helped me to complete the work. I record my sincere thanks to all of them.

BISWAJIT CHATTERJEE

1

Introduction

The window of globalisation was formally opened in India in July 1991, when the new central government introduced market-friendly structural adjustment programme of the IMF to formally integrate the Indian economy with the global economy. Lots of changes have been introduced since then and the worst sufferers has been the social sector in the country. There has been a sharp contraction of government spending on social sector infrastructure and greater reliance was placed on private intitiatives and private sector expenditure on health and education—the two most important social sectors in the country covering the welfare of millions of our people. Health of the population is indicative of the ability of the people to participate in the labour process and live a decent nutritionally efficient, disease-free wealthy life, which contributes to human development and welfare. While the link between per capita SDP of the states and per capita health expenditure is found to be strongly co-related, the efficiency of health outcomes and the distribution of health facilities across regions and income groups have remained poor and the scenario has deteriorated since the introduction of economic reform measures in India. To link the performance of the health sector in India to the forces of globalisation is not easy, and seem tenuous; it would be possible, however to compare the pre and post-reform period's performance of the health sector to gauge the impact of economic reforms on that sector.

Few subjects can be more important than health as a constitutive element of the well-being and freedom of a nation. And yet health care has been one of the most neglected aspects of development in India. Despite repeated statements in the successive plan documents on the centrality of health and health care, the field has suffered from persistent neglect in public policy in general and development planning in particular, with the consequence that the Indian population continues to be exposed to a high incidence of communicable diseases and readily preventable illnesses. Many basic illnesses had radically declined in large parts of the developing world in recent decades, but they continue to be common in India and the burden of disease falls very unevenly on different sections of the population. The incidence of undernourishment and nutrition-related ailments in India is also very high by international standards. Health *inequalities* are very sharp in India, in comparison with many other countries, even poor ones. Class differences in health achievements, in particular, are large by international standards. The same applies to gender-based inequalities in health. India's share of worldwide leprosy cases is estimated to be as high as 68 per cent. These features of the health situation in India are closely related to the state of health services, and to the persistent neglect of health matters in public policy. One symptom of this neglect is the abysmally low level of public expenditure on health-around 0.8 per cent of GDP. Among 142 countries for which the relevant data are available, only six (Burundi, Cambodia, Georgia, Indonesia, Myanmar, and Sudan) have a lower figure for public expenditure on health as a proportion of GDP. The low level of public expenditure on health in India is aggravated by (1) a highly inefficient use of available resources, and (2) sharp inequalities in access to health care based on region, class, caste, and gender.

The emphasis in the context of structural adjustment policy of World Bank in placing the basic task to market mechanism and gradual withdrawal of state in the field of health services seems misplaced in view of the fact that the role of the state in this field has been pathetically low and market mechamisms continue to dominate in health care sectors in our mixed economy framework. In fact, international comparisons reveal the share of public expenditure in India in total health expenditure is only around 15 percent, compared with 75 per cent in Western Europe's 'market economies', and 84 per cent in Thatcherism-ravaged Britain. The following table sums up the picture in India compared to different other countries of the world. In fact, the share of public expenditure in total health expenditure is lower in India than in any other major region of the world.

TABLE 1.1

Health Expenditure : Selected Indicators

	Public expenditure on health, 1990-98[a]		
	In absolute terms (PPP$ per capita)	*As a share of total health expenditure (%)*	*As a share of GDP (%)*
India	14	15	0.8
South Asia	16	18	0.9
Sub-Saharan Africa[b]	36	40	1.7
East Asia and Pacific[b]	60	40	1.7
Middle East and North Africa[b]	114	50	2.3
Latin America and Carribbean[b]	221	49	3.2
Europe and Central Asia[b]	251	77	4.0
High-income countries			
Europe EMU	1,485	75	6.7
All	1,604	62	6.0

Notes : (a) Latest year for which the relevant data are available.

(b) Low and middle income countries only.

Source : Calculated from World Development Indicators, 2001, Table 2.15, reported as Table 6.1 in Dreze and Sen.

It is true that in social sector activity like health care for all, the incentive of private investment and initiatives are clearly low and concerted state action and the allocation of adequate public resources, are badly needed in view of the fact that the incidence of basic communicable diseases and related illnesses is still extremely high in this country. The vast possibilities of low-cost public intervention in the fields of basic health and child nutrition have been highlighted for many years by UNICEF. It would however be a mistake, however, to confine the effectiveness of public health measures to a few 'model' states like Kerala, Tamil Nadu or Himachal Pradesh, where the social or political context happened to be favourable. Indeed, despite the low standards of government activity in most Indian states, there are many other examples of successful initiatives in this field. As for example, the installation of simple, well-designed public hand-pumps in most Indian villages have improved the access to safe drinking water and diminished the incidence of communicable diseases. Child vaccination rates have increased at an impressive rate since the Universal Immunisation Programme was initiated in 1985. Oral rehydration therapy has protected millions of children from diarrhoea at very low cost. Salt iodization has successfully reduced iodine deficiency in several states, notably Himachal Pradesh. The latest success story is the all-India polio immunization programme, which involved unprecedented feats such as the vaccination of about 100 million children in a single day. While the overall record of public health initiatives in India is quite dismal in general, there are cases of success in selected fields and therefore the importance of state intervention and investment with efficient use of resources cannot but be emphasized.

As far as the overall performance of health services is concerned, the picture is far from encouraging in most states. While health services have steadily expanded in quantitative terms, there is much evidence that their *quality* has deteriorated. In many states, health centres are dilapidated, medicines are not available, doctors are chronically absent, and patients are routinely charged for services that are meant to be free (when they are treated at all). The dismal state of public health services is the main reason why most patients turn to private providers, however unreliable or expensive. Private provision of health care poses its own problems, which is often no less serious than those of public health facilities, depending on the context and the type of health care being considered. Even for curative services, the private provision of health care poses well-known difficulties, relating in particular to informational asymmetries between user and provider. In principle, these problems can often be addressed through well-aimed regulation. Indeed, in many countries (including the so-called 'market economies'), private provision of health care is highly regulated, not only by the state but also by the professional associations. Similar regulatory mechanisms also exist in India, but their effectiveness has been extensively undermined for a number of reasons, ranging from the informal nature of a large part of the health-care sector to widespread corruption. The outcome is a highly differentiated 'market' for health services, which combines reliable but expensive facilities (e.g. elite hospitals in major cities) with a large informal sector where patients are exposed to the hazards of unregulated, uncoordinated and exploitative marketing of 'cures'.

There is no denying the fact that under a globalised market friendly regime, provisions of international supply would aggravate the deterioration in the supply of health care facilities in a developing economy like India. The various provisions of the GATS treaty, which makes the health services internationally tradeable, would encourage flow of private investment from foreign country to this sector and would provide international link to strengthen our knowledge in the field of medical care and disease prevention, but these services, being imported in the country would not be within the affordable reach of poor patients and would exclude them mostly from these provisions and support. Infrastructural facilities, being weak and not much cared for by the public support through the budgets of central and state governments, would lose out in the competition for scarce resources to the more advanced and high technology-based service providers, from domestic and foreign enterprises. This is likely to have adverse effects on the state of illness and efficiency of human labour power, and thereby on the long-run growth potentials of the economy. Globalisation in its present form needs to be controlled by the interventions and regulations by the state to weed out these adverse consequences. Available evidences suggest that during the post-reform period, although there have been increases in performance indicators of health outcomes, the state of abject human poverty and morbidity has continued to elude the prospects for a healthy disease free-India. The adverse consequences are reflected in the rise in the prices of essential drugs, and a concomitant decline in health sector allocations in the budgets of central and state governments. For example, in 2001-02 public health, which included four vertical programmes and AIDS control, accounted for 34 per cent of the total for health and 12 per cent of the ministry's entire allocation. In 2000-01, the various programmes, however, returned an unspent amount of Rs. 67 crores out of the meagre Rs. 847 crore budgeted in earlier years. The malaria control programme,, which accounted for 29.5 per cent of the total allocation for public health, has registered a sharp decrease in 2001-02 from Rs. 250 crore to Rs. 173 crore which is 21 per cent of the total provision for public health. The structures that had been created over the last 50 years became too huge, unresponsive and ineffective, and studies indicate that the ratio of expenditure on materials and services to staff and infrastructure had become increasingly un-remunerative, suggesting to disbanding some of the programes and replacing them by effective state regulated programmes depending on regional disease patterns.

It is important to recognize that our health status is intimately linked to the condition of our lives and the livelihoods that we pursue. It is at these levels—condition of living and livelihoods—that any intervention to improve health status would have the most permanent effect. However, over the decades it has been pointed out repeatedly that that road to health is a long-term one and, in the immediate future, what is needed is good accessible, affordable medicare and disease prevention and control. If these were effective, it is argued, then the up scaling of the condition and quality of people's lives would become much easier. In the last few years there has been growing concern over the creation of social safety nets such that the poor and vulnerable sections of the population could be protected until presumably the benefits of the new economic programmes filter down. This would mean that the state, even as it pulls out of certain sectors, would enhance its investment in these areas of health, drinking water and education, so as to create resources and security measures for the possible victims of change. This too has now been part of the Washington Consensus. Unfortunately, the allocations in central budgets do not reflect adequate concern of state intervention in these sectors. Even if we take a broad definition and include allocations made to the ministries of health and family welfare, human resources development which includes the department of education, rural development, urban development and poverty alleviation, social justice and empowerment, tribal affairs, labor and the department of youth affairs and sports, the government deems about 10 per cent of the total central budget sufficient for the creation of support and relief. And worse, these ministries are in charge of areas, which directly affect the condition of living and therefore the health status of people—the newly created departments of drinking water, of rural sanitation and water supply, and of housing and nutrition supplementation. The contraction of the government health sector over the last decade has been a consequence of the falling state inputs into health care, as well as the rapidly expanding private and corporate medicare infrastructure. The shrinking transfers to the states from the centre had imposed austerity in the state budgets, which had translated itself as smaller health care budgets. The budget for 2000-01 had allocated Rs. 5,852.83 crore for the ministry of health and family welfare, of which about 60.5 per went to the department of family welfare. The allocation for the health ministry in terms of capital grants for infrastructural investment remained alarmingly low, and insufficient to the requirements. The annual exercises of the ministry of health for budgetary allocation in India is myopic to the dismal state of health status in the country, and allocations for public health continue to rise at an abysmal low rate. Admittedly, health is a state subject and the central budget only defines the contours of a small part of the health plan for the year. Nevertheless, in the context of the changing epidemiological profile of the country, it is the most important that central provisions for disease control programmes in most states, and provisions for health infrastructure, although to be supplemented by corresponding allocations from the state governments, must play a major role in defining priorities and implementing programmes for improvement of living conditions of the majority of our population, who are poor and vulnerable to illness. Given the disparities in levels of development across the country, it is not likely that Gram Panchayats will be the ones who will come forward to set-up primary health facilities, and in the least developed regions, which lack the minimum services, this task must be borne by the state through its budgetary support. Unfortunately, the response of the central government to undertake this task seems to be lukewarm and sluggish, the rhetoric of inclusive growth notwithstanding.

According to the Washington Consensus, the structural adjustment policies of the IMF and the World Bank provide the panacea of all ills in development, and emphasize the introduction of market-friendly policies with withdrawal or shrinkage of state sector in different domains being filled up by the participation of private initiatives and investments under a deregulated economy with a decline in public investment in general under the norm of fiscal prudence. The proponents of SAP placed their faith in the process of globalisation, mechanisms of free market and international cooperation, and argued that only such policies would encourage quality and efficiency of technology growth and delivery of services to foster long-term growth and well-being of these poor nations. Multilateral institutions, particularly the World Bank, have, in the last two decades, aggressively promoted wide-ranging reforms in health sector, in both the developing and transitional economies. The record of these efforts, especially in respect of the poor, has been mixed. In many cases the benefits did not really reach the poor, and in some, they seem to have been adversely impacted. Examples of the latter include indiscriminate privatization, introduction of cost recovery without safety nets for the poor and hasty decentralization. The focus of many of these efforts was not necessarily the health of the poor, but macro-economic stabilization and fiscal compression. Part of the problem was a serious misunderstanding of the role of the state in the wake of economic liberalization and euphoria about the markets following the collapse of the socialist model. However, there is now a clearer perception of the central role of the state in the health sector in general and in protecting the vulnerable population in particular. The World Development Report, 1993, devoted exclusively to health, set the ball rolling by defining the role of the state in providing public goods, merit goods and provisioning essential health services. The World Development Report, 1997 greatly helped to clear the air by squarely placing the responsibility for protecting the vulnerable on the state. Finally, the World Health Report, 2000 brought out forcefully the stewardship role of the state in steering the health system.

Despite the recognition of the central role of the state in health, doubts still persisted about its importance in the context of development and poverty alleviation. The Millennium Development Goals (MDGs) adopted by the Millennium Summit of the United Nations in September 2000, which put health of the poor in the forefront of the global battle against poverty and disease, and thus represents an unprecedented global consensus on the subject. The WHO commission for Macro-economics and Health (2001) represented a pioneering effort to understand the linkages between economic growth and poverty on the one hand, and health status on the other. It not only underscored the importance of investments in health for economic growth and alleviation of poverty, but also laid out a blueprint for both the developing countries and the donor community to move forward towards the achievement of the MDGs.

What poor countries need urgently is not only greater investment in health sector along with wide ranging systematic reforms, but also that these specifically target the poor. The donor agencies have often shied away from investing in the backward areas on account of poor governance, weak health infrastructure and consequently higher risk of failure. Such investments directed towards the poor is justified not only on moral grounds, but also on economic grounds. The poor are subjected to a disproportionate, and to a large extent avoidable, burden of disease (BOD) from pre-transition diseases (infectious diseases, perinatal and maternal conditions and nutritional disorders). The BOD in low and middle-income countries on this account was estimated at 44% as against 7% in high-income countries (World Health Report, 1999). All these conditions are capable of being controlled very cost effectively with relatively simple and easily available technologies. Investment in the health of the poor could, therefore, not only yield quick results but also maximize the returns on such investments. If the world desires to move ahead rapidly towards the MDGs, the poor would be the best place to direct the efforts. Besides the pre-transition diseases, the new pandemic of HIV/AIDS is causing unimaginable consequences in the poorest regions of the world. A recent World Bank study (2001) in India has also shown the poorest quintile to be having almost double the exposure to lifestyle risk factors like tobacco use and smoking as compared to the richest 20% of the population. The poor are often concentrated in backward and remote areas having very weak infrastructure, degraded environment, poor sanitation, lack of access to safe drinking water, which combined with under-nutrition and poor hygiene makes them highly vulnerable to ill-health. Investment in these areas would definitely improve the health status and living conditions of the poor population. However, the proportion of GDP spent on health in general and on health sector investment in particular, continue to remain very low in India, and that makes this sector a weak participant in global trade process.

The plan of the present book is as follows. Chapter 2 provides a review of GATS provisions regarding the globalisation of health services and the implications for developing countries. Chapter 3 provides a critical review of the literature on health and economic development and cross-country evidences on health care services and health sector outcomes, including India. Chapter 4 provides an account of the Health sector in India and in major states, the link between income, health outcome indicators and distribution of health facilities across states and socio-economic groups. Chapter 5 outlines the health status of Indian population and provides an analytical exercise on the efficiency of health outcomes in the rural areas of Indian states. Chapter 6 deals with poverty, under-nutrition and the link between health sector outcomes in selected Indian states, burden of diseases and socio-economic factors that affect the morbidity of Indian people in rural and urban areas. Chapter 7 summarises the main conclusions of the study, including the implications of globalisation on the health sector of the Indian economy.

2

Globalisation, GATS and Health Sector

I. GLOBALISATION

The term "Globalization" in general refers to a set of processes leading to the integration of economic, cultural, political, and social systems across geographical boundaries, with worldwide integration of markets for goods, services and capital, and compression of both the temporal and spatial dimensions of planet into a global village providing wide human interactions and interplay of forces among different players located in alternate places. In economic terms, the process of globalisation involves generalized expansion of international economic activity, which includes increased international freer trade, growth of international investment (foreign investment) and international migration, and increased creation of technology among countries, indicating development of extensive worldwide patterns of economic relationships between nations. It also involves an increased role for large corporations (MNCs) in the world economy and increased intervention into domestic policies and affairs by international institutions such as the IMF, WTO, and World Bank. A typical-but restrictive-definition of globalisation can be taken from the International Monetary Fund, which stresses the growing economic interdependence of countries worldwide through increasing volume and variety of cross-border transactions in goods and services, free international capital flows, and more rapid and widespread diffusion of technology. Globalisation relies on three forces for development: the role of human migration, international trade, and rapid movements of capital and integration of financial markets. While being a complex and multifaceted array of phenomena, globalization can be broken down into separate aspects:

- *industrial* globalization (alias *transnationalization*)—rise and expansion of multinational enterpriseses;
- *financial* globalization—emergence of worldwide financial markets and better access to external financing for corporate, national and sub-national borrowers;
- *political* globalization—spread of political sphere of interests to the regions and countries outside the neighbourhood of political (state and non-state) actors;
- *informational* globalization—increase in information flows between geographically remote locations; and
- *cultural* globalization—growth of cross-cultural contacts.

The process of globalization is a manifestation of the natural process of capitalism, constrained by the cost of transport and information and accelerated by technologies that make it cheaper to move goods, services and ideas. It has benefits as well as costs and these costs are asymmetrically distributed across regions, nations and people with social and political ramifications including dissents, misery and inequity across different sections of the world community.

A few numbers tell the story of the world's march toward globalization:

- Trade as a percentage of gross world products has risen from 15 percent in 1986 to nearly 29 percent today.

- In the past two decades, the stock of foreign direct investment has nearly quadrupled as a percentage of gross world products.
- More people than ever are crossing national bordersfor business and pleasure. On average around the globe, countries received just one foreign visitor for every 100 people in 1950. By the mid-1980s there were six, and since then that number has doubled to 12.
- Since 1991, international telephone traffic has more than tripled. The number of cell phone subscribers has grown from virtually zero to 1.8 billion—30 percent of the world population—and Internet users will soon hit 1 billion.

The pro-globalisation groups highlight its benefits-the gains from trade, specialization and productivity that come with expanding markets.These gains accrue to private sector more compared to public sector. Because factors of production become increasingly mobile in an era of globalization, governments vie to gain and hold onto them. Mobile factors flee economies that burden them with high taxes, excessive regulation and capricious administration. They gravitate toward countries that offer the best opportunities to increase profits or paychecks. The economic benefits of productive factors give nations incentives to pursue freer economic policies. The USA is the world's fourth most globalised country, behind Singapore, Switzerland and Ireland. In countries with a higher degree of globalization, policies tend to support more accountability in the private and public sectors. These nations are more likely to maintain courts that recognize property rights and enforce the rule of law. Policies in these more globalized countries tend to be more stable, essential for long-term planning by business.

The integration with the world economy does not provide unqualified benefits to all nations, particularly the less developed ones with age-old structural problems. The gradual withdrawal of governments particularly from the social sectors accentuates the pains to the vulnerable and poor sections of the society resulting in illfare as opposed to national welfare and the financial vulnerability through capital flight becomes a threat to the pursuant of independent of macro-economic policies by the governments who have to withdraw regulations and subsidies causing serious damages to the living conditions of the poorer and weaker sections of their population. Nations that fail to control inflation find they cannot retain their own capital or attract money from other countries, except at high interest rates. They end up not only with high inflation but also with lower investment, higher interest rates and slower growth. Likewise, labor market flexibility does not generally improve as economies open up to the rest of the world. As long as workers refuse to acknowledge that they are competing in a global economy, they petition wealthy governments to protect their jobs. Labor market rigidities slow job growth and raise unemployment, in turn creating a greater demand for expensive safety nets for idle workers and poor workers and in poor developing countries the problems get compounded with large stock of ever-growing unemployment.

The Washington Consensus between the US Treasury, International Monetary Fund and the World Bank speeded up the globalisation process in the world economy by the introduction of the famous Structural Adjustment Programmes (SAP) in poor countries of Latin America, Africa and Asia during the 1980s. In brief, the Structural Adjustment programme (SAP) was designed to:

- Cut government spending—this means big cuts in health care, education and subsidies to farmers and the poor.
- Privatisation—state owned industries and services must be sold off to private corporations. Often foreign multinationals are the buyers. Many workers lose their jobs, as Government industries close down. Services like transportation and power become more expensive.
- Devalue the local currency—for example in India the rupee should be worth less and less compared to American Dollar. The World Bank and IMF demand this to be implemented so as to make the devaluing country's exports cheaper in the international market.
- Introduction of market-based reforms in the domestic economic policies of the loan receiving poor countries.

- Export more—the country should export more to pay back loans.
- Open the door to foreign multinational companies.
- Reduce duties and tariffs on imports—in this way foreign multinationals can more easily sell their products in countries like India.

According to the World Bank and the IMF, the SAP prescription is applicable to all countries and are supposed to provide *pancea* to all economic ills facing the poor nations. Recorded information suggests that implications of SAP have been detrimental to many nation states : rising prices, inflation, rising unemployment, change in cropping patterns, loss of food security, withdrawal of subsidies on public welfare services such as public health, public education and public distribution system. The Structural Adjustment Programs had far-reaching consequences for the vulnerable sections for two reasons: first, it was well accepted in official circles that the brunt of the negative effects—be it shrinking job opportunities or rising prices—were to be borne by the poor sections; second, the cuts in investments in the welfare sector too were to affect the poor the most. As a result, these policies directly and selectively affected the already 'disadvantaged' people indifferent developing countries, apart from the loss of sovereignty to pursue independent domestic economic policies. Changes, such as the gradual dismantling of public sector health institutions, their receding resource base, introduction of user fee in public hospitals, and opening up of medical care to the private sector, meant that the interests of the poor would not be safeguarded any more. On the contrary, their problems were to increase, notwithstanding the rhetoric of so-called "safety net".

After the second oil crisis in 1975, the advanced northern countries introduced restrictive monetary and trade policies to protect their domestic industries from the onward march of export growth by the developing countries. The falling prices of goods exported by these developing countries, and rise in global interest rates pushed these poor vulnerable economies of Latin America, Africa and South Asia to debt trap. Their external debt continued to rise, as did their acceptance of the debt management strategies of the eighties. In 1997, the total external debt of developing countries rose to US $ 2173 billion, and of South Asia region to US $ 150 billion, of which India accounted for US $ 94 billion. The crisis in their economies put these South Asian countries' experiment with autonomous industrial development out of gear and they had to accept the terms of IMF and World Bank for support to bail out of the crisis. From creating politically and economically independent industrial base with self-sufficient and less inequitable societies, these LDCs had to accept the terms of Structural Adjustment Policies of the IMF and World Bank and adopt the uniform model of so-called reforms. By the eighties, the International Monetary Fund and World Bank were freely using the debt trap of Third World countries to compel them to accept a set of new economic deals, of which health sector reform was a part. By the early nineties, South Asian countries were made to agree to plans which were conceived for them, but not necessarily by them (World Bank, 1993). They adopted bank-driven, narrow, technocentric interventive strategies in the area of population control, reproductive and child health, and treatment of communicable diseases. They opened up medical care to the private sector and introduced a slow dismantling of the public sector, first by depriving it of funds and second by taking advantage of people's dissatisfaction with it. The cuts in subsidies for food and basic services further marginalized the role of the public sector in health care. The justifications for the World Bank induced reforms was provided by highlighting the existing state structures and failure of the promises of nation-states such as democratic governance, individual rights and efficiency in administering the development programmes under regulated state-controlled regimes. The supporters of the reforms argued that there were not enough resources to invest in public provision and that the only way forward would be to privatise as the quality of public services could never be improved. The move further distorted the access and enhance existing inequities in the provision of health services, ignoring the non-affordability of these market driven facilities for the bulk of poor and vulnerable in these countries.

Public health is an obvious casualty of this process. There is a clear contradiction between the principal tenets of public health and neo-liberal economics theory that permeates policy-making today. The former posits that public health is 'public good', i.e. its benefits cannot be individually appropriated or computed, but have to be seen in the context of benefit that accrue to the public. The public health outcomes are shared, and their accumulation lead to better living conditions. Such goods never mechanically translate into visible economic determinants, viz. income levels or rates of economic growth. Kerala, for example, has one of the lowest per capita incomes in the country but its public health parameters rival those in many developed countries. The infant mortality rate in Kerala is less than a third of any other large state in the country. But neo-liberal economic policies are loath to even acknowledge such benefits. Contrary to the very essence of PHC, in India, health was officially declared a "non-essential" service (Ghosh, 1997). Inevitable for the sake of stability of reforms, a theoretical rationalization had to be found for this restructuring.

The current economic policies would view health as a private-good that is accessed by the medium of the market. SAP induced economic policies had the following specific consequences for the health sector:

- A cut in the welfare investment, leading to gradual dismantling of the public health services.
- Introduction of services charges in public institutions, which has now making the services inaccessible to the poor.
- Handing over the responsibility of health service to the private sector and undermining the rationality of public health. The private sector on the other hand focused only on curative care. India for instance, was forced to reduce its public health expenditure in health and to recover the cost of health services from its users by international banks.
- The voluntary sector, which has also helped in to provide health services is forced to concentrate and priorities only those areas where international aid is made available—like AIDS, population control, etc.

Multilateral institutions have aggressively promoted wide-ranging reforms in health sector, particularly the World Bank, in the last two decades in the developing and transitional economies. The record of these efforts, especially in respect of the poor, has been mixed. In many cases the benefits did not really reach the poor, and in some, they seem to have been adversely impacted. Examples of the latter include indiscriminate privatization, introduction of cost recovery without safety nets for the poor and hasty decentralization. The focus of many of these efforts was not necessarily the health of the poor, but macro-economic stabilization and fiscal compression. Part of the problem was a serious misunderstanding of the role of the state in the wake of economic liberalization and euphoria about the markets following the collapse of the socialist model. However there is now a clearer perception of the central role of the state in the health sector in general and in protecting the vulnerable population in particular. The World Development Report, 1993, devoted exclusively to health, set the ball rolling by defining the role of the state in providing public goods, merit goods and provisioning essential health services. The World Development Report, 1997 greatly helped to clear the air by squarely placing the responsibility for protecting the vulnerable on the state. Finally, the World Health Report, 2000 brought out forcefully the stewardship role of the state in steering the health system. What poor countries need urgently is not only greater investment in health along with wide ranging systematic reforms, but also that these specifically target the poor. And even donor agencies have often shied away from investing in the backward areas on account of poor governance, weak health infrastructure and consequently higher risk of failure. Needless to say, that the poor generally lack political influence and are unlikely to receive the desired attention without a special focus. The poor are subjected to a disproportionate, and to a large extent avoidable, burden of disease (BOD) from pre-transition diseases (infectious diseases, perinatal and maternal conditions and nutritional disorders). The burden of diseases (BOD) in low and middle-income countries on this account was estimated at 44% as against 7% in high-income countries (World Health Report, 1999). Investment in the health of the poor could, therefore, not only yield quick results but also maximize the returns on such investments. If the world desires to move ahead rapidly towards the MDGs, the poor would be the best place to direct the efforts. Besides the pre-transition diseases, the new pandemic of HIV/AIDS is causing unimaginable consequences in the poorest regions of the world. A recent World Bank study (2001) in India has also shown the poorest quintile to be having almost double the exposure to lifestyle risk factors like tobacco use and smoking as compared to the richest 20% of the population. The poor are often concentrated in backward and remote areas having very weak infrastructure, degraded environment, poor sanitation, lack of access to safe drinking water, which combined with under-nutrition and poor hygiene makes them highly vulnerable to ill health.

These fundamentals were more sharply focused upon in 1987 by the World Bank document titled "financing Health Services in Developing Countries". The document recommended that developing countries should:

- Increase amounts paid by patients
- Develop private health insurance mechanisms (this requires a dismantling of state supported health services as if free or low cost health care is available there is little interest in private insurance).
- Expand the participation of private sector.
- Decentralize government health care services not real decentralization but a euphemism for "rolling back" of state responsibility and passing on the burden to local communities.

These recommendations were further "fine-tuned" and reiterated by the Bank's World Development Report, 1993 titled "Investing in Health". This document represents the bank's major foray into health policy formulation. Today the bank is the decisive voice in this regard, and the organisations such as the WHO and UNICEF have been reduced to playing the role of "drum beaters" of the Bank's doctrine of market penetration and globalisation, with emphasis on social safety nets and proactive role of the state in the provision of health services for the poor and the vulnerables.

Despite the recognition of the central role of the state in health, doubts still persisted about its importance in the context of development and poverty alleviation. The Millennium Development Goals (MDGs) adopted by the Millennium Summit of the United Nations in September 2000 put health of the poor in the forefront of the global battle against poverty and disease, and thus represents an unprecedented global consensus on the subject. The WHO commission for Macro-economics and Health (2001) represented a pioneering effort to understand the linkages between economic growth and poverty on the one hand, and health status on the other. It not only underscored the importance of investments in health for economic growth and alleviation of poverty, but also laid out a blueprint for both the developing countries and the donor community to move forward towards the achievement of the MDGs.

II. GATS

After World War II, the task of coordinating trade in goods across nations had been placed under the international organization called General Agreement on Tariff and Trade (GATT) in 1947, which tried to liberalize international trade in industrial and primary goods among nations through eight rounds of negotiation. A multilateral treaty entered into in 1948 by the intended members of the International Trade Organization, the purpose of which was to implement many of the rules and negotiated tariff reductions that would be overseen by the ITO. With the failure of the ITO, the GATT became the principal institution regulating trade policy until it was subsumed within the WTO in 1995. In 1995, GATT was replaced by World Trade Organization (WTO) and a decision was taken to broader its participation in trade in service, which was hitherto considered as non-tradables. The agreement, negotiated in the Uruguay Round brought international trade in services into the ambit WTO. The General Agreement on Trade in Services (GATS) was designed to facilitate trade in services. GATS explicitly provides for successive rounds of negotiation with a view to achieving a progressively higher degrees of liberalization. The GATS provides for countries to provide national treatment to Foreign Service providers and for them to select and negotiate the service sectors to be covered under GATS. In the first phase, education, health services and financial services were put under the ambit of trade in services.

GATS committed the WTO members to achieve a progressively higher level of liberalization in their services sectors and enter newer markets. To achieve this, WTO members made liberalization requests to member countries in bilateral meetings at Geneva to open up competition in those sectors, which are of most interest to their service providers. For instance: India has requests from countries like Singapore, China, Brazil, Australia, Turkey, Poland, Thailand, Peru, Jordan and Oman, for full market access and national treatment commitments in Modes 1, 2 and 3 and horizontal commitments in Mode 4 for both the professional services. Requests are there for India to allow joint ventures and permit foreign doctors with national licenses in the country of origin to practice for three years or more. Requests are also there for taking commitments in social services delivered through residential institutions to old persons and the handicapped.

Under GATS, services trade—including health services—the member nations are bound by two guiding principles. First, is to disallow bestowing 'most-favoured-nation status', the degree to which a WTO member opens a sector of its service market to any country must be the same for all member countries. The second is 'principle of national treatment', this requires all members to treat service providers, whether domestic or foreign, in the same way by the member Governments. However, the degree to which individual members commit to open their markets to foreign health services providers is quite flexible. However, GATS commitments do not explain whether they represent liberalization from previous policies, thus, does not capture how trade policies have changed over time and also do not consider the range of DR that often has a strong effect on services' trade. To address the latter problem of DR, the World Bank is developing a database on measures affecting trade in services. This would allow researchers 'to address a range of questions about services trade policy, including identification of barriers to trade; how such barriers differ across services sectors and across countries; and the implications of liberalizing trade in services for overall economic performance'.

GATS commits WTO members to successive rounds of negotiations "with a view to achieving a progressively higher level of liberalization" in their service sectors. Although developing countries officially have the right to choose whether to commit a sector to GATS, in practice they come under intense pressure in these negotiations to meet the demands of more powerful WTO members—pressure which the smaller and poorer countries are often powerless to resist. In this way, GATS is primarily a mechanism for the service corporations of developed countries to expand their reach into new markets around the world. This is widely acknowledged by official negotiators: the European Commission has confirmed that GATS is "first and foremost an instrument for the benefit of business, and not only for business in general, but for individual service companies wishing to export services or to invest and operate abroad."

GATS defines the scope of the agreement as follows:

- "Services" includes any service in any sector except services supplied in the exercise of *governmental authority*. It may appear therefore that in countries where health care is mostly provided by government may be exempted from implementing GATS in the health sector." However, "a service supplied in the exercise of governmental authority", means any service that is supplied neither on a commercial basis nor in competition with one or more service suppliers. In most countries health services are also provided by the private sector and even the government sector charges for certain services. Therefore, under these sections of the agreement, the health sector is invariably covered by GATS. Unlike many other services, however, the direct impact of liberalization on the priorities of the public health sector makes this kind of trade a critical issue in terms of people right to health.

Under GATS, supply can take four modes: one, Cross Border Supply, where the service is provided remotely from one country to another (e.g., international telephone calls, Internet services, telemedicine); two, Consumption Abroad, where individuals use a service in another country (e.g. tourists traveling abroad, patients taking advantage of health care in foreign countries); three, Commercial Presence, where a foreign company sets up a subsidiary or branch within another country in order to deliver the service locally (e.g. banks, private health clinics); four, Presence of Natural Persons, where individuals travel to another country to supply a service there on a temporary basis (e.g. software programmers, nurses, doctors).

III. GATS AND HEALTH SERVICES

Globalization has brought in, over the past decade, a spurt in technological advances and emergence of new forms of business opportunities, process and organizations, impacting a wide range of sectors including healthcare. Globalization of health services involves various modes of transaction. It involves cross-border electronic delivery, such as telediagnosis, teleconsultations, and transmission of medical images. As well as traditional shipments of medical reports and samples and, more recently, outsourcing of clinical trials. It also involves cross-border movement of consumers to avail of healthcare services in another country, often because such treatment is not available or is too expensive in the patient's home country. These may also be combined with tour packages, giving rise to the term 'medical tourism', and focusing attention on countries like Thailand, aggressively marketing it. Globalization of health sector is also evident from the growing foreign equity participation in this sector and establishment of joint ventures, alliances and management tie-ups among care establishments, resulting in the transfer of technology, skills and practices. Finally there is the global movement of doctors, nurses and technicians, and the resulting networks of healthcare professionals that are sources of investment and know how.

The health care sector is today among the most rapidly growing sectors in the world economy. It was estimated to generate US $ 3 trillion per year in countries in the Organization for Economic Co-operation and Development alone and was expected to rise to US $ 4 trillion by 2005. The globalization of health services is reflected in the growing cross-border delivery of health services, through movement of personnel and consumers (by electronic and other means), and in an increasing number of joint ventures and collaborative arrangements. Using the General Agreement on Trade in Services (GATS) definitions, trade in health services occurs via four modes of supply. There are strong regional and bilateral patterns to these flows, involving North-South and South-South transactions, making this a truly globally integrative process. There are considerable linkages across the different forms of transactions.

When GATS was adopted in 1994, few countries were aware of the challenges it would bring. Very few government departments other than trade and finance ministries were involved in the negotiations, and several countries committed all or part of their health services to GATS liberalization without the knowledge of their health ministries. Health services are also included under the GATS heading of 'professional services', which covers medical and dental services as well as the category of 'services provided by midwives, nurses, physiotherapists and paramedical personnel'. Already 52 countries have made liberalization commitments in the former category, and 28 in the latter. GATS also covers insurance services, including health insurance, and 78 countries have already committed those services to liberalization under GATS. This has caused particular concern in those countries, which base their health systems on social insurance programmes, since few health ministries were informed that their trade negotiators had committed their health insurance sectors to GATS.

Modes of Supply Under GATS

Cross-border Delivery

Cross-border delivery includes shipment of laboratory samples, diagnosis, and clinical consultation via traditional mail channels, as well as electronic delivery of health services, such as diagnosis, second opinions, and consultations. Countries use a variety of telehealth services, including telepathology, teleradiology and telepsychiatry. Many cross-border telemedicine initiatives have also emerged. For example, telediagnostics, surveillance and consultation services are provided by hospitals in the United States of America (USA) to hospitals in Central America and the eastern Mediterraneanan, and Indian physicians provide telepathology services to hospitals in Bangladesh and Nepal. Telediagnosis services are also provided by hospitals in China's coastal provinces to patients in Macao, Taiwan, and some South-East Asian countries.

The most important example of cross border supply or trade in health services is telemedicine: the provision of medical services from a practitioner in one country to a patient or practitioner in another, predominantly via the Internet or satellite transmission of medical images. While still at an early stage, the potential benefits of telemedicine are already evident, especially for remote diagnosis and treatment. Based on evidence of its use among remote rural communities in Japan and Australia, telemedicine could expand the capacities of doctors in developing countries.

But the effective implementation of telemedicine projects presupposes a communications infrastructure developed to a level far higher than is currently found in most remote areas of the developing world. However, several examples already exist of non-commercial telemedicine projects working within developing countries on an experimental basis. While a growing body of evidence attests to the clinical benefit and cost effectiveness of telemedicine, there is less proof of its commercial sustainability.

Telemedicine includes the remote provision of medical education. Teleconferencing has already been established between institutions in Canada, Kenya and Uganda to enable health care workers in Africa to benefit from the latest medical knowledge. Internet sites such as the University of Iowa's Virtual Hospitals provide free online information on a wide range of adult and child health problems—a valuable resource for doctors otherwise reliant upon outdated collections of medical journals. In all these cases, the expansion of cross-border supply of telemedicine offers potential gains for health care. However, concerns remain about the confidentiality of patients and the applicability and relevance of medical information generated in industrialized countries to situations in the developing world.

In addition, there is the problem of regulatory control over telemedicine, as noted by the 50th World Health Assembly in its 1997 resolution on the uncontrolled sale of prescription drugs over the Internet. The resolution focused on the public health hazard of counterfeit products being passed off as genuine, and on the inappropriate use of potentially dangerous medicines without medical supervision. (The WHO had already exposed four companies selling prescription drugs over the Internet without the detailed information that should accompany the sales). Telemedicine poses regulatory challenges on the demand as well as the supply side. Even the most advanced regulatory systems will be unable to prevent doctors or clinics from ordering medicines over the Internet which are not included in a country's essential drugs list. Such practices might give those practitioners a perceived commercial edge over rivals who keep within treatment guidelines, but would undermine national policies promoting the rational use of drugs.

The potential drain which commercial cross-border trade in telemedicine could have on limited health care budgets in developing countries is also a matter of great concern. At present almost all trade in remote health care is from North to South, and the expense of entering into commercial relationships would be prohibitive for poorer nations. While the technology of telemedicine offers potential benefits in some cases, few would suggest its commercial development offers more general solutions to the health problems of the majority.

Of more immediate significance is the development of cross-border private medical insurance and managed health care. Companies mostly provide private health insurance with a commercial presence in the country (and thus covered by mode three, or Commercial Presence, under GATS), and the potential is increasing for such services to be provided across national borders. However, the issues remain substantially the same as those discussed later in connection with mode three: the increased commercialization of health care and the growing involvement of the private sector.

As far as India is concerned, a foreign investor can come into India by two routes: Foreign Investment Promotion Board (FIPB) route, which is already existing and is a 100 per cent autonomous route wherein there is no check. The second route is established entity route wherein there is a need for a holding company in India with the present equity of 49 per cent and 51 per cent with the foreign and Indian collaboration respectively. There is a move to increase this to 74 per cent and 26 per cent with a condition that newer technology is brought in along with the investment by the foreign company and later 100 per cent, if some member country asks for more liberalization.

Here the catch is to define "latest technology". Different experts have their own definition to call a technology as 'new'. However, here the prerogative lies with the Ministry of Health to accept Genetic Engineering Council's (GEC) restrictions or intervene with more restrictions for a Foreign Service provider. Logically therefore, till such time that 'latest technology' is categorically defined, the best route of entry into the healthcare service delivery is Route 1.

Consumption of Health Services Abroad

Consumption abroad refers to the movement of consumers to the country providing the service for diagnosis and treatment. Under this mode, affluent patients in developing countries seek specialized high quality treatment overseas in hospitals in industrialized countries or in neighbouring developing countries with superior health care standards. Patients from industrialized countries seek affordable, high quality treatment or alternative medicines and treatments in developing countries.

Several developing countries export health services via consumption abroad. Cuba, for example, has made a conscious effort to attract foreign patients from Latin America, the Caribbean, Europe, and Russia to specialized hospitals which provide high quality care at competitive prices. It has also differentiated itself by focusing on treatment of certain skin diseases, which are incurable in countries, and on the development of new procedures and drugs, such as for pigmentary retinopathy or vitiligo. In 1995-96, more than 25,000 foreign patients went to Cuba for treatment, generating an estimated US $ 25 million in sales of health services to foreigners.

India also exports health services through consumption abroad. Patients come from industrialized and developing countries (including Bangladesh, the Eastern Mediterranean, Nepal, Sri Lanka, the United Kingdom and the USA) for surgery and specialized services in areas such as neurology, cardiology, endocrinology, nephrology, and urology. They are attracted by India's pool of highly qualified health care professionals and by the country's ability to provide good quality and affordable treatment. In India, a coronary bypass operation costs Rs. 70,000-100,000, compared to Rs. 1.5-2.0 million in Western countries. A liver transplant in India costs one-tenth of that in the USA. Specially hospitals, such as those in the Apollo group in India, get surgery cases from the USA, foreign tourists, non-resident Indians, and foreign residents for such treatments. Each year an estimated 50,000 patients come to India from Bangladesh and spend over US $ 1 million per year on the specialized treatment of diseases.

Several developing countries have also diversified into areas such as medical and paramedical education, health tourism, and alternative medicines and treatments. India and Thailand, for example, reserve places in medical colleges for students from other developing countries, and Cuba provides training for specialists, paramedics and students from selected countries under bilateral agreements. Cuba and Thailand have also combined health care with tourism and recreational services. India is exploiting its niche in traditional medicines like Unani, Ayurveda and Homeopathic forms of treatment and has developed holistic health care centres, such as the Ayurvedic school in Kottakkal, Kerala, where it attracts patients from the Eastern Mediterranean, Germany Malaysia, the United Kingdom, and the U.S.A. Patients consuming medical services abroad represent a more significant source of international trade in health services. They may have traveled abroad especially to seek medical treatment in another country or happen to need treatment while visiting that country for other reasons. The majority of the USA's estimated $ 872 million in health care exports in 1996 came from foreigners being treated in the country.

The potential for developing countries to gain economic benefit from attracting foreign consumption of their health services is limited. However, certain countries have identified the provision of health services to foreigners as a potential growth area. India offers significant cost advantages for patients traveling from industrialized countries, with major treatments such as liver transplants or coronary bypass surgery priced at a tenth of what individuals would be charged in the USA. In addition, certain countries offer culturally specific health services. Traditional medicine draws a substantial number of patients to China every year, the majority of them overseas Chinese but also a growing number of individuals who have turned away from the western medical tradition. India has a similar advantage in its extensive network of Ayurvedic practitioners, who attract a steady trickle of foreigners every year. States like Kerala are already encouraging health tourism based on traditional knowledge.

Another aspect of consumption of health services abroad is the training of medical students at foreign educational institutions. Countries such as the UK and USA have long traditions of providing such education to foreign students on a commercial basis. Certain countries have the ability to attract foreign students for culturally specific courses, such as training in Ayurvedic or traditional Chinese medicine. Some German universities now give students credits for courses taken in institutions in China. In these limited cases, the consumption of domestic services by foreigners represents a potential source of export earnings for the host countries.

However, these benefits will be outweighed by the social costs if limited investment is drawn away from national health priorities. In the vase majority of countries, an expanding private sector will draw medical personnel away from the public sector. Favoring foreign patients will come at the expense of the local population. While extra investment financed by charges on foreign consumers has the potential to upgrade services for local users, in practice the two groups often use separate facilities, with little opportunity for crossovers. Worse still, the public sector often has to bear the cost of building the new hospitals and clinics to treat foreign patients, which is a further diversion of resources away from public health needs.

A lesser threat applies to those countries, which provide education to foreign medical students, given that there is greater elasticity of supply than in the case of health care. However, the economic imperative to raise numbers of paying foreign students has the potential to drive down the quality of training as a result of declining teacher to student ratios and rising pressure on resources.

Ultimately there may emerge a parallel threat to that experienced by patients: reduced opportunity of access for domestic students and a consequent contraction in the numbers of qualified nationals. The reverse situation pertains for those countries, which send medical students for training abroad. In such cases the training represents an import in balance of payment terms, but can be seen as an investment in terms of the obvious potential for skills transfer. However, the extent to which those skills can be deployed to the benefit of the wider society depends on how many of the trainees return to their home country once their courses are over. Only half of the Indian doctors trained in Europe and the USA return home at the end of their training.

Commercial Presence

Commercial presence involves the establishment of hospitals, clinics, diagnostic and treatment centres, and nursing homes. Countries such as India, Indonesia, Nepal, Sri Lanka, and Thailand have become increasingly open to foreign direct investment. For example, approval has been given to a German company to have 90% foreign equity ownership for setting up a 200-bed hospital in Delhi. Several speciality corporate hospitals are being built in collaboration between Indian and foreign companies, including a US $ 40 million cardiac center, set-up under a consortium between Australia, Canada and India. Corporate hospitals in developing countries are also establishing commercial presence overseas. For example, the Apollo group of hospitals in India has established a hospital outside the country and plans to invest roughly US $ 4 billion to build 15 new hospitals in Malaysia, Nepal, and Sri Lanka.

Health care companies in industrialized and some developing countries are increasingly engaging in joint ventures and alliances resulting in several regional health care networks and chains. For instance, the Singapore-based Parkway Group has acquired hospitals in Asia and the United Kingdom, to create an international chain of hospitals, Gleneagles International. In partnership with host country investors, the Raffles Medical Group in Singapore has formed global strategic alliances with health care organizations from industrialized countries, to develop an integrated network of health care companies that offers a range of high quality and cost effective health services.

The establishment of commercial presence in a foreign country differs from the other three modes of GATS in that it is essentially an issue of investment. In health care, this investment relates primarily to foreign commercial presence in hospitals, health clinics and health insurance, and to a lesser extent to the provision of medical education. As noted, GATS aims to generate new opportunities for companies to invest and operate in the service sectors of other countries. But the prospect of increased foreign commercial presence in the health sector has raised serious concerns about people's right to health, given the negative experience of fees in the sector.

In developing countries, much of this experience has come as a result of the liberalization process, which has involved structural adjustment programmes under the IMF and the World Bank. The introduction of cost recovery programmes in the health sector is now widely accepted to have been disastrous, forcing many poor families and their children into a "medical poverty trap" characterized by untreated illness and long-term impoverishment. Even the World Bank, while it continues to support user fees for health in it national poverty-reduction strategy papers, has acknowledged that they are responsible for denying poor families access to health care.

Structural adjustment programmes have introduced cost recovery principles into the health care sector in many countries. Yet GATS goes one stage further, as it represents the commodification of health care for trade on the open market. Just as internal liberalization prepares the way for commercialization of the health sector, so too external liberalization locks in commercialization through the long-term presence of foreign investment.

For developing countries with failing health systems, this foreign investment may seem an attractive source of capital and medical technology at a time when other sources are thin on the ground. Yet involvement by the foreign private sector in health care has the potential to marginalize the poor even further. Companies seek markets in which they can be assured sufficient returns, and this typically concentrates investment in more affluent areas. Loans granted to private health care providers by the World Bank's International Finance Corporation, for instance, are predominantly directed towards facilities for the richer communities of the country or for expatriates, not the majority of the population. This practice of "cream skimming" by the private sector is already familiar in the field of private health insurance, where insurance companies and health maintenance organizations (HMOs) typically favour the healthy and wealthy over high-risk customers, excluding the latter by means of prohibitive premiums.

In terms of direct health care provision, similarly, the private sector's profit-making imperative limits its relevance to those sections of society which are unable to pay for its services, even though it is they who need the extra investment the most. Yet private investment in health care is not irrelevant to poor people. In many countries, as noted, an expanding private sector will draw personnel away from public health systems and exacerbate shortages of trained and qualified staff. Often it is the most skilled staff that makes the move to the private sector, lowering the overall quality of personnel in the public health system. Worse still, cream skimming undermines the very ability of public health systems to sustain themselves financially, as it denies the basic principles of cross-subsidization and risk pooling by which the healthy support the ill, the young the old and the rich the poor.

Foreign investment also brings with it the risk of domination by transnational corporations to the exclusion of domestic development. In the hospital sector, the overwhelming majority of these corporations are powerful companies based in Europe and the USA. Only Singapore's Parkway Holdings and South Africa's Afrox Healthcare are exceptions.

As well as the equity issues raised by commercialization, liberalization also risks compromising the quality of health care delivery. The introduction of private sector companies into public health systems raises potential conflicts of interest between commercial pressures and public health goals. In industrialized countries this has commonly meant a reduction in quality as a result of cost cutting, often through a substitution of casual for skilled labor amongst nursing and ancillary staff. It has also led to the planning of hospitals on the basis of financial rather than clinical need, with accompanying reductions in the clinical workforce and service capacity.

In the USA, where the health care market has become increasingly competitive over time, HMOs have responded by pressurizing doctors to withhold treatment from their patients. By means of performance-related pay mechanisms linking their incomes directly to the clinical costs they incur, doctors are encouraged to refer the lowest possible number of patients to specialists or to hospitals. The HMO awards bonuses to those who minimize such expenditure, while doctors who generate above-average costs risk expulsion.

In developing countries, commercial pressures lead to similar profit maximization strategies. One study of private clinics in Malaysia revealed that many fail to assess new clients properly in their provision of family planning services, and cervical screening is undertaken only if requested. Conversely, private practitioners in Egypt have been found to be less likely than public sector workers to administer (inexpensive) oral rehydration solution, and more likely to prescribe anti-diarrhoeal drugs even though the latter are contraindicated in the country's national programme.

The decision to involve foreign companies in the health sector requires very definite structural conditions if it is not to damage the quality of health care delivery in systems which are already under severe strain. As many commentators have stressed, national and regional health authorities need highly developed regulatory, analytical and managerial capacity if they are to see any benefit from the challenges of working with foreign companies.

In the majority of poorer countries, however, this capacity is simply non-existent. As a result, the introduction of private sector investment threatens to divert care away from public health priorities and to further compromise the quality of health care delivery. Concerns that profit-led health care is excessively focused on curative rather than preventive measures are familiar and longstanding, as are fears of over-prescription and unnecessary treatment undertaken for financial motives. Even joint public-private initiatives based on donations or price discounts have revealed their own shortcomings, distorting national health strategies and diverting funds towards non-priority areas, as well as hindering the development of national health systems as a whole. The acknowledged difficulties of integrating private sector companies into public health care have sown doubts among even the most pro-liberalization commentators.

Moreover, as far as the objectives of health services are concerned, the efficiency of the private sector is unsubstantiated. Patterns of health care consumption resemble those for luxury goods, with high-income households spending a higher proportion of their income on health care than poor households. Poor households therefore account for the majority of health needs but a disproportionately minority share of health expenditure, so that the use of resources in the private health care market is doubly skewed away from need. Precisely this inverted relation between supply and demand renders the market inefficient.

Presence of Natural Persons

If the establishment of commercial presence is primarily of interest to transnational corporations from industrialized countries, the temporary movement of "natural persons" to provide a service abroad has generated most interest among developing countries. There is already substantial movement of medical personnel from South to North and between countries of the developing world (health services, unlike many other professional services, being largely based on universal principles). However, the perceived economic benefits of this trade raise serious concerns about people right to health, especially in the poorest countries.

The potential for exchange of medical personnel between countries is attested by experience from across the world.

Developing countries—particularly in Asia—supply over half of all migrating physicians, with about 100, 000 doctors of Indian origin settled in the USA and UK alone. Active international recruitment by national health systems has generated a particularly high level of cross-border mobility among nurses. A large number of countries which export doctors or nurses experience severe shortages themselves, and can ill afford to send their services abroad. Increased trade in health services risks exacerbating this transfer of medical personnel from poor to rich countries, thereby placing an even greater strain on health systems in the poorest. Since these are often the countries with the most acute health crises, the public health consequences of expanded trade can be considerable. Weighed against these losses, the remittances that medical personnel send home and the enhanced skills they bring with them if and when they return are poor compensation.

Movement of Health Personnel

Health service are also traded via the movement of health personnel, including physicians, specialists, nurses, paramedics, mid-wives, technicians, consultants, trainers, health management personnel, and other professionals. The movement of health care professionals includes both temporary and permanent flows, each having different legal, social and economic implications for both source and host countries.

Short-term flows have mainly been driven by conscious strategies to promote health services exports, in order to earn foreign exchange and foster cooperation between governments. For instance, China and Cuba send health personnel abroad on short-term remunerated contracts to countries in Africa, under government supervision. There is also a short-term flow of health care professionals from Ghana to Jamaica, and from India to the Eastern Mediterranean. The Eastern Mediterranean is an important host market for physicians, nurses, X-ray technicians, laboratory technicians, dental hygienists, physiotherapists, and medical rehabilitation workers from many developing countries.

Permanent migration of health professionals occurs mainly from developing to industrialized countries. It is driven by wage differentials between countries and a search for better working conditions and living standards; a search for better training possibilities; and demand supply imbalances in the health sector between host and source countries. A 1998 United Nations Conference on Trade and Development/WHO study estimated that 56% of all migrating physicians flow from developing countries to industrialized countries, while 11% migrate in the opposite direction; the imbalance was even greater for nurses. The most prominent source countries for health personnel are India, the Philippines, and South Africa, whose nurses, physicians and technicians emigrate to Australia, the Eastern Mediterranean, the United Kingdom and the USA.

Countries have adopted different policies towards the migration of health care professionals. To deter permanent outflows of personnel, countries like India and South Africa have required their health care professional to provide a period of service in their own country after graduation. Some destination markets have actively encouraged inflows of specific categories of foreign health care professionals. The USA, for example, has introduced special visa schemes and changes in immigration policy to encourage inflows of nurses and technicians from India, Jamaica, and the Philippines and inflows of specialists from Canada and the United Kingdom. Changes in immigration policy in the USA greatly increased the emigration of nurses and physicians from developing and industrialized countries to the USA between 1990 and 1996. Between 1970 and 1993, the number of foreign medical graduates in the USA rose from 57,000 to 150,000, with India, Pakistan, and the Philippines accounting for 45% of all international medical graduates by 1993. By 1996, there were 110,000 nurses employed or residing in the USA who had been educated outside the USA: 43% of them came from the Philippines, 19% from Canada, 15% from the United Kingdom, and 9% from India.

IV. IMPLICATIONS OF TRADE IN HEALTH SERVICES

Many factors must be considered when assessing the implications of trade in health services, but ultimately the net impact of the trade depends on the specifics of a country's national health care system, the regulatory environment, and government policies. Each supply mode has associated benefits and problems. However, many of the problems would exist even in the absence of globalization. The question is, therefore, whether globalization of health service is likely to aggravate such problems and pose additional challenges.

Cross-Border Delivery

Cross-border delivery of health services through telemedicine can enable health care providers to cater to remote and undeserved segments of the population; help alleviate human resource constraints; enable more cost-effective surveillance of diseases; improve the quality of diagnosis and treatment; and help upgrade skills through interactive electronic means. However, these gains are possible only if the requisite infrastructure is present. Given the lack of telecommunications and power sector infrastructure in many developing countries, telemedicine may not be cost-effective. In such cases, public sector resources for tele-medicine may be better invested in improving basic health care facilities for disease prevention and cure, and in areas where there is a direct impact on the poor. The risk is that tele-medicine will channel revenues away from rural and primary health care and towards specialized centres, thus concentrating technologies, which cater to the affluent few in developing countries.

Consumption Abroad

Trade in health services via consumption abroad also has mixed implications. On the positive side, it may enable exporting countries to improve their national health systems, by generating foreign exchange and additional resources for investment in health care. It can also help in overcoming shortages of physical and human resources in the importing countries, particularly for specialized health services. But consumption of trade abroad could also result in a dual market structure, by creating a higher quality, expensive segment that caters to wealthy nationals and foreigners, and a much lower quality, resource constrained segment catering to the poor. Availability of services, including physicians and other trained personnel, as well as the availability of beds may rise in the higher standard centres at the expense of public sector, resulting in a crowding out of the local population.

Commercial Presence

As for consumption abroad, commercial presence in health services can generate additional resources for investment in and upgrading of health care infrastructure and technologies; generate employment; reduce unemployment of health personnel; and provide expensive and specialized medical services. The availability of private capital could reduce the total burden of government resources, helping to reallocate government expenditure towards the public health care sector. Affiliations and partnerships with reputed health service institutions in industrialized countries can also help to improve service facilities in developing countries and introduce superior management techniques and information systems.

However, the gains from reduced pressure on government resources may be offset by the huge initial public investments that may be required to attract foreign direct investment into the health sector. Furthermore, if specialist corporate hospitals are established using public funds and subsidies, this would divert resources from the public health system and could lead to a two-tiered health care system with a corporate segment and a public sector segment, the former concentrating on high level technology and services which do not address broader social needs. A two-tiered system may also result in an internal "brain drain", as better quality health care professionals flow from the public health care segment to the corporate segment, with its better pay and superior infrastructure. It may also cause "cream skimming", whereby those who need less but can pay more are served at the expense of the poor and more deserving. These problems have occurred in countries such as Thailand, where there has been an increased outflow of service providers from the public to the private health sector, partly in response to the emergence of joint venture private hospitals formed by local and foreign companies. This internal brain drain has aggravated the shortage of health personnel and worsened the existing inequitable distribution of health care resources within the country.

Trade in Water and Sanitation

In addition to trade in health care, trade in water and sanitation services also raises significant issues for people right to health. In India the Pepsi and Coca Cola companies have already been marketing "mineral water". Here there are no balance of payment incentives encouraging developing countries to engage in increased trade: almost all the transnational corporations in the water and sanitation sectors are European and none are from the developing world. Clean water and proper sanitation facilities play a particularly important role in maintaining health during infancy and early childhood. Yet 1.1 billion people across the developing world still lack access to safe drinking water and 2.4 billion people—two-fifths of the world's population—do not have adequate sanitation. As a result, more than two million children die from sanitation-related diseases every year.

As with health care, commercialization has further restricted poor families' access to water and sanitation in many parts of the world. Cost recovery and water privatization schemes have typically involved significant price rises, often putting water beyond the reach of low-income households. Such developments raise similar problems of equity to those encountered in health care-except that with water, as with education, demand for the service is continual, not intermittent.

Most Favoured Nations and National Treatment

Apart from the problems discussed above regarding the various modes of supply, there are other provisions in GATS that can adversely affect the interests of poorer nations. According to the WTO agreement, if favoured treatment is given to one country it should be extended to all the countries which have signed the agreement under WTO. The principle is: *favour one—favour all*. Most Favoured Nation means treating each trading partner equally. Under this provision of the GATT, if a country allows foreign competition in a sector, equal opportunities in that sector should be given to service providers from other WTO member countries. This in effect means that a country cannot be selective in permitting a foreign country in offering services based on its national interest.

The principle of National Treatment relates to treating one's own nationals and foreigners equally. In services, it implies that once a Foreign Service provider has been allowed to provide a service in one country there should be no discrimination between Foreign Service supplier and the national/local service provider. For example, if a foreign group is allowed to set-up a hospital in India, it should be given the same treatment that is given to national/local health service providers in the country. This means that they may have to be given all the facilities like the subsidies a national institution is entitled to. Since the public health system is already starving for funds this provision can further take away the meagre government funds they receive. In this situation the easier option for the government would be to withdraw subsidy altogether from public sector.

A Balance Sheet

GATS aims to increase the global trade in services with progressive liberalization. An increase in trade in health services offers a handful of developing countries a limited set of export opportunities, predominantly in attracting foreign consumers to their health facilities and in sending their own health professionals abroad. Yet these gains look trivial when compared with the effects, which increased, trade in health services could have on people's right to health. While there may be individual cases in which patients benefit from the development of telemedicine, the potential impacts of increased trade in health services are overwhelmingly negative. If developing countries divert health care resources and personnel towards foreign consumers for the sake of balance of payment gains, whether in their own health facilities or abroad, it can only lead to increased pressure on health systems which in most countries are already overstretched.

Attracting foreign investment in the health, water and sanitation sectors may initially seem like a more promising option. Yet the commercial presence of private sector companies is unable to address the central problems of access and quality, which challenge health, water and sanitation systems across the world. Instead of adding extra capacity to beleaguered public services, the private sector threatens to undermine them by taking over the most profitable parts of the system and drawing key personnel away from the public sector. In addition, it threatens to increase existing inequalities, given that the poor are commonly excluded from services provided on a commercial basis.

Trade in health services, then, risks exacerbating many of the problems, which already plague health systems across the world. The main thrust of GATS towards increasing trade and greater liberalization seems inappropriate for the health sector and the damage may outweigh the benefits, particularly for those with little ability to pay more for publicly provided health care.

GATS provides the countries the flexibility to manage trade in health services in ways that are consistent with national health policy objectives. The countries can choose to make commitments only in some sectors and can set the limits as required to deal with various policy concerns. But both the novelty of the concept and the concerns about appropriate regulatory enforcement have caused member not to undertake commitments with ease.Only about 88 countries have made specific commitments on medical, health-related, and social and health-related services including medical and dental services, veterinary services, services of nurses and mid-wives, hospitals services, other human health services and health insurance. In the case of Europe, only 12 countries have initially made commitments and additionally, the EU itself has made commitments on behalf of the 12 members who had been EU members prior to Australia, Finland and Sweden joining the Union.

The health care sector, one of the most rapidly growing sectors in the world economy, has brought in new kinds of healthcare organizations, systems and methods of health services. Globalization of health services is reflected in the emergence of new kinds of healthcare organizations over the past decade and in the emergence of cross-border delivery of health services through movements of consumers, personnel and services. Globalization or liberalization of international trade within the context of multilateral international trade agreements such as GATS (General Agreement on Trade and Services) and TRIPS (Trade Related Aspects of Intellectual

Property Rights), have not been well anticipated and prepared for, and as a result in many countries like India have impeded efforts towards improving equity in access to health care. Making the free movement of health personnel to and from other countries possible through GATS, might accentuate the present imbalance of human resources for health, especially those needed for rural areas, thereby affecting the access to health care by the poor. With the prices of pharmaceuticals increasing considerably in many developing countries due to the TRIPS becoming effective, the already scarce health resources in many such countries have been strained.

Providing basic services for all requires strong government regulation and a proper understanding of where liberalization may be beneficial, and where it may not, is of special concern in the case of health services, where the market-based model of competition threatens the integrity of health systems themselves. Health is a human right and a public good whose positive externalities cannot be captured through market mechanisms. Even in countries where the public sector already faces competition from domestic private hospitals, the additional challenge of hospital services provided by foreign private sector health providers exerts extra pressure on public health systems, which are already under severe strain. For those patients who can afford them, high-tech foreign hospitals may offer an unparalleled level of health service. They also offer medical personnel an opportunity to practice their profession in the most modern and fulfilling environment, and often at far higher rates of pay. For the vast majority who are unable to afford the high costs of foreign private sector health care, the promise of 'increased choice' as a result of liberalizations becomes therefore a hollow one. Rural communities in particular, risk seeing their access to health care undermined by the expansion of the private sector, as foreign hospitals draw away their remaining doctors, nurses and mid-wives to serve the urban elite. By attracting the most experienced staff and the most affluent patients away from the public sector, expansion of the private sector undermines the integrity of the health system as a whole. As WHO affirmed in its World Health Report, 2000, leaving the public sector to provide services only to the poorest and most needy patients undermines the possibility of cross-subsidization and risk pooling on which sustainable health systems are based.

The financing of health systems faces a similar challenge from GATS liberalization. National health insurance systems can be seriously undermined by such liberalization, as competition from foreign providers threatens the sustainability of programmes designed to spread costs across society and provide affordable health care for all. This is because WTO agreements are designed to bind liberalization commitments for the future so as to give foreign investors increased security—even if this means exposing vulnerable communities and their children to increased levels of risk. Many commentators see this 'lock-in' mechanism as the most dangerous aspect of GATS, since it closes down the possibility of reversing excessive or damaging liberalization in the future

Migration and health are inter-related in a number of ways. The movement of human populations can obviously promote the spread of diseases, and place migrants in positions where their health suffers. However, migration may be a form of livelihood diversification and so ill health may deny some individuals the opportunity to migrate. For example, remittances generated by migration may be critical in promoting access to essential treatment and drugs. This may also promote health-seeking behaviour and the spread of knowledge of health and technology. In addition to the establishment of hospitals, clinics or insurance offices, trade in services also covers the movement of individual people to provide services abroad. In the case of health services, this 'trade' takes place when doctors, dentists, nurses, mid-wives or other health personnel move to other countries in order to practice there.

V. CONCLUSIONS

The expansion of trade liberalization poses sericus challenges to people's right to health. While some people may benefit from the increased economic opportunities which globalization brings, many more stand to remain marginalized from its gains. Communities whose food security is undermined by exposure to international markets are directly at risk from increased trade liberalization, and measures need be taken to protect their livelihoods, as the risk is most for the most vulnerable and poor in society. Increased international trade in health services may offer meagre economic benefits to a handful of developing countries. Diverting resources and personnel towards foreign consumers threatens to put extra pressure on health systems, which in many countries are already at breaking point. The commercial presence of transnational health corporations risks exacerbating existing problems of equity, quality and capacity. Given the low level of regulatory capacity in many countries, increased foreign investment in the health sector may well be a potential danger. Within just 10 years of its adoption, the General Agreement on Trade in Services (GATS) has become one of the most controversial elements of the international trading system. More and more countries are becoming aware of the threat posed by the scope of the GATS agreement, and there is a growing call for governments to defend essential services from the GATS liberalization agenda. GATS poses threats to health services themselves, including the potential for increased inequity, fragmentation of health systems and further marginalisation of the public sector as a result of the increased mercerization of health care. The health risks, which come with liberalization of other service sectors such as water and insurance, pose challenge to national health regulations from current negotiations at the WTO. For a poor country like India with very poor health services, and weak regulatory mechanisms, committing the health services to GATS, would be immiserizing.

3

Health and Development—Survey of Literature

I. HEALTH AND DEVELOPMENT

Health is not just an attribute of individuals; it is also a reflection of the social environment in which an individual experiences life. How a society values and understands health will determine in great part how the individuals in society experience health. Even more, it will determine what society and individuals can do about health, how health will be measured and how the society's medical care services will be evaluated.

There are certain measurement requirements that are necessary in order to both assess the health status of a population and to ascertain the relations of health services to outcomes in health status. The measures must be relevant to the phenomenon under assessment of health status, and they should also be relevant to the health problems of the society. Our health status measurement strategies have mainly focused on these latter criteria of relevance-relevant to the health problems of society that is death, disease, disorder, dysfunction, discomfort and dissatisfaction. The importance of health in its own right cannot be overstressed. Good health consistently ranked as the number one desire of men and women around the world. The wisdom of every culture also teaches that 'health is wealth' in a more instrumental sense as well. For individuals and families, health brings the capacity for personal development and economic security in the future.

According to W.H.O. conference (1987), by 2000 every one should enjoy 'a level of health that will permit them to lead a socially and economically productive life'. Achieving this goal would require economic and social development, as well as action within the health sector. The declaration views better health as a 'most important world-wide social goal'. Health is essential to building strong societies, with improved health leading to social development, improved quality of life and conditions more conducive to world peace. The importance of a socially-based understanding of health—with health having social determinants, social impacts and social remedies—is advanced by recent research.

Health, in other words, is thought to be influenced by relative income, suggesting that levels of health can be regarded as a signal of the socio-economic development within which people live, as well as to how rich or poor as society is on average. Inequality can affect health through a variety of social factors, such as access of life opportunities, levels of social cohesion and psychosocial explanations, such as hopelessness, lack of control, isolation, and chronic stress (Kawachi, *et. al.*, 1999). Poor health, in turn, further contributes to these social factors, draining social capital and creating conditions where sections of a society become trapped in a cycle of self-reinforcing social exclusion. On a macro level, health is a major cornerstone of economic development, while at the micro-level, health is essential to ensure that people can achieve a more 'economically productive life'. Increasingly, research is showing that a healthy population is an engine for economic growth. This new thinking supplements and to a certain extent re-aligns, the traditional justifications of spending on health, which were rooted in humanitarian and equity arguments.

The classical view of the relationship between health and economic development is that wealth leads to health, with health an output of the development process. This view is supported by the broad correlation between average GDP and life expectancy at the national level. There is little evidence that periods of rapid health improvement follow periods of high income growth (Bloom and Canning, 2001). The higher a country's average income per capita, the more likely its people are to live long and healthy lives. Of course, this effect tapers off as income rises: a doubling of income per capita (adjusted for purchasing power parity) from, say, $ 1,000 in 1990 corresponds to a gain of eleven years in life expectancy, whereas a doubling from $ 4,000 is matched by a gain of only four years (World Development Report, 1993). Income growth has more impact in poor populations because additional resources buy basic necessities, particularly food and shelter, which yield especially large health benefits. Because poverty has a powerful influence on health, it is not just income per capita that is relevant; the distribution of income and the number of people in poverty matter as well. In industrial countries life expectancy depends much more on income distribution than on income per capita. Research has also highlighted the importance of health improvements to human development; better health itself contributes to economic growth. Indeed, while economic growth is not essential for health, health may be crucial for economic growth. Numerous studies have demonstrated that healthier the people the more productive they are. The role of health, education, and experience in the form of human capital in fostering economic development is well recognized in the growth literature. Human capital has been identified not only as the key determinant of growth and poverty alleviation, but as critical for human development in general (Squire (1993), Ravallion and Chen (1997), and Schultz (1999)). The growing focus on the Millennium Development Goals (MDGs) has further highlighted the importance of making tangible progress in indicators of human capital measured on the basis of key education, nutrition and health indicators.

Conceptually, a healthy person can not only work more effectively and efficiently but also devote more time to productive activities. Based on micro-economic evidence,

Strauss and Thomas (1998) argue that health explains the variations in wages at least as much as education. Research at the macro level can better capture the potential externalities of health sector interventions, and the existing studies are supportive of the positive contribution of health capital to growth. Bloom and Canning (2003) and Gyimah-Brempong and Wilson (2004) found that health capital indicators positively influence aggregate output. They found that about 22 to 30 percent of the growth rate is attributed to health capital and improvements in health conditions equivalent to one more year of life expectancy are associated with higher GDP growth of up to 4 percentage points per year. Cross-country studies have demonstrated that reductions in adult mortality accounted for 10 to 15 percent of economic growth between 1960 and 1990. (Jamison, *et. al.*, 2006).

In developing countries, the number of people in poverty is especially an important reason for differences in health. One study looked at twenty-two developing countries with comparable data on poverty (defined as the share of the population consuming less than $1 a day at 1985 purchasing power parity prices) and found that variation in the prevalence of poverty and in per capita public spending on health is important in explaining cross-country variation in life expectancy. Differences in income per capita became unimportant once these two factors were taken into account. This does not mean that income growth is irrelevant to increased life expectancy; rather, its main effect lies in how much it reduces poverty and supports public health services. In the twenty-two countries, roughly one-third of the effect of economic growth on life expectancy came through poverty reduction and the remaining two-thirds through increased public spending on health. In Sri Lanka, an increase in per capita public spending on health was twenty-two times more effective in reducing infant mortality than was the same increase in average income (World Development Report, 1993).

Improvements in health set off a demographic transition from high to low fertility and mortality. However, the lag between decline in mortality and fertility results in a 'baby-boom' generation, which can kick start a period of economic growth as it enters the workforce. This effect is called the demographic dividend and its realization is heavily reliant on policies that allow extra workers to be absorbed into the workforce (Bloom, *et. al.*, 2002a). Healthy children attend more school and are better able to learn when in a school. Nutritional deficiencies, infectious diseases, disabilities, reproductive problems, injury, poisoning and substance abuse all have measurable effects on learning (Ruger, *et. al.*, 2001). Most importantly, lower mortality provides greater security that investment in a child's education will not go waste and rising life expectancies offer a longer horizon over which to recoup the benefits of investments in education, thus acting as a fundamental driver of economic growth and human development. Healthy people expect to live longer and are more likely to save for retirement, increasing the amount of investment available to the domestic economy (Bloom, *et. al.*, 2002). The Human Development Index, introduced in 1990 by Mahbub ul Haq and colleagues, reflects achievements in 'the most basic human capabilities leading a long life, being knowledgeable and enjoying a decent standard of living (UNDP, 1990)'.

Good health, as people know from their own experience, is a crucial part of well-being, but spending on health can also be justified on purely economic grounds. Improved health contributes to economic growth in four ways: it reduces production loses caused by worker illness; it permits the use of natural resources that had been totally or nearly inaccessible because of disease; it increase the enrolment of children in school and increases their learning and it frees resources for alternative uses that would otherwise have to be spent on treating illness. The economic gains are relatively greater for poor people, who are typically most handicapped by ill health and who stand to gain the most from the development of underutilized natural resources.

Non income inequalities matter as well. Discrimination by gender and ethnicity in the allocation of public spending for education and health or in the operation of education and health facilities can lead to differences in education and health achievements. Cross-country studies have also identified geographic factors, ethnic fragmentation, and especially female educational attainment as important in explaining differences in health outcomes at a given income (US Census Bureau, 1999). Finally, the quality and quantity of public spending matter as well, though the size of the impact on poor people depends greatly on supportive policies and institutions.

The empirical literature has not shed much light on the link between public spending and health outcomes. Earlier studies (Musgrove in 1996) find no evidence that total spending on health has any impact on child mortality. Filmer and Pritchett (1999) find that government health expenditures account for less than one-seventh of one percent of the variation in under-five mortality across countries, although the result was not statistically significant. They conclude that 95 percent of the variation in under-five mortality can be explained by factors such as the country's per capita income, female educational attainment, and choice of religion. Finally, using a model similar to that of Filmer and Pritchett, Wagstaff and Claeson (2004) showed more recently that good policies and institutions (as measured by the World Bank's Country Policy and Institutional Assessment or CPIA Index) are important determinants of the impact of government health expenditures on outcomes. In particular, as the quality of policies and Institutions improves (as the CPIA Index rises), the impact of government health expenditures on maternal mortality, underweight children under age five, and tuberculosis mortality also increases and is statistically significant. However, the impact of government expenditures on under-five mortality remains not significantly different from zero.

There are evidences that growth depends on education and life expectancy, particularly at lower incomes. For example, it has been shown that female literacy and girls' education are good for overall economic growth (Hammer and Naschoed, 1999; Mcgee, 1999). Evidence is also available about the negative association between rapid population growth and per capita GDP growth and that the changing age structure of the population can also affect growth (World Bank, 2000a).

There is strong evidence that better health and education outcomes contribute to faster economic growth. Across countries, and across individuals within countries, there are strong correlations between health and education outcomes and income. Richer countries and richer individuals within countries have lower rates of mortality and malnutrition (Liu, Haiso and Eggleston, 1999). Within and between counties both the quantity and the quality of education improve with income-although quality is difficult to measure (Vella, 1997). Disparities in educational attainment also decline with income.

Furthermore, many studies concentrated essentially on education, and has often focused on the impact of the initial stock of education capital on growth. Among these, Levine and Renelt (1992), Mankiw and others (1992), Barro and Sala-i-Martin (1995), Barro (1996a and 1996b), and Sala-i-Martin (1997) find a positive relationship between enrolment and/or schooling and growth. Also, using a more refined measure on skills, Coulombe and others (2004) find that a country with literacy scores 1 percent higher than the average, experiences an increase in per capita GDP growth of 1.5 percentage points.

Benhabib and Spiegel (1994) and Pritchett and Summers (1996), however, find that some macro-economic evidence conflicts with the findings at the micro-economic level on the returns to education and conclude that the positive link between education attainment and output growth is, at best, weak.

The strong correlations reflect reinforcing causal effects form higher income to better health and education outcomes-and from better health and education to higher income. For individuals, this is not surprising. Ill health and malnutrition reduces productivity and time spent working, effects that vary with the level of education. Conversely, individuals with higher incomes can better afford to invest in health and education (Filmer, 1999). Many studies document the positive effects of parental education on children's health and education. Similar patterns hold for countries, with positive effects of higher per capita income on infant mortality (World Bank, 1998). Other studies have documented the benefits of lower mortality for faster growth, with most of the growth payoff at low levels of income (World Bank, 2000).

Moreover, there is some evidence that these relationships are not linear, with stronger increases in health associated with growth in poorer countries and regions. Fairly small differences in economic growth rates can thus have large impacts on human development outcomes in such countries. One study estimated that had growth rates in the developing world (excluding China and India) been as high as in the 1980s as they re in the 1960s and 1970s, 656,000 deaths could have been averted during the 1980s among children under five (Paschatiopoulos and Patrinos, 1994).

Alongside the intrinsic importance of health as a dimension of welfare, poor health can directly influence individual's opportunities—his or her earning capacity, performance at school, ability to care for children, participation in community activities, and so on. This important instrumental function of health implies that inequalities in the health outcomes often translate into inequalities in other dimensions of welfare. And these inequalities are reproduced over time. Education is of great intrinsic importance when assessing inequalities of opportunity. It is also an important determinant of individuals' income, health (and that of their children), and capacity to interact and communicate with others. Inequalities in education thus contribute to inequalities in other important dimensions of well being.

The other important aspect of health is nutrition. Without nutritious food there will be no health. So nutrition also plays an important role in a country's economic development. The subject of nutrition is not only of theoretical interest but it has tremendous importance in practical life. It may, however, be remembered that this problem is not a new one. It is infact as old as the civilization itself. The quantity and quality of food available determine in an important way, the physical and mental health and well-being of the nation. Until World War-I, the discussion of balanced food, that is, food rich in essential nutrients was discussed. Since a wide awareness has emerged of the role that nutrition plays in promoting the work efficiency of the individual on one hand and the economic development on the other.

In simplest terms, science of nutrition has been expressed as the science of nourishing the body properly or as the one concerned with analysis of the effect of food on living organisms. Yudkin (1969) defines 'Nutrition as the relationship between man and his food which includes psychological, biochemical, social and physiological aspects. And, the term food embraces those substances, which are taken into the body to support growth, maintains body functions, repair or replace tissue and provide energy.' Robinson (1965) says, 'Nutrition is the science of foods, the nutrients and other substances there in, there action, interaction and balance in relationship to health and disease, the process by which the organism ingests, digests, absorbs and utilize nutrients and disposes of their end products.' Health has been defined by WHO as the 'state of complete physical, mental and social well-beings and not merely the absence of disease or infirmity.' What is more important for us is that 'in addition nutrition must be concerned with social, economic, cultural and psychological implications of food and eatings'. There may be so many other definitions but all imply that nutrition is science of nutrients, which are the constituents in food that must be supplied to the body in suitable amount. In brief, we find that along with biochemical and physiological aspects, social and economic dimensions too are inherent in nutrition.

Malnutrition remains a formidable global development challenge. Worldwide, more than 180 million children under age five—nearly one in three—are stunted. Malnutrition is implicated in half of all child deaths and is a major contributor to child ill health and cognitive underdevelopment (Schroeder, 2001). About 1 billion adults in developing countries are underweight, and an estimated 1.6 billion are anemic. They suffer from lower resistance to infection, impaired work capacity, and reduced economic productivity (Horton, 2002). In addition, fetal malnutrition threatens survival, growth, and development in childhood—and increases the risk of chronic diseases later in life (Allen and Gillespie, 2001). Although nutrition has improved steadily in most developing countries, progress has been slow. In South Asia, the high rates of child malnutrition are declining only sluggishly, while in East Africa malnutrition has increased (ACC/SCN, 2000). The vast majority of countries have not met the goal-set at the 1990 World Summit for Children—of halving the prevalence of underweight children under age five by 2000. Unless action against malnutrition is intensified, 140 million preschool children nearly one in five—will be malnourished in the year 2020 (Smith and Haddad, 2000). Beyond its serious direct consequences, malnutrition may also limit further reductions in infant and child morality (Pelletier and Frongillo, 2003). Malnutrition is both a cause and manifestation of poverty. It also represents a violation of the fundamental right to adequate food, health and care as enshrined in international human rights declarations and conventions. Thus addressing malnutrition is both a developing and ethical imperative. Simply put, the Millennium Development Goals for poverty, education, and health cannot be reached unless global malnutrition is addressed.

The causes and effects of malnutrition can be easily understood by the arguments given by Sparton (1976). According to him poverty causes malnutrition, high fertility, poor infrastructure, i.e. poor water supply, sanitation and housing. Poor infrastructure and high fertility cause ill health which further causes high child mortality. He concludes that malnutrition is both the cause and the affect of ill health.

Measuring resource flows for nutrition is difficult. Yet, by any reasonable standard, nutrition spending is clearly inadequate—both nationally and internationally when judged against the magnitude of the problem that it addresses. The limited resources invested in nutrition translate to low coverage and intensity, and in turn have a low impact.

The initiative, adopted at the 1995 World Summit for Social Development in Copenhagen, urged industrialized nations to devote at least 20 percent of their aid budgets to basic social services, including nutrition, primary education, safe water supply, and reproductive health care. Few countries achieve this target. Moreover, although aid for health has grown, little goes to nutrition. Member countries of the Development Assistance Committee (DAC) of the Organization for Economic Cooperation and Development (OECD) have increased their aid allocations for health by about 3 percent a year in real terms since 1975, from a few hundred million dollars a year to $ 3.5 billion today. The share for health has also increased, from about 4 percent in the early 1990s to around 7 percent of total aid in 2000 (GECD, 2000). Nonetheless, DAC countries direct only 10 percent of their aid for health to basic health care, the component that includes nutrition. For multilateral aid, this share is 8 percent. The amount actually spent on nutrition is minimal. To actually improve the health and nutritional status of people in developing countries, donors would need to increase the aid available for country-level health and nutrition-related programs substantially over the next few years (WHO 2001).

The initiative asked developing nations to commit about 20 percent of their national budgets to basic social services. Few are meeting this target. A 1999 survey by United Nations Children's Fund (UNICEF) and the United Nations Development Programme (UNDP) found that only three countries in Africa namely Namibia (30 percent), Mali (23 percent), and Kenya (20 percent) were doing so. (1999) In India, for example, spending for direct nutrition activities by the central and state governments amounted to less than 0.2 percent of GDP during the 1990s and India is a country where one child in two is malnourished. Even if budgeted, it is not certain that funds are actually available, much less that they go to community-based programmes effective in improving nutrition. Gender disparities in educational attainment are especially pronounced in poor countries. In the Indian state of Kerala—which has a long history of equitable gender relations—education and mortality differed little between men and women. But in such states as Uttar Pradesh—where gender discrimination is high—the female literacy rate is less than half the male rate and the female to male ratio in the population is a disturbing 87.9 to 100 (Gragnolati, 1999).

Malnutrition increases the risk of illness and death; it impairs physical and mental development; and therefore it reduces the productive capacity of individuals. Because of its effect on productivity, a high rate of malnutrition reduces the potential of national economies to grow. Simply stated, this is the understanding that drives development agencies to invest in programs to combat malnutrition. Beyond this, malnutrition and ill health are synergistic, so that both malnutrition and illness can be seen as components of any measure of human well-being. Agencies whose primary concern is human welfare, therefore invest in improved nutrition for its own sake and for its effects on other direct measures of welfare: healthy development and longer healthier life.

The basic understanding of malnutrition as a force affecting survival, health, and productive capacity has persisted for 50 years, though the emphasis has shifted as research has contributed to a greater understanding of the precise ways in which malnutrition—both protein energy malnutrition (PEM) and specific micronutrient deficiencies—affects individuals, their households, and the larger economy. Specifically, as research has elucidated the effects of specific micronutrients, there has been a shift in focus from a concern with general lack of food (PEM due to poverty) to efforts to address individual micronutrients deficiencies, sometimes through interventions such as micronutrients supplements or food fortification that do not address household food supply or individual food consumption. At its most general, though, the basic underlying narrative linking nutrition with health and productivity has not been fundamentally changed; rather, it has been strengthened as evidence has mounted concerning the connections between nutritional status and human capacities.

Of course, human capacity is also a determinant of nutritional status. An individual's productive capacity determines, to some extent, his or her command over resources (that is, over income); and to a large extent, an individual's income determines the household's ability to obtain adequate food, live in a healthy environment, and even to obtain the education that may guide the choice of health-promoting behaviors.

The causal connections between nutrition and health and productivity are clear and relatively direct. Children who are well nourished grow bigger and stronger, and as adults they have a higher capacity for work and output. Their cognitive capacity—ability to learn, remember, and perform complex tasks—is also greater. Well-nourished children are more resistant to disease; when they are infected, severity and duration of illness are short, and the children are less likely to die. Children who are healthy and energetic are able to learn better, both in school and through active play; better learning capacity and school absence due to illness affect their likelihood of completing formal education. Adults whose food intake is adequate are generally more productive in work than those whose intake is insufficient. Moreover, malnutrition is the result of a complex of factors reflected in the UNICEF framework of food, health, and care, and food, to be effective in reducing malnutrition rates, must be provided, if at all, in the context of interventions that addresses the other aspects of nutrition problem. Adequate incomes and effective health-promoting practices are both essential to ensuring good nutritional status of poor populations. These two concerns are united in the relatively recent concept of household food security, which includes three components: availability of food (in the market or through home production), access to food through adequate income or productive resources, and use of food, which includes growth and preparation of food to maintain nutrient quality; second, allocation of food among individuals within households; and third, the ability of individuals to make biological use of the food, and reflection of their illness status and activity level.

Conference on nutrition and development in 1971 provided an opportunity for senior nutrition and development professionals to interact with academics studying the relationship of nutrition to economic development. This focus on nutrition as an input to development was advanced further with the 1973 publication of The Nutrition Factor by Berg (1973), a publication whose preparation was used strategically to advance the idea that nutrition was an essential input into economic growth. Professor Robert Fogel, whose seminal studies have elucidated the relationship between body size and food supply, had shown it to be critical for long-term labour productivity (Fogel 1991). The secular declines in mortality that have been observed over the past 200 years in Europe have been importantly boosted by the increased availability of calories in the diet, as well as by advances in public health and medical technologies. Fogel states "the increase in the amount of calories available for work over the past 200 years must have made a non-trivial contribution to the growth rate of the per capita income of countries such as France and Great Britain." The economic costs of avoidable disease, when taken together, are staggeringly high. Disease reduces annual incomes of society, the lifetime incomes of individuals, and prospects for economic growth.

In the 1970s and 1980s, Amartya Sen's work on famine and entitlements received considerable attention in the development community. Sen focused on the importance of entitlements in ensuring food adequacy. He made a persuasive case that income distribution and poverty alleviation must be explicitly considered in economic policy if adequate nutrition is to be ensured and contributed to the shift in focus from economic growth *per se* to growth with equity. According to Reutlinger and Selowsky (1976), relying on economic growth alone to ensure dietary adequacy among the poor would take an unreasonable amount of time. With a focus on poverty alleviation came an explicit commitment within the World Bank to address basic human needs, including health.

II. REVIEW OF LITERATURE

According to Wilson, Fisher and Fuqua (1971) nutrition is the Science of nourishing the body. Nutrient substances for this purpose are provided by food. An individual's nutritional status is dependent on the provision of sufficient nutrient substances and the good utilization of these nutrients. Poor status of nutrient may be caused by eating food that is inadequate in amount or kind or it may be caused by failure in digestion and the utilization of these nutrients. The individual's selection of food is influenced by many factors, such as the habits of his family and associates, his religion, where he lives, and his attitude as to the appropriateness of the substance for use as food. Some of the benefits of good nutrition are readily recognized. Good pasture, from muscle, and abundant vitality are the results of an adequate diet over period of time. A good diet helps to ensure more vitality in health. It is bulwark against illness and essential in recovery from illness.

According to Aggarwal (1977), persistent high fertility causes important health problems not only because economic improvements which are essential for good health get restricted, but also because it posed an immediate health problem for the mother and the child. In most of the developing countries married women, aged between 17-37, are characterized by continuous nutritional drain from repeated pregnancies and lactation resulting in material depletion and measured risk of maternal mortality, which increases with every pregnancy beyond the third. Study concludes that in recent years there has been a growing concern about the widening gap between population growth and food supply in developing countries, in view of rapid population growth. Available food supplies are inadequate in nutritive quantity for a healthy and active life. Retarded development and poor health are responsible for low stamina and low physical activity. Low physical activity results in low productivity, which in turn causes more poverty and more inadequate food supply. Unless this vicious circle is broken, future generations will have reduced stature, lower body weights, lower level of physical capacity and consequently reduced working efficiency.

The study on 'Global Strategy for Health for all by the year 2002' conducted by World Health Organization (1981) shows that nearly 1000 million people are trapped in vicious circle of poverty, malnutrition, disease and despair that saps their energy and reduces their work capacity. Study states that most deaths in many developing countries result from infections and parasitic diseases. Literacy is of major importance for health because it enables people to understand their health problems and ways of solving them. Study highlighted that in many countries the health personnel are not appropriately trained for the tasks they are expected to perform. The proportion of GNP spent on health ranges from far less than 1% in many developing countries. Empirical evidence regarding world health and socio economic situation is presented by means of a number of indicators like infant mortality rate, life expectancy, adult literacy rate, coverage of safe water supply and per capita public expenditure on health.

According to Teresa (1982) there is a close interactive relationship between health and level of income. The attainment of a higher income level affords an individual to have access to better health. He may not necessarily choose to maximize his health status but he at least has the means to attain improved health. Differences in mortality rates among rich and poor countries are paralleled by differences in diseases patterns. In the early stages of development, infectious and parasitic diseases coupled with malnutrition predominate, affecting infants and children. As income level, environmental conditions and life styles change, problem of infectious diseases and malnutrition are contained and non-infectious diseases such as diseases of the circulatory system emerge as principle causes of illness and death, affecting children less and adults more. Study concludes that improved health relates to income level not only as an outcome of improved living condition but also as an input to income generation itself. Together with education, health is the most significant form of investment in human capital that can be made, and improvement in productivity generally follow improvements in health status.

Musgrove (1983) uses data collected from several household surveys in six Latin American countries between 1966 and 1975, to investigate how the availability of public services and the way they are provided and paid for appear to affect family expenditures. The study compares family health spending versus total family spending, by Income Quartile, in ten South American cities. An analysis of household income to private health pending shows constant elasticity. Moreover, at any level of total spending, rural families spend the most on health care, families in small and medium sized cities spend less and households in the largest urban areas spend the least. The study shows that regional differences are significant because spending is higher in some regions than other regions. It is observed that expenditure on drugs tends towards saturation, irrespective of region and location. Spending is higher in metropolitan or other urban areas, but at low levels in rural areas.

Grand (1987) demonstrated the relevance and importance of applying some of the techniques of inequality measurement developed in the income distribution literature to the problem of international comparisons of health inequality. Moreover, he has shown that techniques do not rely on the vagaries of classification systems and are easier to apply to this task than measures of health inequality being relied on. However, study emphasized that, they do not answer the same kinds of questions and therefore should be viewed as complement to them, not as a substitute.

Berlarge and Terncedeive (1988) classified countries on·the basis of country characteristics using cluster and factor analysis. The results of the study are in particular, compared with the categorization of the countries into least developed countries (LLDCs) and of newly industrialized countries (NICs) by international agencies. The study concludes that the LLDCs clearly emerge as a separate group from the analysis but some countries presently included do not belong to this group, while some countries not included have LLDC characteristics. The NICs do not emerge as a separate homogenous group. Study observed that criteria presently used for NICs are quite narrow as there is pragmatism in the selection of criteria and arbitrariness in determining the critical values for each of them. They observed that cluster and factor analysis have the advantage that many variables can be included in order to make the selection procedure more general and there is no need to establish an arbitrary demarcation of time for each variables.

Wagstaff, Paci and Doorslaer (1991) in their paper "On the measurement of inequalities in health" offers a critical appraisal of the various methods employed to measure inequalities in health. The main objectives of this study are to provide a critical review of the various measures of inequality that have been employed in the literature on inequalities in health and to identify which of these measures are best suited for measuring health inequality. The author has identified six measures of inequality: the range, the Gini coefficient and the associated Lorenz curve, a pseudo Gini coefficient, the index of similarity, the slope index of inequality, and the concentration index. It is pointed out that only the slope index of inequality and the concentration index meet the minimal requirements of an inequality measure in this context; that it reflects the socio-economic dimension to inequalities in health; that it reflect the experiences of this entire population rather than social classes, and that it may be sensitive to the changes in the distribution of the population across socio-economic groups. The other objective of the study is to illustrate the importance of having a reliable measure of inequality in comparative studies of inequalities in health. In several cases, the authors find that the use of concentration index leads to quite different conclusions concerning the extent of inequalities in health.

Grifin (1992) in his study entitled, "Current Health Conditions: World Comparisons"examines the health and population outcomes, the intermediate outputs, physical inputs and expenditure in comparing the performance and activity levels of different countries and regions. The comparisons are made in both the current state of these variables and changes in them. The study indicates that the progress in improving health and reducing population growth rates has been strong in Asia over the last 20 years. Asia is not exceptional; the same could be the case of Latin America and Europe, the Middle-East, and North Africa. Small differences in regional averages for most outcome measures, despite large differences in spending and inputs for these three regions, suggest that there are many different methods that can achieve similar results. Africa lags behind the other regions and is the outlier for every measure. Study found that there is large percentage improvement in health outcomes in industrial countries during the last 20 years despite the high levels of good health they had already achieved by 1965. Continued improvement in health outcomes in industrial countries is consistent with the notion of decreasing returns to additional spending on health care because the improvement has been purchased at extra ordinary cost.

Ravallion (1997) in his study entitled "Good and Bad Growth: The Human Development Reports" examines the human development reports' (HDRs) main messages concerning economic growth. His study is concerned about both the analytics, and the rhetoric of the human development reports. The impact of these reports has clearly come from both, and they are not always in agreement. Study begin by examining what these reports say about the objective of development, after which it looks at the measure they use for assessing progress in attaining that objective. This is followed by an assessment of their views on economic growth. The study observed that the HDRs are right that there is no guarantee that economic growth will benefit the large numbers of people in the world who lack the access to market and non-market goods needed to lead enjoyable and fulfilling lives. The benefits of growth might be fully captured by those for whom that access is already assured (of which there are many people, even in poor countries). The HDRs are also right by saying that there are ways for poor countries, to promote human development. The study concludes that these observations, however, should not deflect attention from the fact that economic growth typically does reduce absolute poverty and promote human development. There have been exceptions. Growth has helped more, under some country circumstances than others and there are policies, which can make it more pro-poor, some of which may come with little or no growth cost. But arguably the biggest problem facing the world's poor today is not "low-quality growth" but too little growth of even quite normal quality.

Schultz (1997) examines how household survey data from individuals on child health, nutrition, child schooling, anthropometrics, fertility, wage rates and other sources of income and household expenditure can be usefully combined with regional data for the residential area on pubic expenditure on human resources programs. These merged data provide a flexible basis for assessing the success of human resource programs to help individuals increase their health and productivity and families to cope with the challenges of economic and demographic change in the low-income world. Nutrition programs may be evaluated by comparing the productivity of individuals who have benefited from a program to the productivity of smaller individuals who have not benefited. To perform such an evaluation a model of the demand for several distinct forms of human capital may be required which include how public agencies and private firms work with households to produce human capital and of how these investments increase the productivity of individuals. An integrated wage function with endogenous human capital might then be estimated that provide policy-makers with a tool for simulating the private and social returns to nutrition.

Bidani and Matin Ravallion (1997) try to address two questions; Are the poor less healthy? And does public health and spending matter more to them? A random coefficients model was estimated, regressing aggregate life expectancy and infant/parental mortality rates across 35 countries against data on the distribution of consumption per person, allowing for differential impacts of public health spending and primary schooling. The results suggest that those living under $ 2 per day can expect to live nine years less on an average than the rest, and that their children are fifty percent more likely to die before their birthday. Thus the incidence of consumption poverty is an important determinant of aggregate health outcomes. Cross-country differences in public health spending and primary school enrolment also matter, though for more to explaining the cross-country differences in health status of the poor than of the non-poor. The better-off appear to be protected from those differences, presumably because they are in a better position to substitute private for public health spending. This finding reinforces efforts to protect public spending on basic health and education during times of fiscal contraction; not doing so could entail large costs to poor people.

Thomas and Strauss (1997) examine low different dimensions of health affect the wages of men and women in urban Brazil. According to the study, height has a large and significant effect on wages, i.e. taller men and women earn more. Study used four distinct measures, height, body mass index, per capita calories intake and per capita protein intake for representing health. Study found that in Urban Brazil, height is clearly an important determinant of wages of men and also of those women who work in the market sector. Body mass is a significant positive predictor of male wages, even after controlling for height and nutrient intakes, and these impact are generally larger among the less educated. This suggests that body mass is important in a particular types of work. For women, body mass is only related to wages for the least educated. Per capita calories and protein intakes are also significantly related to wages of both men and women who work in the market sector. This is true even after holding height and BMI constant. The positive effect of calories disappears rapidly, with calories being important only for the very malnourished. With calories constant protein intakes do positively influence wages, more so at higher levels of intake. This probably represents an effect of diet quality of which protein and its quality is an important dimension. If the assumptions of the empirical model are correct, then taking these results together, the evidence suggests that health yields a substantial return in the formal sector of Brazilian labour markets. Different dimension of health affect wages differentially, and a nutritional part of the impact of education on wages appears to operate through these measures of health.

Osmani and Bhargava (1998) examines the quality of health and nutrition in emerging Asia. The objective is to assess the likely prospects for the early 21st century and identify the policy responses that may become necessary to meet new challenges or to deal with the persistent ones. The study begins by assessing past achievements and failures in the areas of health and nutrition in Asia in comparison with the rest of the world, and then analyzes the differentials that exist within Asia—differentials between sexes, between urban and rural location, and between countries. Some simple models are then developed to explain inter country differences in health outcomes. Among the persistent problems, the study highlights the excessive incidence of malnutrition in south asia. Among the emerging problems, special attention is given to the general problem of "overlapping health transition" and the specific problems of smoking-related diseases and a potential AIDS epidemic. The study concludes by drawing out a number of policy implications.

Prescott (1998) analyses how differences in physical and intangible capital can account for the large international income difference that characterize the world economy today. Study finds that savings rate differences are of minor importance, what is important is total factor productivity (TFP). Besides, the study presents industry evidence that TFP differ. across countries. Study accounts for the differences in TFP that arise for reasons other than growth in stock of technical knowledge. Study tries to find answer to the question: Why are total factor productivities different? One reason for the factor is the strength of the resistance to the adoption of new technologies and to the efficient use of currently operating technologies and this resistance depends upon the policy arrangement a society employs. What is needed is a theory of how arrangement affects total factor productivity. Once there is a successful theory of total factor productivity, the next level of theorizing is to explain why a society chooses the arrangement it has. The author lays emphasis on the importance of the effectiveness of resistance to the use of better technologies in understanding economic development.

Mason, Hunt, Parker and Jonsson (1999) observes that child malnutrition is pervasive and persistent in Asia, and at present rates it will take decades to halve the prevalence—a goal common to many national plans. Nutrition-oriented programs are familiar in most countries, but have far too low coverage and resources, which is wasteful as well as ineffective. A massive expansion of community-based programs is feasible, with well-established activities (usually including support to:

antenatal care, breastfeeding, caring practices including complementary feeding, growth monitoring, access to health care). Study suggests that networks of local workers, ensuring individual contact with families, are the essential feature. Micro-nutrient deficiency control programs must also be expanded towards universal coverage. Context is crucial to success, important examples being women's status, social exclusion, political commitment, community organizations, and literacy, and the policies should be directed at improving these. Assessing and building local capacity, and resolving certain generic issues, are early priorities.

World Health Organization (2000) provides an overview of selected aspects of the reproductive and sexual health of women in the countries of South-East Asian region. This study examines the key components of reproductive behavior that effect women's reproductive and sexual health. These include the ages at which the sexual activity and reproduction begin, levels and trends in fertility over the past decades and adolescent pregnancy and child bearing. Study found that every country in the region has witnessed a steady decline in fertility levels over the past two or three decades. Higher proportion of births to women below 20 years is not necessarily associated with high total fertility rates. Contraceptive prevalence rates (CPR) among married women in the 15-49 year age group vary widely among countries. Study points out that the gap between the total fertility rate and the total wanted fertility indicates the average level of unwanted or unplanned child bearing prevailing in a particular setting.

Seguino (2000) investigates whether gendered outcomes in labour markets and education have macro-economic effects and in particular, whether gender inequality affects the rate of economic growth. Study indicates that across-countries there is a positive link between gender wage inequality and growth via both channels. In particular, the evidence is consistent with the argument that gender inequality stimulates investment, but also enhances the productivity. The author stresses that while cross-country regressions can highlight some useful factors that are statistically correlated with economic growth, a richer understanding of the dynamics of growth at the country level it needed and require an investigation of institutional structures.

His research results show that gender inequality is a casual factor in investment and economic growth for the semi-industrialized countries in the sample used in the study. Moreover, there is little evidence to suggest that gender inequality has dissipated to any marked degree even in the most successful of these countries. One might even question whether supporting this strategy in its current form as on gender inequality can successfully lead to a more equitable distribution of labour and resources over time. Further, study states that future research might consider alternative macro-economic strategies and policies that can raise productivity and material well being. But international factors clearly play an influential role as well, suggesting that the scope of analysis must also be enlarged to consider how global trading system and its institutions might be transformed to make gender equity re achievable during the process of growth.

Bhargava, Jamison, Lau and Murray (2001) in their paper investigate the effects of health indicators such as Adult Survival Rates (ASR) on GDP growth rates at five year intervals in several countries. Panel data were analyzed on GDP series based on purchasing power adjustments and on exchange rates. First, they developed a framework for modeling the inter-relationship between GDP growth rates and explanatory variables by re-examining the life expectancy-income relationship. Second, models for growth rates were estimated taking into account the interaction between adult survival rates and lagged GDP level-issues of endogeneity and reverse causality were addressed. Lastly, they computed confidence intervals for the effect of adult survival rates on growth rate and applied a test for parameter stability. The results showed positive effects of adult survival rates on GDP growth rates in low income countries.

The link between nutrition and morbidity in developing countries is another important issue that needs serious attention. This is important since improvement in nutrition status ultimately manifest in better health status, especially for diseases directly related to poor nutrition. According to the study improvement in nutritional status is a formidable challenge, but a more challenging task is to convert it into an instrument for improving health status in developing countries.

It requires not only an effective integration of nutritional care with public health care and education programmers, but also a policy shield for increasing security and safety of food. Bloom, Canning and Sevilla (2001) examine economic growth by the growth of factor inputs, technological innovation, and technological diffusion. They extend production function models of economic growth to account for two additional variables that micro economists have identified as fundamental components of human capital-work experience and health. Their result, consistent with their theoretical argument and with the microeconomic evidence, is that health has a positive sizable and statistically significant effect on economic growth. They found that a one-year improvement in a population's life expectancy contributes to an increase of 4 percent in output. This is a relatively large effect, indicating that increased expenditures on improving health might be justified purely on the grounds of their impact on labour productivity. They found no evidence that the macro-economic effects of education and experience are greater than those found in micro-economic studies. This suggests the absence of externalities at the aggregate level and calibration studies provide reasonable picture of the proximate sources of economic growth. They found little variation across countries in average work experience, thus differentials in work experience account for little variation in rates of economic growth. Finally, they found that the effects of average schooling on national output are consistent with micro economic estimates of the effects of individual schooling on earnings, suggesting that education creates no discernible externalities. A fully specified model of economic growth would be multidimensional, showing not only how inputs and technology affect output, but also how the growth rates of inputs and their productivity are themselves determined.

Bloom, Canning and Sevilla (2001a) examine whether population growth restricts, promotes, or is independent of economic growth. All of these explanations, however, focus on population size and growth. In recent years, however, the debate has under-emphasized a critical issue, the age structure of the population (that is, the way in which the population is distributed across different age group), which can change dramatically as the population grows. Because people's economic behavior varies at different stages of life, changes in a country's age structure can have significant effects on its economic performance. Nations with a high proportion of children are likely to devote a high proportion of resources to their care, which tends to depress the pace of economic growth. By contrast, if most of a nation's population falls within the working ages, the added productivity of this group can produce a "demographic dividend" of economic growth, assuming that policies to take advantage of this are in place. In fact, the combined effect of this large working-age population and health, family, labour, financial, and human capital policies can create virtuous cycles of wealth creation. And if a large proportion of a nation's population consists of the elderly, the effects can be similar to those of a very young population. A large share of resources is needed by a relatively less productive segment of the population, which likewise can inhibit economic growth. After tracing the history of theories of the effects of population growth, this study reviews evidence on the relevance of changes in age structure for economic growth. It also examines the relationship between population change and economic development in particular regions of the world: East Asia; Japan; OECD, North America and Western Europe; South-central and Southeast Asia; Latin America; Middle-East and North Africa; Sub-Saharan Africa; and Eastern Europe and the former Soviet Union. Finally, they find that reduced fertility and increased working-age population have contributed to economic growth in some areas of the developing world.

Dolan and Olsey (2001) aims, first, to develop a framework within which to discuss different types of equity-efficiency trade-off within the domain of health and second to find the extent to which a person's health is the result of previous benefits from care is a morally relevant attribute to this trade-off. Study shows that the distribution of the benefits from health care can be analyzed according to four different of health. According to them, the sole objective of health policy was to maximize gains. However, there is evidence that the no-treatment health profile is important to policy-makers. And recently, economists and others have focused attention on the level of health that people have experienced prior to the point at which a prioritization decision is made. Study discusses these considerations simultaneously rather than in isolation of another. In doing so, it appears to them that the relevant literature today has overlooked the importance of identifying the health frontier. They feel that it would be wrong to have a general principle that gave less weight to the future health gains of people whose previous gains were the results of 'own actions'. They also think that it would be wrong to 'blame' someone for their previous actions if their current actions are different, since the lessons learned from a past 'mistake' cannot be expected to have much impact upon a different 'mistakes' now. Whatever the conclusion others may reach regarding these issues, the framework study developed, provides a background against which these issues, can be discussed. It might also serve to enhance the understanding of factors that policy-makers take into account when making resource allocation decisions. Finally ,their conceptual framework highlights possible ways in which future empirical research into equity-efficiency trade-off could be conducted.

Peter (2001) in his study entitled "Health Equity and Social Justice" outlined an approach to health enquiry that proceeds indirectly and embeds health equity within the general pursuit of social justice. Building on Rawls' theory of justice as fairness, the study argued that social inequalities in health are unjust or inequitable if they result from an unjust basic structure of society, i.e. a basic structure that imposes sacrifices to the worse-off only to benefit the already better-off groups. Study observes that to be able to form a judgment on social inequalities in health, one needs an understanding of the underlying causes. At the same time, information about these important information are needed to assess the justice of social arrangements. Understanding the effects the basic structure has, on people's prospects of health, may help us to decide whether or not these institutions ensure the social bases for self-respect for everybody. Study concludes that while justice as fairness cannot offer a complete blueprint of what a just society would look like, it certainly provides a framework for thinking about issues related to social justice.

Zon and Muysken (2001) presented a simple model of endogenous growth based on the Lucas (1988) model in which a good health functions as necessary condition for people to be able to provide labour services. At the same time, health is produced under conditions of decreasing returns, whereas human capital is produced under conditions of increasing returns. Study found that health is a pure complement to growth, and any re-allocation of labour from health sector towards human capital accumulation activities would cause a decline in growth. Research found that, since the steady-state growth rate rises linearly in the average health-level of the population, the productivity of the health sector is as important determinant of growth as the productivity of the human capital accumulation process itself. They arrived at the conclusion that there may be circumstances regarding the provision of health-services and life expectancy, in which it may be hard for growth to take place at all. Aid meant to improve the productivity of the health sector or the net availability of human capital resources for non-health activities in the poorest developing countries, could actually lead to growth taking off on its own. Growth can even become self-sustaining if the rate of discounts falls and the intertemporal elasticity of substitution rises in the face of structural gains in life expectancy.

Bloom, Canning and Sevilla (2002) in their study, analyse the effect of the growth of factor inputs, technological innovation and technological diffusion on economic growth. They found no evidence that the macro-economic effects of capital accumulation and schooling are any greater to those found in micro studies. Study suggests the absence of externalities at the aggregate level and observes that calibration studies based on micro economic evidence on private returns provide reasonable pictures of the proximate resources of economic growth. They also found evidence of conditional convergence in the growth data, but their framework allows them to interpret this specifically as evidence of technological diffusion. The fact that they found no externalities puts the emphasis in explaining cross-country differences in income levels on how and why total factor productivity (TFP) varies across counties. Their results suggest that steady state TFP varies systematically across-country with their geography : this steady state level, through technological diffusion, is quite slow.

Thorbecke and Charumiling (2002) observed that income inequality is of fundamental interest not only to economists, but also to other social scientists. A substantial literature in economics and the social science has investigated the relationship between income inequality and economic growth and a variety of social phenomena. The link between inequality and economic growth are explored as well as those between inequality and such key social variables as political conflict, education, health and crime. The analysis of their study follows a two-step process. First, a review of the empirical evidence relating inequality to growth and to each of the above social variables is undertaken. Second, the various causal mechanisms that have been proposed in the social science literature to explain those links are surveyed.

Wagstaff (2002) in his study tries to quantify the trade-off between the health costs of rising incomes against the health benefits. Results show that reducing income inequality and raising the share of health expenditure financed publicly might reduce health inequalities, but neither effect is at all strong and nor is statistically significant. Study found that economic growth tends to increase health inequalities. Countries that are successful in raising their per capita incomes will typically pay a price in terms of higher health inequalities. Another finding of the study is that the countries with the lowest average rates of under-five mortality and malnutrition have the largest gaps between poor and non-poor children. Evidence from trends in health inequalities show that health inequalities have tended to grow both in developing and developed countries at times of economic growth. The study suggests that this is probably due to technological change going hand-in-hand with economic growth, and a tendency for the better-off to assimilate technology ahead of the poor.

Anne, Darran and Christina (2002) observed that the positive association between health and income in adulthood has antecedent in childhood. Study found that a family's long run average income is a powerful determinant of children's health status. The results highlight the role of chronic conditions in the relationship between income and health. It is likely that parents with high income are better able to manage chronic health problems. As regards the implications of poor health in childhood, in addition to the direct welfare and financial costs of illness, poor childhood health results in lower levels of human capital accumulation. Less healthy children spend more days in bed and miss more schools. Poor children also arrive at the doorstep of adulthood with lower health status and with less education.

Bommier and Stecklov (2002) analysed the reasons, why the classical welfare foundation of income inequality analysis fails to provide a framework for health inequality analysis. The study evaluates the appropriateness of the classical social welfare (SW) approach to the development of a conceptual definition of health inequality. Several measurement and ethical criticism to the analysis of health inequality that reduces the desirability of the classical approach. The SW approach treats income and health as comparable variables—an important drawback in terms of ethical considerations. The authors propose a alternative approach which appears to be more closely linked to the World Health Organization (WHO) concept of equity in health and is also consistent with the principles espoused by them. This concept is closely related to be concentration curve as soon as it is assumed that health and income are positively related. The criterion presented in their study 'does an important theoretical foundation for empirical analysis using the concentration curve. Besides, the authors have provided an additional measure, which is theoretically more appealing, but further study is needed in order to determine its relevance in empirical research on health inequality.

Anand (2003) highlighted the use of social choice and welfare theory in health economics by developing and applying the 'integration of claims framework' to healthcare rationing. Related to Sen's critique of neo-classical welfare economics, the claims framework recognizes three primitive sources of claim consequences, deontology and procedure. Taxonomy was presented with the aid of which it is shown that social welfare functions reflecting these claims individually or together, be specified. Some of the resulting social choice rules can be regarded as generalizations of health-maximization and all have normative justifications, though the justification may not be universally acceptable. The study shows how non-linear programming can be used to operationalise such choice rules and illustrates their differential impacts on the optimal provision of health-care. The study concludes that the integration of claims provides a viable framework for modelling health-care rationing, is technically rigorous, general and tractable, as well as is consistent with the moral considerations and citizen preferences.

Barro and Lee (2003) presents a data set on educational attainment for the population over age 15 and over age 25 at five-year intervals between 1960 and 2000 for number of countries. The data provide the distribution of education attainment of the population at seven levels of schooling and show a breakdown by sex. The data set provided by them is improved data set on educational attainment and will continue to contribute to empirical research in many areas. Their data set have been widely used to 'get the effects on economic growth of educational attainment, measured by years of schooling as well as by the composition of attainment at various levels of health and so on. The data set has also been useful for studying the linkage across countries between education and other important economic and social variables, such as fertility, income inequality, and political freedom. It will be very useful in improving international measures of human capital. International test scores of students at the primary and secondary levels provide useful information on the quality of education. The study also shows that it would also be possible to study further the effects of human capital on economic performance and to see how these effects interact with the level of economic development.

Wildman (2003) developed a framework to analyse the impact of the distribution of income on individual health and health inequality, with individual health modeled as a function of income and the distribution of income. It was demonstrated that the impact of inequality could generate non-concave health production functions resulting in a non-concave health production possibility frontier. In this context, the impact of different policies are considered and its is argued that if the distribution of income affects individual health, any policy aimed at equalizing health, which does not account for inequality, will lead to unequal distributions of health.

Meer, Douglas and Harvey (2003) found that causal links between health and economic resources have long concerned social scientists. They use four waves of the Panel Study of Income Dynamic (PSID) to analyze the impact of wealth upon an individual's health status. The difficulty in approaching this task that has bedeviled previous studies is that wealth may be endogenous; a priori, it is just as likely that in health affect wealth and *vice versa.* They argue that inheritance is a suitable instrument for the change in wealth, and implement a straightforward instrumental variables strategy to deal with this problem. Their results suggest that the causal relationship running from wealth to health may not be as strong as it first appears. In the data, wealth exerts a positive and statistically significant effect on health status, but it is very small in magnitude. Instrumental variables estimation leaves the point estimate approximately the same, but renders it insignificantly different from zero. And even when the point estimate is increased by twice its standard error (S.E.), the quantitative effect is that the wealth-health connection is not driven by short-run changes in wealth.

Pradhan, Sahn and Younger (2003) explored the global inequality in health status decomposed it into within and between country inequalities. The authors rely on standardize height as health indicator since it avoids the measurement pitfalls of more traditional measures of health such as morbidity, mortality and life expectancy. The results show that within country variation is the source of most inequality rather than the difference between countries. The reason why results on health inequality differ so dramatically from income inequality is that relationship between income and health is a strongly concave function, which implies that as income, improves from low levels, the associated improvements in health tipper-off quickly.

Savedoff (2003) has identified at least four different approaches for answering the question of "how much" a country should spend on health. These four approaches ranges from rough comparisons with other countries to a full budgeting framework. In general, the peer pressure approach is the easiest to quantify but probably the least informative. The political economy approach focuses attention on the process of political decision-making but is least likely to produce a quantitative estimate of requirements. It will probably take years before a satisfactory and robust health production function can be estimated with the precision required for policy analysis. Only the budget approach appears to be both feasible and quantifiable, although it requires directly confronting the current and desired health status, prices, effectiveness, and tradeoffs. According to author, fundamentally there is no shortcut.

Martens and Huynen (2003) examines the health dimensions and socio-cultural, economic, and ecological determinants of health in existing global scenario studies. Not even half of the 31 scenarios reviewed gave a good description of future health developments and the different scenario studies did not handle health with consistency. Most of the global driving forces of health are addressed adequately in the selected scenarios, however, and it therefore would have been possible to describe the future developments in health as an outcome of these multiple driving forces. To examine how future wealth can be incorporated in existing scenarios, we liked the socio cultural, economic and environmental developments described in three sets of scenarios i.e. special report on emission scenarios (SRES), global environment outlook-3 (GEO3) and world water scenarios (WWS) to three potential, but imaginary, health futures. The paper offers useful insights into how to deal with future health scenarios and shows how comprehensive picture of future health evolves when all important driving forces and pressures are taken into account.

Alison and Foster (2004) in their study found that objective data on individuals are often unavailable or incomplete, especially for populations with very low mortality. Their study made use of self-reported health status (SRHS) data, which record people's own perceptions of their health status. SRHS has been shown to be a strong indictor of objective health outcomes and indicators, including mortality. Nevertheless, the qualitative or categorical nature of SRHS data prevents the straightforward use of traditional tools of distributional analysis such as the Lorenz curve, in evaluating inequality. The study presents a methodology for evaluating inequality, where the data are qualitative rather than quantitative in nature. A partial inequality ordering is defined to indicate when a distribution is more "spread out" than another, a second partial ordering (first order dominance) is used to indicate when the overall health level rises. Both are applicable to qualitative data, such as SRHS, in that results do not depend on the numerical scaling assigned to the categories. The approach is illustrated by data from the National Health Interview Survey (NHIS), State Data Files for using on the distribution of SRHS within states.

Asada and Ohkusa (2004) observed that research conducted over the past decade has increasingly focused on health inequality. The goals of improving the health of a population are now often expressed as the increase in the average level of health and the in health inequality as clearly specified in the Healthy People 2010 and the World Health Report 2000. Using a nationally representative sample of the 1989 and of the Japanese Comprehensive Survey of Living Conditions of the People and Welfare (CSLC), the study examines the average health-related quality of life and its distribution. The study departs from previous health inequality analyses in the following two ways-construction of a measure of HRQL in the CSLC and its relation to health inequality analysis, and inclusion of the dead in health inequality analying a cross-sectional survey. It found that between 1989 and 1998, the average HRQL in Japan slightly reduced its inequality by income slightly, and inequality measured by Gini-coefficient slightly increased. Women's HRQL was almost always lower than men's, except in earlier ages. Younger than 10 years old Health Related Quality of Life (HRQL) was more unequally distributed among women than men and in older ages. The result shows that the success in the improvement in the length of life in Japan did not always coincide with the improvement in HRQL and provides a future population health research.

Baldalli, Clements, Gupta and Cui (2004) in their study the finds that number of policy interventions could be effective in moving countries' Millennium Development Goals (MDGs). Study found that education spending have a positive and significant direct impact on accumulation of health capital and a positive and significant indirect impact on growth. Study reveals that an increase in education spending of 1 percentage point of GDP is associated with 3 more years of schooling on average and a total increase in growth of 15 years. Similarly, an increase in health spending of 1 associated with an increase of

0.6 percentage points in the under-five child survival rate and a rise of 0.5 percentage point in annual per capita GDP growth. Furthermore, the study found that there is significant time lag between increases in education spending and the realization of their full effects on social indicators and growth. Two-thirds of the direct impact of education spending is felt within five years, but the full impact materializes with a significant time lag of to 15 years. Study suggests that such a lag needs to be kept in mind when designing policy interventions. According to the study, the impact of health spending, however, is immediate. The positive effects of both education and health spending are strongly influenced by the quality of governance. In countries suffering from poor governance, the positive effects increased spending on education are reduced and those of higher health spending can be completely negated. Study includes that there are substantial difference in the effects of social spending on social indicators and growth among different country groups. The positive effects are the highest in low-income countries and sub-Saharan Africa. This supports the view that social spending can be more effective in such countries in achieving MDGs, as the marginal returns to social spending tend to decline for countries high levels of social outlays.

Banerjee, Deaton and Duflo (2004) discusses the report on delivery of health care and the impact it has on the health status of the largely poor population of the region. The reveals that the quality of public service is extremely low and that unqualified private providers amount for the bulk of health care provision. The low quality of public facilities has also had an adverse impact on the people's health. It is suggested that the state should take up the task of being the provider or regulator.

Bloom, Canning and Sevilla (2004) estimated a production function model of aggregate economic growth including two variables that have been identified as fundamental components of human capital, work experience and health. Study found that health has a positive and statistically significant effect on economic growth and is a lively large effect, indicating that increased expenditure on improved health might be justified purely on the grounds of their impact on labour productivity, quite apart from direct effect of improved health on welfare. Further study found that good health has positive, sizable and statistically significant effect on aggregate output. Furthermore, study revealed that the life expectancy's effect in growth regression appears to be a real labour productivity effect and is not the result of life expectancy acting as a proxy for worker experience. Study observed that in a fully specified model, life expectancy may influence life cycle savings and capital accumulation and the expected returns and investment in education. Furthermore, the study highlights that improvements in health may increase output not only through labour productivity, but also through the accumulation of capital. Study concludes that a fully specified model of economic growth would be dimensional, showing not only how inputs and technology affect output, but also the growth rates of inputs and their productivity are themselves determined.

Chen and Ravallion (2004) provided new estimate of the extent of poverty in the developing world. According to them, by the frugal $ 1 a day standard, there were 1.1 billion poor people in 2001—almost 400 million fewer than 20 years earlier. During the period the number of poor people declined by more than 400 million in China, half the decline was in the early 1980s and the number outside China rose slightly. The study found that there has been a marked bunching up of people living between $ 1 and $ 2 a day. It is found that sub-Saharan Africa has become the region with the highest incidence of extreme poverty and the greatest depth of poverty. If these trends continue, the 1990 aggregate $ 1 a day poverty rate may well be halved by 2015, meeting the millennium development goal, though only East and South Asia will reach this goal.

In order to know whether health system in the central government is misdirecting its efforts or is it badly designed, Das Gupta and Rani (2004) have used the framework of the essential Health Functions. The results indicate that the reported strengths of the system lies in having the capacity to carry out most of the public health functions. Analysis also shows that the health system in India has overlooked fundamental public health regulations and their enforcement. Besides this, deep management flaws hinder effective use of resources such as inadequate focus on evaluation, on assessing quality of services, openness to learning and innovation. Their study further points out that resources could also be much better used with small changes such as the use of incentives and funds and greater flexibility to reassign resources as priorities. Also the central government functions too much in isolation and needs to work more closely with other key factors such as private sector and sub-national governments. Study concludes that reassessment of priorities and better management practices would significantly improve health in India.

Musgrove (2004) states that the fundamental idea of equity is equal treatment for all the population. The objective should be to assure good health for all and this is to be pursued through preventive or curative treatment. Inequality results from differences in the ability to obtain health care that prevents some people and not others from getting medical assistance. The analysis clearly brings out that the physicians are very highly concentrated. Nurses on the other hand, are equally distributed and access to safe water still more. In general, the study shows that expensive resources seem to be more concentrated than cheaper ones, e.g. physicians versus nurses and sanitation *versus* water supply. It is pointed out that the relatively full assessment of equity must draw on population-based data and cannot be constructed only from the information available to ministry of health. The study points out the fact that given a baseline assessment of how equitable a system is and where its principal problems are, changes over time can give a good idea of whether the system is becoming more or less equitable.

Macinko, Shi and Starfield (2004) in their study assess the impact of health variables on the relationship between wage inequality and infant mortality in 19 countries over the period 1970-96. The data was derived from the OECD's world value surveys, and Luxemburg Income study and political economy databases. There are many potential conclusions suggested by the research. First, an alternative measure of inequality, offers several advantages over more commonly used LIS Gini-coefficient. These include the fact that the Theil index available for many more countries and years than the Gini; there is evidence that the Theil is based on more reliable data than are most Ginis; and the Theil is highly correlated with the Gini. At the same time, the Theil appears to exhibit other properties that make it particularly suitable for international comparisons such as the finding that it is not highly correlated with GDP per capita or with other commonly used economic measures. The second finding is that the Theil is associated with IMR within the sample of 19 wealthy OECD countries included in this analysis. This relationship holds even while controlling for the most powerful ecological predictor of infant mortality, GDP per capita. Another important finding is that health system components particularly equity of health care financing—significantly reduced the magnitude of the inequality measure. The study reiterates for the international evidence that suggests the improving aspects of the health care system may be one way to compensate for the negative effects of social inequalities on health outcomes. This policy response is likely be more amenable to decision makers than some of the other solutions to the problem of social inequalities, such as the redistributior of income through more progressive taxes.

Bloom (2005) in his study entitled "Public Health in Transition" explores the epidemiological transition of countries with rapidly expanding economies where chronic diseases are becoming the greatest challenge to health systems. In these countries, people are living longer and developing diseases such as obesity, diabetes and heart diseases, which occur more typically in developed nations like the United States. Bloom illustrates the economic benefits of using measures to prevent or reduce both infectious and chronic diseases. According to the study, although health threats often cross national boundaries, there is no global organization in place to develop and coordinate an integrated response to such threats. The study lists eight recommendations that, if implemented, would have significant impact on health around the world.

World Development Report (2006) observed that inequalities in incomes, in health and in educational outcomes have long been a stark fact of life in many developing countries. When such inequalities in outcomes arise from unequal opportunities, there are both intrinsic and instrumental grounds for concern. The report presents evidence on the inequality of opportunity, within and across-countries, and illustrates the mechanisms through which it impairs development. The Report advocates taking explicit account of equity in determining the development priorities: public action should aim to expand the opportunities of those who, in the absence of policy interventions, have the least resources, voice, and capabilities. Domestically, it makes the case for investing in people, expanding access to justice, land, and infrastructure, and promoting fairness in markets. Internationally, the Report considers the functioning of global markets and the rules that govern them, as well as the complementary provision of aid to help poor countries and poor people build greater endowments. Drawing on the World Bank's 60 years of development experience, the World Development Report, 2006 is essential reading for understanding how greater equity can reduce poverty, improve health, enhance economic growth, advance development, and deliver increased opportunities to the poorest groups in our societies.

III. STUDIES ON INDIA

Gandhi (2002) observed that most of the countries in the world including India and other countries in the South East Asia Region have recorded impressive gains in and development during the 20th century. The green revolution in India has increased the consumption of horticultural produces and leafy vegetables, which along the national programme of administering vitamin A as oil to young children, iron folio acid during pregnancy, after delivery and for pre school children, have reduced important micro-nutrient malnutrition. Despite overall movements in control of some communicable diseases, many are still deep rooted in country and are still the major causes of mortality. Health problems are arising due to rapid urbanization of environmental degradation. The nationwide health infrastructure and the on going national health programmes have failed to provide adequate and quality health care to meet the need of the population. Study suggests that effective health information system should be established. Good quality and adequate drugs, vaccines and equipment should be manufactured and made available at affordable prices. Balanced development of basic, clinical and problem-oriented health research be encouraged. So in order to meet the challenges of 21st century and to achieve the objectives of National Health Policy 2001, it is necessary that health should be attached higher priority on political and the development agenda.

Barun (2001) found that the poor nutrition remains a significant challenge to the developing world. Malnutrition seriously constrains people's ability to fulfil their potential, and significantly contributes to the morbidity status, and the challenge has indeed become a fundamental issue linked to overall development of the world. The global picture of nutritional status, as presented in the Fourth Report on the World Nutrition Situation, sends a signal in the new millennium. His study observed that on the one hand, prevalence of several malnutrition problems (such as stunting and under weight) has been showing declining trends in the last two decades, on the other, the size and gravity of the problem is still vast, and progress in most regions is all too slow. India is a good example of slow progress. Citing from the first National Family Health Survey (NFHS-I) in the early 1990s and the second (NFHS-II) in 1998-99, study points that there is little progress in basic nutritional indicators. Poor nutrition remains a significant contributor to morbidity and mortality in developing counties. There is a broad agreement that all other things remaining the same, a higher level of malnutrition could lead to higher burden on diseases in a society and *vice versa.* The extent of these diseases and their interaction with infection, make nutrition the single most important host factor underlying the health status of the world's population. The achievements of nutrition improvement programmes in developing nations are often influenced by a number of worldwide trends such as the increasing globalization of trade, rapid urbanization and the rapid spread of HIV/AIDS. The concept of chronic malnutrition is often used interchangeably with poverty and consequent food insecurity among a majority of the population. Higher income allows people to buy a more balanced diet, as well as better hygiene and reduced case.

Devadas (1977) in his study entitled 'Need for Nutrition Education' examines the India's food and nutrition problem. Nutrition education is a mean of translating nutritional requirements into food, and adjusting the food choices to satisfy nutritional, cultural, psychological and economical needs. Nutrition education is the process by which beliefs, attitudes, environmental influences and understandings about food are converted into practices which are nutritionally sound and consistent with an individual's needs, purchasing power, available food sources and socio-cultural background. The aims and objectives of nutrition education are to impart knowledge that enable people to make proper choice of food, keeping nutrition in mind. The general objectives of imparting nutrition/health education are to enable children and their caretakers understand that proper nutrition is essential for good health, normal physical and mental development. For this purpose, it is essential to have an understanding of the simple principles of good nutrition and basic food values and knowledge of locally available foods and their nutritive value.

Vijayaraghavan, *et. al.* (2000) examines the current diet and nutritional status. The objective of the study was to develop database on the diet and nutritional status of the elderly from different parts of the country to enable the government and NGOs to formulate policies and initiate strategies, which would contribute to the well being of elderly population. The results of the study indicate that the twentieth century has seen an unprecedented transition from high birth and death rates to low fertility and mortality rates, resulting in increased longevity. Thus aging of the population is one of the important developments of the 20th century during which there has been a considerable increase both in absolute and relative numbers of older people in both developed and developing countries. This new development could be attributed to decline in the mortality rates due to improved health care facilities, changed life styles and diversification of food habits. The study also indicated that the overall intake of various foods except cereals and mullets was less for males. Similarly, the average intake of all the nutrients except calcium and vitamin C was also less. The prevalence of chronic energy deficiency (CED) decreased over the period, with a concomitant increase in the prevalence of overweight among males and females. There is however a need to conduct comprehensive surveys including information on diet-related chronic diseases and behavioural aspects, in addition to diet and nutritional status.

Ghosh (2006) evaluates relative performance of fifteen major Indian states on human development, and examines the two-way nexus between economic growth and human development. Study addressed the issue of convergence and examined to what extent measures of human well-being alternative to real capita income are converging across the states. The estimates of cross-sectional growth regressions provide strong evidence of regional convergence in human development despite considerable divergence in real per capita income, indicating that the poor states that have failed to catch up with the rich ones in terms of per capita income have managed to catch up in terms of human development. The classification of the states based on their performance on human development and economic growth reveals that while only four states have been in the virtuous cycle category, as many as seven states have been in vicious cycle. The results suggested that the sequencing of policy should be such that the human development induced growth process has to be strengthened for lifting the states from the vicious to virtuous cycle category.

Barn, Rana, Imrana and Ritu (2000) throws light on the efficiency of the private sector in providing health services to the people. Study says that though it is assumed that private sector is more efficient and provides better quality care, it does not stand up to empirical scrutiny. According to the study, Delhi's private hospitals follow questionable management practices with regard to workers as well as patient care. Expenditure on wages in these hospitals are kept low through contractualisation of fourth class employees and by gradually undermining the established rights of permanent workers due to which over worked, ill trained and insecure workers are likely to make more mistakes and hide them too. Thus these private hospitals are having many loopholes like more emphasis on profit motive leading to cutting of costs which has a direct bearing on the quality of care, practice of discharging patients early in order to ensure quick turnover and increased intervention. Study concludes by saying that it is imperative for these hospitals to ensure certain minimum working conditions expected in all industries for the employees. State should have effective administrative mechanisms that will ensure that these private hospitals comply with conditionalities for receiving subsidies like quality and equity in the provision of services. Regulatory framework for medical care would certainly help in improving the performance or medical industry in health services delivery.

Randall and Gupta (2000) found that health expenditure in India as a percentage of its GDP is higher than the level in many underdeveloped countries in Asia and a greater part of this comes from the private sector. In other words, public sector expenditure on health care is rather under-funded and also suffers from quality and access problems resulting in higher dependence of consumers of the expensive private treatments. The main contention of the paper is that the higher financial burdens of consumers on account of health arise because of lack of or inadequate insurance to meet their health care expenditure. Study presents a comprehensive review of the existing pattern of health care financing while examining the diversity of financing methods currently in vogue in India. Their analysis of various schemes and policies towards meeting health care expenses for various segments of population suggests that the low income households engaged in informal economic activities have to shell out much more towards meeting their health care needs. It is this segment that goes uncovered by any health care plans and policies. According to the study even those covered by health care plans experience growing inefficiencies and low quality of services. Study suggests that besides revamping the public health care system there was an urgent need to restructure the existing schemes, including the mediclaim policies. The authors believe that there is an enormous potential for health care insurance that needs to be tapped through public and private initiatives.

Rao and Bhat (1991) in their paper "Estimation of A Community Health Status Index on the Basis of MIMIC Model" have presented a Multiple Indicators Multiple Causes (MIMC) model, which treats the health status of the community as an unobservable variable. On the basis of this model, a community health status index (CHSI) has been estimated for 15 states of India using cross-section data on health indicators and health causes separately for the year 1971 and 1981. The index used by him is very useful in ranking the states in terms of their health status and in monitoring their progress. The estimated values of the structural coefficients in the model throw light on the differential marginal impact of improvement in health causes on the CHSI and also on the different indicators.

Rao (2004) recognizes that health status is related to and determined by numerous factors such as per capita income, way of life, martial status, housing, sanitation, water supply, infrastructure, social organization, structure of the economy, nutrition, education, health services provided by the government, political and administrative set-up, geography, climate, religious beliefs etc. Study found that during 1986-99, the birth rate declined significantly by 10.10 percent while the death rate also climbed down from 9.9 percent. Another significant feature of health status is a significant fall in the infant mortality rate. Expansion and extension of health facilities to improve their accessibility and availability yielded positive results. The effective birth control programmes and family welfare efforts made by the government in the previous two decades forced the death rate downwards. The decline in the death rate indicates the improved standard of health facilities that control the deaths caused by communicable disease. However, the findings of the study that the stagnant or marginally negative infant mortality rate during 1990-2000, particularly in rural areas, is a matter of greater concern that needs to be addressed immediately. Though per capita income influenced the death rate to decline, the rate of decline was not significant. Perhaps, the present level of per capita income is the minimum required to cause a decline in death rate. Hence, a higher rate of per capita income seems to be necessary to bring down the death rate considerably in future, particularly in rural areas. The influence of per capita income and number of hospitals in Andhra Pradesh on the infant mortality rate, though not significant, is debatable. The rural-urban variations in the health status are significant. Higher rate of literacy, high of levels of per capita income, larger expenditure on public health, improved medical facilities both in the public and private sectors contributed to an improvement in the health status in urban areas. The inadequate and unsatisfactory health facilities available resulted in high rate of infant mortality in rural areas.

Sankar and Kathuria (2004) attempts to analyze the performance of rural public systems of 16 major states in India in improving the health indicators of their population. In order to measure performance, the study used techniques from the stochastic production function and panel data estimation using data for the period 1986-97. Efficiency of health programmes reflects not only whether health programmes and interventions are produced at the lowest possible cost (technical efficiency), but also whether the health system achieves the most within the given level of expenditure (sometimes called allocative efficiency in health economics literature). Both technical efficiency and allocative efficiency together give the economic efficiency of the health system. In this paper, they focus only on the technical efficiency aspect. The econometric estimation of the frontier is done from a sample of observed infrastructure and accessibility inputs and outputs from various provinces of India. The estimation is done in two stages. In the first stage, data on health inputs and outcome of the health inputs are employed to generate a vector of state-specific efficiency indices for each state using techniques from the stochastic production frontier and panel data. In the second stage, these efficiency indices are compared with the most efficient state (MES) to generate the relative efficiency of the states and then the paper looks into the factors determining the relative efficiency of the states. One of the most important findings of the paper is that health outcomes in the rural areas of Indian states is positively related to the level of health infrastructure in terms of access to facilities and availability of skilled professionals such as doctors. However, the efficiency of the health systems depends on the extent of education in the state. Secondly, unlike the aggregates, which are often deceptive, the disaggregated figures at the state level show disparities in terms of area coverage as well as population coverage, adding to the inefficient management of the rural health systems. States vary enormously in their levels of health outcomes such as mortality levels, and in particular, in the levels of infant mortality. States also differ in their levels of health system efficiencies, which result in varied health system performance. Differences in literacy levels (as revealed in the study) account for much of such variations. Income does not seem to be a possible explanatory variable in the regressions designed to estimate efficiency dispersion. It is important to note that contrary to the belief that all the so-called 'bimaru' states perform poorly, Bihar was not a badly performing state in the efficiency analysis. On the other hand, states like Tamil Nadu and Karnataka, which are believed to have improved their health indicators, showed poor efficiency in performance. It is also incorrect to say that the most efficient states do not have scope to improve further in health indicators. The performance of Kerala is better only in comparison with the other 15 states in the analysis, and though health attainment levels are high and comparable with other developed or developing countries, the efficiency/performance of the health systems need not be comparable with other countries of similar attainment levels. It is indeed revealing that literacy is the only non-health infrastructure-related variable that contributes to the dispersion of relative efficiencies across states and none of the income or expenditure related aspects. Based on the sign and significance level, it can be argued that as literacy level in the state increases, the relative efficiency of health systems also increases, and hence the variations across states get widened as well as the interlinkages between health and education outcomes.

The question of how to improve efficiency then becomes paramount and in view of resource limitations, it is important that the resources are used wisely and efficiently. Certainly reducing waste and inefficiency is one way, and choosing the appropriate mix of intervention is another important way. Increase in efficiency as well as providing more facilities implies that both qualitative and quantitative measures need to be taken for the health system performance to produce results. The analysis points to the existing variations across states in the health systems in rural areas to suggest that there are two critical measures to improve health outcomes. The first is to increase the efficiency of the health sector, that is, moving further to the frontier. The second is to create more health infrastructure and thus provide better access to rural health facilities and making more physicians available in rural areas. Thus it was found by Sankar and Kathuria that relative efficiencies differ across states and this is due to differences in not only in the health sector endowment, but also its efficient use. They argue that states should not only increase their investment in health sector, but also manage it efficiently to achieve better health outcomes.

Vani Borooah (July 2004) has used unit-record data on over 50,000 rural children for the year 1993-94, drawn from 16 major states of India to analyse the determinants of risks of severe stunting and of being severely underweight. Given the shockingly high incidence of undernourishment in India, the study uses anthropometric measures for each children to relate to the household circumstances of the children, including the quality of of the living conditions of the households, and the birth order of the children, the circumstances of the mothers including their literacy, quality of infrastructure in which children live, namely quality of water supply, and facilities of sanitation, availability of hospitals and mother-and-child centers like *anganwadis,* and the degree of food security that the childrens' households enjoy. His estimates of bivariate probit model provide the following conclusions, ceteris paribus: (a) The likelihood of being stunted and underweight was lower for girls than boys.; (b) The higher the birth order of a child, the greater the likelihood of it being stunted/underweight.; (c) Children living in female-headed households were less likely to be stunted/underweight than children living in male-headed households; (d) the later a child was introduced to solid foods, the greater the likelihood of it being stunted/underweight; on the other hand, the longer it was breast-fed, the smaller the likelihood of it being stunted/underweight.; (e) Household poverty had no significant effect on the likelihood of a child from that household being stunted, but it did significantly raise the likelihood of a child from that household being underweight.; (f) The size of a household's stock of food grains and its access to a fair price shop were inversely related to the likelihood of a child from that household being stunted, but neither variable had an effect on the likelihood of being underweight; (g) Poor housing conditions—in the sense of poor cooking conditions—affected the likelihood of being underweight but not the likelihood of being stunted; (h) Children from households with one, or more, empowered females, defined earlier, were less likely to be stunted and to be underweight than children from other households in India; (i) The greater the spacing of a mother's pregnancies, the more likely it would be that her children were stunted. This study is a small exception: even though data on the medical past of the mother is sketchy, the results are able to point to the importance of foetal malnutrition (caused by births following each other too closely) on child development.

Among these effects, there were three instances where the influence of a variable varied according to the literacy of the mother: (a) Although the likelihood of a child being stunted/underweight increased with its birth order, the effect of birth order on stunting, compared to a situation in which the mother was illiterate, was moderated when the mother was literate, though not when the mother was proximate literate; (b) The presence of *anganwadis* in a village and the easy access to hospital facilities both reduced the likelihood of stunting, even when the mothers were illiterate; however, the reduction in this likelihood, flowing from the presence of these facilities, was particularly marked when the mothers of the children were literate; (c) Easy access to hospitals only reduced the likelihood of children being underweight when their mothers were literate; the presence of village *anganwadis* only reduced the likelihood of children being underweight when their mothers were literate or proximate literate, the influence of literacy being stronger than that of proximate literacy.

Findings (b) and (c), above, are consistent with and, indeed, corroborate Caldwell's (1993) observation that, in the context of developing countries, three areas are of critical importance to a child's health. Firstly, an educated mother assumes the responsibility of taking a sick child to a health center: by extension, educated mothers, more than illiterate mothers, take advantage of the advice and information on child care and health available from *anganwadis*. Second, the time that mothers spend discussing their child's illness with a doctor is almost directly proportional to their level of education; in consequence, illiterate women (and their sick children) get much less out of visiting a doctor than do literate women. Lastly, when a currently prescribed course of treatment for a child proves to be ineffective, illiterate mothers, relative to literate mothers, are less inclined to report this to their doctor. Collectively, these observations imply that the effectiveness of health-care organizations to child health is enhanced when their services are complemented by mothers who are literate.

Govindaraj *et al.* (1997) looked into the factors governing health spending based on a cross-section of 106 countries from the whole world for 1990. A unique feature of their study was that it determined the determinants of public and private health expenditure (both expressed as a share of gross domestic product (GDP) separately. The public health expenditure regression showed that gross domestic product per capita and government consumption as a share of GDP have a positive significant impact. Socio-demographic factors, for e.g., proportion of urban population, literacy, average years of schooling, etc. and institutional factor like hospital beds per capita indicating infrastructure were found to be non-significant and hence dropped from the final model. Surprisingly, per capita income was found to have no significant impact on private expenditure on health. The share of the government in total GDP, average years of schooling and the dummy variable for oil producing countries exerted a negative significant impact while the infrastructure variable namely hospital beds per capita had a positive significant influence.

A majority of the studies, analysing the relationship between health care expenditure and income, have confined themselves to the developed countries, particularly OECD nations. However the question of link between income and health spending is of paramount importance for a developing country like India. Although there exists considerable variation among the states in India in terms of real per capita health spending, the degree to which this discrepancy can be explained by the differences in (real) per capita income of the states needs to be explored. One would envisage that as per capita income increases, the pressure on the state machinery to provide better and varied health services increases (for instance this may be due to increasing incidence of the so called "lifestyle" diseases such as diabetes, cancer and cardiovascular diseases) and the government is required (in face of its increased ability) to spend more to meet this demand. Testing of this phenomenon in the Indian scenario is the object of the paper by Anindita Chakrabarti and D.N. Rao (2005) who have examined the role played by income in determining the extent of fund allocated by Indian states for improvement of health of its population. Drawing data from the fourteen major states of India over a time span of twenty-three financial years (1974-75 to 1996-97) and using recent advances in panel data time series econometrics, they find the presence of a long-run relationship between income and health expenditure. The long-run elasticity estimates reiterate that publicly provided health services should be considered as "necessities". Results from the panel error correction model demonstrate that ageing of the population and proportion of rural population are the only non-income factors, which exert a significant positive impact on real per capita health expenditure. This is particularly important given the demographic transition that India is passing through.

Chakraborti and Rao (2005) have applied the available techniques to explore the nature of the two series namely real per capita health care expenditure (HCE) and real per capita state domestic product (SDP) before estimating the role played by the latter in determining the former. Although the existing literature acknowledges income as a predominant determinant of health expenditure (in most cases with elasticity greater than one), no such consensus could however be reached regarding the relationship between health spending and the non-income factors. Their study have explored the role played by the latter in explaining the variations in health expenditure across the major Indian states. The study comprises of fourteen major states of India and spans over twenty-three financial years starting from 1974-75 to 1996-97. They have included expenses on medical (medical relief, education and research, hospitals and dispensaries, etc.), public health (communicable disease control, primary health care centre, etc.), family welfare (family planning, maternal and child health, immunization) and water supply and sanitation. Figures on total expenditure on health (incorporating expenses on revenue and capital account) were taken from the various issues of Reserve Bank of India Bulletin. The data on state domestic product for the period of study were taken from the various issues of National Account Statistics, Central Statistical Organisation, Government of India. Both health care expenditure and state domestic product are measured in real (1960-61 price) per capita terms and in keeping with most of the aforementioned work expressed in natural logarithm. Summary statistics on the two series, namely real per capita health care expenditure (hereafter HCE) and real per capita state domestic product (hereafter SDP), are provided in Table 3.1, which throws light on the considerable discrepancy

TABLE 3.1
Descriptive Statistics on Real Per Capita Health Care Expenditure (HEX) and Real Per Capita State Domestic Product (SDP)

State	*Mean (HEX)*		*Mean (SDP)*		*Growth (HEX)*	*Growth (SDP)*
	1974-75 to 1985-86	*1986-87 to 1996-97*	*1974-75 to 1985-86*	*1986-87 to 1996-97*	*1986-87 to 1996-97*	*1986-87 to 1996-97*
(1)	(2)	(3)	(4)	(5)	(6)	(7)
Andhra Pradesh	5.60	7.04	350.29	446.63	0.03	0.02
Bihar	3.02	4.78	221.89	257.25	0.05	0.01
Gujarat	6.53	9.75	474.56	685.47	0.04	0.03
Haryana	7.27	10.61	527.11	767.94	0.04	0.03
Karnataka	5.90	9.62	416.93	586.72	0.04	0.03
Kerala	6.94	9.15	334.30	430.08	0.03	0.02
Madhya Pradesh	4.83	7.40	295.84	380.26	0.04	0.02
Maharashtra	7.27	9.37	553.10	798.27	0.03	0.03
Orissa	7.69	10.32	450.46	527.16	0.03	0.01
Punjab	7.34	10.88	653.64	917.31	0.03	0.03
Rajasthan	8.27	14.65	316.06	434.22	0.05	0.03
Tamil Nadu	7.41	11.47	426.38	613.15	0.04	0.03
Uttar Pradesh	3.31	5.56	269.68	345.36	0.05	0.02
West Bengal	6.10	8.11	446.54	578.10	0.03	0.02
Average	6.25	9.19	409.77	554.85	0.04	0.02

among the states with respect to both their income and pattern of public spending on health.

During the first half, i.e. 1974-75 to 1985-86 the average per capita health care expenditure (in 1960-61 prices) was as low as 3.02 for Bihar. On the higher side it varied between 7 and 8 for six of the fourteen major states. The range widened in the latter half of the study, i.e. 1986-87 to 1996-97. Bihar once again registered the lowest average HCE (4.78) while Rajasthan recorded a high of 14.65. The surprisingly high figure for Rajasthan is explained by its spending on water supply and sanitation. The imbalance amongst the states is particularly striking when we compare the per capita state domestic products expressed in 1960-61 prices (SDP). Over the period 1974-75 to 1985-86, the average SDP of states like Punjab (653.64) and Maharashtra (553.10) far surpassed that of Bihar (221.89) and Uttar Pradesh (269.68). The gap widened during the succeeding decade (1986-87 to 1996-97) with Bihar's mean SDP rising marginally to 257.25 while Punjab attaining a mean of 917.31. However, a common feature emerges when we compare the rate at which HCE and SDP has grown over the entire time span. For each of the states' public spending on health (captured by HCE) has grown at least as fast as its income (captured by SDP). In fact, apart from Punjab and Maharashtra all other states display a higher growth in HCE as compared to SDP.

In their paper, Chakraborti and Rao (2005) have tried to estimate the role played by income in determining the health expenditure variation across the major Indian States and in the process quantify the income elasticity of health expenditure. They have found both of the above-mentioned series to be non-stationary, not only in individual state-by-state analysis but also for the panel of fourteen states. Using recent developments in time series econometrics, they obtain that the real per capita public health expenditure and real per capita state domestic product are cointegrated in a panel context or in other words there exists a long-run equilibrium relationship between the two. In the short-run, the concerned variables are found to deviate from the equilibrium relationship because of external shocks. The FMOLS estimates reveal that in the absence of contemporaneous shock the long-run income elasticity is significantly greater than one. This is primarily because of the comparatively higher elasticity values for the BIMARU states *vis-a-vis* the other states. However, in the presence of time dummies public health expenditure is inelastic to changes in income for the fourteen major states on the whole and the BIMARU group in particular. This highlights the importance of including time specific effects while testing for non- stationarity and cointegration-an issue hitherto not addressed in the literature. Using the panel error correction mechanism ,they have also analysed the short-run dynamics and have tested for the significance of other non-income factors in determining the health care expenditure growth differentials across the Indian states, like the ageing of the population, and proportion of population residing in rural areas which are the only other factors found to have a significant positive impact. This is particularly important for the policy-makers in view of the demographic transition that India is going through.

Gita Sen, Aditi Iyer, Asha George (2002) presents preliminary results of an analysis of data sets on morbidity and health care utilisation from two NSS surveys in the 1980s and 1990s together with empirical results of other studies, which points the worsening of class-based inequalities in access to health services for both men and women. They argue that although morbidity in general, and particularly for poor men and possibly all women, is undercounted in the NSS surveys, and despite the fact that data by economic class and gender are incomplete, this comparison of two NSS Surveys shows some disturbing trends. Despite attempts to develop a wide ranging set of institutions and to provide a floor of basic services through the public system in order to meet the goals of affordable and accessible health care for all, the reality was rather different. Public health services were poor in terms of access and quality. As a result, by the 1980s the bulk of health expenditure was out-of-pocket, and a largely unregulated private sector in health was becoming increasingly dominant. Gender and class inequity in access and cost continued to be severe. Nevertheless the public sector, and especially public hospitals, did act to provide an important if inadequate alternative, especially for the poor. They have shown that by the mid-1990s, the private sector had become dominant in terms of both out-patient and in-patient services, and that the average cost of all care (and particularly of in-patient care) has gone up significantly. Although the extent of untreated morbidity overall appears to have declined, this may be partly a statistical artifact resulting from under counting of morbidity among the poor and declines in untreated morbidity among the rich. Untreated illness among the poor has clearly increased. Inequity by economic class appears to have worsened, and the divide between rich and poor in terms of untreated illness and expenditures on health services, as well in the use of both public and private health care institutions, has grown. Thus class-based inequalities in access to health services have clearly worsened for both men and women. While gender inequity, particularly in untreated morbidity, appears to have remained severe, also seen is a relative worsening of access for poor men over this period, even though in absolute terms men are better off than poor women.

Gupta, Parasuraman, Arokiasamy, Singh and, Lhungdim, (2006) presented preliminary findings from the Third National Family Health Survey, 2005-06 for the states of Chhattisgarh, Gujarat, Maharashtra, Orissa, and Punjab, from the National Family Health Survey (NFHS-3) to show that some health and family welfare indicators have improved markedly in the past seven years, while nutritional deficiencies remain a major challenge. The following is a summary of key findings from the five states.

Fertility and Family Planning

Overall, during the past 13 years, since NFHS-1, there has been continuous fertility decline among the five states. The states of Punjab and Maharashtra have reached the replacement level of fertility, i.e., around two children per woman. Women in Chhattisgarh, Gujarat, and Orissa are expected to have an average of about 2.5 children at current fertility rates. The urban areas of all the five states have reached below replacement level fertility. There is a difference of one child between the fertility of women with no education and those with 10 or more years of schooling. Consistent with decline in fertility, the use of contraceptive methods, particularly modern methods and that too of spacing methods is rising. The contraceptive prevalence rate shows that about two-thirds of women in Gujarat, Maharashtra, and Punjab are currently using some method of contraception, compared with half of women in Orissa and Chhattisgarh. Also contributing to decreasing fertility is a rise in the average age at marriage and the resulting increase in the average age at the time of the first birth. Since 1998-99, the median age of women at the time of their first birth has increased by about one year in Chhattisgarh and Maharashtra, increased by about half a year in Orissa and Gujarat, and remained about the same in Punjab. The fertility decline and increasing contraceptive use are the result of an increasing desire among women to limit their family size. At least three-quarters of women who currently have two children do not want any more children. Son preference remains a barrier to more rapid decline in fertility. Only about half of women with two daughters and no sons want to stop childbearing, as against 90 per cent with two sons and no daughter want to stop childbearing. However, from NFHS-1 to NFHS-3 there is a continuous increase in the proportion of women, with two daughters and no son, do not want to have any more children.

Maternal Health

According to NFHS-3, antenatal care (ANC) is almost universal in all five states, i.e., almost all pregnant women have at least one contact with health personnel. However, just one contact is not sufficient for effective health monitoring of pregnancy. The maternal and child health programme recommends minimum three antenatal visits during pregnancy period. Women received antenatal care at least three times during their pregnancies. There are also large urban-rural and education-wise differences in women receiving three ANC visits. Institutional births have been steadily increasing over time in all states except Chhattisgarh, where there has been only a slight increase in the last seven years. Only one out of every six children is born in medical institutions in Chhattisgarh, compared with two out of every three births in Maharashtra.

Child Survival and Child Health

The proportion of children who die in the first year of life has dropped substantially in the last seven years in all five states. The largest decline in the infant mortality rate has taken place in Punjab (26 per cent), Gujarat (21 per cent), and Orissa (20 per cent). The infant mortality rate in Orissa has declined by more than 40 per cent in the last 13 years. Nevertheless, 7 per cent of children in Orissa still die before reaching their first birthday. Impressive gains in immunisation coverage have been made in Chhattisgarh and Orissa. But in Maharashtra, Punjab and Gujarat, there has been a substantial deterioration in full immunisation coverage in the last seven years due to the decline in vaccination coverage for both DPT and polio. The urban-rural differences in full immunisation coverage are more pronounced in Chhattisgarh, Gujarat and Maharashtra. In all the five states, mother's education leads to increase in immunisation coverage. The full immunization coverage among children of mothers with 10 or more years of schooling is more than twice that of the immunization coverage among children of mothers with no education.

Nutrition and Anaemia

It is also revealed that many adults suffer from nutritional deficiencies. These five states are struggling with the dual burden of undernutrition accompanied by a substantial problem of overweight and obesity. More than 40 per cent of ever-married women and about one-third of ever-married men in Orissa and Chhattisgarh are thin for their height. In Gujarat and Maharashtra, one-third of women and 20-25 per cent of men are thin. Undernutrition is much lower in Punjab (only 12-14 per cent of women and men are too thin). Except Punjab, a larger proportion (above 40 per cent) of rural women and those with no education are thin. Obesity is emerging as a major problem in Punjab. Thirty-eight per cent of women and 30 per cent of men are overweight or obese. In urban areas of Punjab, close to half of women are overweight or obese.

In all five states, obesity is a growing problem. In the last seven years, the percentage of women who are overweight or obese has increased from 16 per cent to 20 per cent in Gujarat, from 12 per cent to 17 per cent in Maharashtra, from 30 per cent to 38 per cent in Punjab, and from 4 per cent to 7-8 per cent in Orissa and Chhattisgarh. In the urban areas and among women with 10 or more years of schooling, at least one in five women are overweight or obese. The extent of overweight and obesity is greater among women than men. There has been substantial improvement in the nutritional status of young children since 1998-99 in Orissa, Maharashtra and Chhattisgarh, but nutritional deficiencies are still widespread in these states (40-52 per cent of children are underweight). There has also been no improvement in nutritional status in the last seven years in Gujarat, where 47 per cent of children are underweight. Undernutrition is considerably lower in Punjab, but even in that state 27 per cent of young children are underweight. The extent of 10 percentage points among rural children compared to their urban counterparts. Except in Punjab, in all other four states more than 50 per cent of the children of women without any education are underweight. A related problem that is also due primarily to poor nutrition is the high level of anaemia in both adults and children. The percentage of ever-married women who have anaemia ranges from 38 per cent in Punjab to 63 per cent in Orissa. In each of the five states, anaemia prevalence among pregnant women is almost 5 percentage points higher than that among all women. A matter of serious concern is increasing anaemia prevalence among pregnant women in all five states, except Chhattisgarh, in the last seven years, and low coverage (less than 35 per cent) of consumption of iron and folic acid for 90 or more days during pregnancy. Men are much less likely than women to be anaemic, but anaemia level in men are still unacceptably high, ranging from 13 per cent in Punjab to 37 per cent in Orissa. The anaemia situation is most serious among young children age 6-35 months. NFHS-3 found that remarkably high and more women should receive postnatal care within two days, which can help prevent complications after childbirth, but the percentage actually receiving such care ranges from only 23 per cent in or less similar levels of anaemia prevalence in children in all five states. Moreover, except for Chhattisgarh, in the last seven years there has been little or no improvement in anaemia levels of young children.The prevalence of anaemia actually increased in Gujarat and Orissa during that period. A general pattern among the five states is that anaemia levels do not differ substantially by residence and education of the mother.

Knowledge of AIDS

Knowledge of AIDS among women has been increasing rapidly over time, but many women have still not heard of AIDS. Between 1998-99 and 2005-06, the percentage of ever-married women who have heard of AIDS increased from 20 per cent to 41 per cent in Chhattisgarh, from 30 per cent to 49 per cent in Gujarat, from 39 per cent to 62 per cent in Orissa, from 55 per cent to 70 per cent in Punjab, and from 61 per cent to 79 per cent in Maharashtra. In all five states, men are much more likely than women to have heard of AIDS. Two-thirds of men in Chhattisgarh and more than 90 per cent of men in Maharashtra and Punjab have heard of AIDS. Knowledge of AIDS is universal among men and women with 10 or more years of schooling. Majority of women with no education have not heard of AIDS.

David M. Dror (2006), based on a survey in seven locations, finds that most Indians are willing to pay 1.35 per cent of income or more for health insurance and most people prefer a holistic benefit package at basic coverage over high coverage of only rare events. The needs of the poor, and their demand for health insurance, depend on local conditions. for health insurance, and the lower their income, the less they are willing to pay for health. Community-based endeavors can be a powerful resource for process innovation and for gaining acceptance by the target population, because nobody is closer-to-client, and no other body is as effective as communities in implementing the local ethos that makes the local economy run. The communities are also best placed to mediate an optimal balance between needs, costs, resources and supply, all of which are context-specific. Minor adaptations of products developed for richer clients (and often in Europe or the US) are unlikely to find many willing takers in the slums and villages in India. Becoming familiar with the needs and priorities of the poor requires considerable innovation in processes; the logistics for data mining, access to clients, selling and servicing of the health insurance must be adapted to the context-specific social dynamics and local infrastructure. However, the long tail of the cost distribution, implies that outlier costs can be devastatingly high, and it is necessary to link local communities with a financial mechanism of reinsurance and risk equalization, thereby enabling micro-heath insurance schemes to benefit from economies of scale.

Prashanta Pathak and Kamal K. Gaur (2001) have studied specific features of the Indian socio-economic environment, the health and family welfare service facilities and the programmatic efforts, which determine the health status of the Indian community, from the health system angle by constructing several composite indices, constructed objectively by using Principal Component Analysis technique. Based on data on 16 Indian States compiled by the Central Bureau of Health Intelligence [1991], Agarwal *et. al.* [1993] and the Foundation for Research in Health Systems [1993], this study has established the utility of such a composite index-based statistical approach by associating the community health status with the availability of service facilities, the programme efforts and the socio-economic environment by multiple linear regression. The composite indices are presented in Table 3.2 below.

The results of this study suggest a definite approach of identifying the most important factors that are associated with community health and gives their order of importance. The values of the indices measuring degree of unhealthiness (I), social environment status (I_S), degree of weakness in the services area coverage by the existing health service facilities (I_F), achievement out of the programme efforts (I_P) and economic backwardness (I_E), are shown in Table 3.3.

The states have been listed in decreasing order of I values, i.e. the state which is most unhealthy has been put at the top and ranked 1, and the state, which is least unhealthy has been put at the bottom and ranked 16. As per this ordering, the health status of Madhya Pradesh, Uttar Pradesh, Orissa and Rajasthan cause maximum concern. The values of I for these states are above the all India value 1. These states are also socio-economically backward with the values of I_S ranked as 14, 8, 13

TABLE 3.2

Description of Constructed Indices and the Constituent Variables

Name of the Composite Index (Symbol)	*Constituent Indices (Form)*	*Constituent Variables, used in Location Factor or other Appropriate Form*
(1)	*(2)*	*(3)*
(I) Social Environment Index [I_S]	(a) Sex Discrimination [SSR *] (Composite)	(i) Sex ratio for Scheduled Castes (SC) population [SSRC]; (ii) Sex ratio for Scheduled Tribes (ST) population [SSRT]; (iii) Sex ratio for non-SC/ST [SSRN].
	(b) Literacy (SLR*] (Composite)	(i) Male literacy rate [SLRM]; (ii) Female literacy rate [SLRF].
	(c) SC/ST Concentration [SSCT*] (Simple)	(i) Percentage of SC/ST population [SSCT].
(II) Economic Environment Index [I_E]	(a) Poverty [EPL*] (Simple)	(i) Percentage of population below poverty line [EPL];
	(b) Income [EPI*] (Simple)	(i) Per capita income [EPI];
	(c) Scope of Employment [ESW*] (Composite)	(i) Percentage of combined male and female main workers in the population [EMW]; (ii) Percentage of female main workers' participation with respect to male main workers' participation rEFMWl.

(*Contd.*)

TABLE 3.2 (*Contd.*)

(1)	(2)	(3)
(III) Health Service Facility Index [I HI]	(a) Service Coverage by Sub-centre (SC) [HSC*] (Composite)	(i) Average coverage of population by an SC [HPSC]; (ii) Average number of villages covered by an SC [HYSC].
	(b) Service Coverage by Primary Health Centre (PHC) [IHHC] (Composite)	(i) Average coverage of population by a PHC [HPHC]; (ii) Average number of villages covered by a PHC [HYHC].
	(c) Service Coverage by Doctors and Para-medicals [HP*] (Composite)	(i) Average coverage of population by a doctor [HRD] (i) Average coverage of population by a para-medic [HPP].
(IV) Programme Effort Index (I_p)	(a) Achievement in Child Immunisation [PT} (Composite)	(i) Percentage target achievement with Index regard to BCG [PBCG}; (ii) Percentage target achievement with regard to OPT [POPT]; (iii) Percentage target achievement with regard to OPV [POPV]; (iv) Percentage target achievement with regard to Measles [PMS}; (v) Percentage target achievement with regard to Vitamin A [PVA];

		(vi) Percentage target achievement with regard to OT [PDT}.
	(b) Achievement in Immunisation of Pregnant Women with TT [PTT*] (Simple)	Percentage target achievement with regard to TT [PTT]
	(c) Achievement in through Prophylaxis against Nutritional Anaemia among Women [PAW*] (Simple)	Percentage target achievement with regard to prophylaxis against nutritional anaemia among women [PAW]
	(d) Achievement through Prophylaxis against Nutritional Anaemia among Children [PAC*] (Simple)	Percentage target achievement with regard to prophylaxis against nutritional anaemia among children [PAC]
	(e) Achievement in Family Planning (FP) Programme [PCPR*] (Simple)	Achieved couple protection rate [PCPR]
	(f) Reported Prevalence of Diseases of National Concern [PRD*] (Simple)	Percentage of Population having reported diseases of national concern [PRO]
(V) Status of Health Index	1. Life Expectancy [LEB*] (Simple)	(i) Life expectancy of males and females [LEB].
	2. Crude Birth Rate [CBR*] (Composite)	(ii) CBR in rural area [CBRR]; (iii) CBR in urban area [CBRU];
	3. Infant Mortality Rate [IMR*] (Composite)	(i) IMR in rural area [IMRR]; (ii) IMR in urban area [IMRU].

TABLE 3.3

State-wise Values of the Composite Indices, Measuring Social Environment Status, Degree of Weakness in Service Area Coverage, Level of Achievement through Programme Efforts, Extent of Economic Backwardness and Degree of Unhealthiness in India*

States	*Composite Indices Measuring*				
	Social Environment Status	*Degree of Weakness in the Service Area Coverage*	*Level of Achievement through Programme Efforts*	*Extent of Economic Backwardness*	*Degree of Unhealthiness*
	I_S (Rank)	I_F (Rank)	I_P (Rank)	I_E (Rank)	I (Rank)
(1)	(2)	(3)	(4)	(5)	(6)
Madhya Pradesh	0.2497 (14)	I. 1676 (3)	0.8912 (8)	2.2327 (1)	1.6941 (1)
Uttar Pradesh	0.9161 (8)	1.1086 (4)	0.8257 (11)	1.3799 (5)	1.5 128 (2)
Orissa	0.3578 (13)	1.2254 (2)	0.8547 (10)	1.9387 (3)	1.3687 (3)
Rajasthan	0.5219 (12)	0.7725 (I I)	0.7068 (13)	0.8638 (8)	I. I 077 (4)
Gujarat	1.2662 (5)	0.6733 (13)	1.1751 (3)	-0.0067 (13)	0.9186 (5)

Haryana	I. I 829 (6)	0.6764 (12)	1.1172 (4)	-0.8438 (15)	0.9029 (6)
Andhra Pradesh	0.2438 (15)	0.8363 (9)	0.9891 (6)	1.4699 (4)	0.8558 (7)
Assam	-0.9878 (16)	0.9024 (5)	0.4587 (16)	0.7867 (10)	0.8324 (8)
Bihar	0.8788 (10)	0.8438 (8)	0.6410 (15)	2.0442 (2)	0.8297 (9)
Karnataka	1.2808 (4)	0.8569 (7)	0.9808 (7)	1.0592 (7)	0.7978 (10)
Punjab	0.8199 (11)	0.5431 (15)	1.3005 (1)	- 1.3523 (16)	0.6840 (I I)
West Bengal	0.8896 (9)	0.7349 (10)	0.8008 (12)	0.7886 (9)	0.6855 (12)
Himachal Pradesh	1.0080 (7)	2.2302 (1)	0.6184 (14))	-0.1114 (14)	0.5955 (13)
Maharashtra	1.3906 (3)	0.8924 (6)	1.2589 (2)	0.2731 {121	0.5832 (14)
Tamil Nadu	1.4475 (2)	0.5832 (14)	1.0883 (5)	1.3691 (6)	0.4554 (15)
Kerala	2.3731 (1)	0.3596 (16)	0.8637 (9)	0.4804 (11)	-0.2886 (16)
India	1,0000	1,0000	1,0000	1,0000	1,0000

*The value predominantly refer to the year 1991.

and 12, and the values of I_E, ranked as 1, 5, 3 and 8 respectively. All other states have a status of health better than the all-India status. However, it is worth noting that the achievement through programme efforts in Rajasthan is rather poor in spite of much less weakness in the service area coverage by the existing health service facilities. Given that in Rajasthan, the degree of weakness in the service area coverage is low (with I_F = 0.7725 and rank = 11) and the extent of economic backwardness is moderate (with I_E = 0.8638 and rank = 8) in comparison to the all India values, the unhealthy status of the state (with I = 1.1077 and rank = 4) might have something to do with its poor status of social environment (with I_s = 0.5219 and rank = 12) and poor achievement through various programme efforts (with I_P = 0.7068 and rank 13). The case of Bihar is interesting because it is maintaining a moderately unhealthy status in spite of its socio-economic backwardness and poor achievement through various programme efforts under moderate weaknesses in the service area coverage. More in-depth probing is required to understand this phenomenon. Further in-depth probing is required for Gujarat also which has quite a favourable socio-economic environment, service facilities and programme efforts, but has an unsatisfactory health status. The moderately unhealthy status of Andhra Pradesh, on the other hand, seems to be due particularly to its socio-economic backwardness. Punjab has much scope to improve its health status by improving the social environment status. In fact, its health service facilities, programme efforts and economic status are almost the best among all the states, and yet, it is as unhealthy as West Bengal, and worse than Himachal Pradesh, Maharashtra, Tamil Nadu and Kerala. The situation in West Bengal, with respect to service area coverage, achievement through programme efforts and economic status, is comparable to that in Rajasthan, and yet, its health status is better because of better social environment. The importance of social environment in improving health status gets further established when the situation in Assam is compared with that in Himachal Pradesh. Achievement through programme efforts is found unsatisfactory in both these states, may be because of their difficult terrain. The situation in Maharashtra, in comparison to that in Tamil Nadu and Kerala, makes one feel that Maharashtra is capable of performing as well as Kerala if it overcomes its weaknesses in service area coverage.

Measham, A.R., Rao, K.D., Jamilson, D.T., Wang Jia and Singh, A. (1999) have explored the relationship between income, infant mortality and fertility in India from 1975 to 1990, and given the importance of both income and time (or technical progress) as determinants of infant mortality rates (IMR) and total fertility rates (TFR), they have used these rates to assess progress or performance in human development in India after appropriately controlling for income and time. For India, the state time series on infant mortality and total fertility rates are from the Sample Registration System (SRS) of Government of India. They found that between 1975 and 1990, increases in per capita income within each quartile was associated with significant declines in infant mortality and total fertility. States in the richest quartile experienced the biggest increase in per capita income as well as the some of the biggest declines in infant mortality and total fertility, while the poorest quartile achieved equally substantial declines in IMR and TFR despite a much smaller increase in per capita income. Although the inverse per capita income—IMR/TFR relationship is found to be inconsistent in India, the regression analysis nonetheless suggests that income has a significant influence on infant mortality and total fertility. Moreover, in terms of reducing total fertility rate, the income effect is found to be greater in India than in other low—and middle-income countries. In general, these authors find that in most Indian states, income growth is only about one-third as important as improvements over time in reducing infant mortality and fertility. The relatively weak correlation of per capita income on IMR and TFR in India may also be due in part to non-income, state-specific factors which are weakly correlated with income. Indeed, the contribution of income in infant mortality and fertility declines between 1975 and 1990 was found to be much smaller than that of technical change, implying thereby that while income is important, technical change combined with other factors has a stronger influence on these indicators—every state's performance on infant mortality and total fertility would improve even if their incomes did not (in this period). Interestingly, relative performance on total fertility exhibited a stronger association with achievements on the poverty indices, and both Kerala and Haryana are found to have lower levels of poverty and generally reduced their poverty levels faster than the states that had declining relative performance.

Levels of female literacy, age of female marriage and access to medical facilities are found to have a much higher degree of association with trends in relative performance than the poverty indices. All states which improved relative performance on infant mortality, excepting Uttar Pradesh, did substantially better on these indicators than states where relative performance worsened between the period. Kerala, Gujarat and Tamil Nadu had a greater proportion of literate women, their women married later and their populations had much better access to medical facilities than states in which relative performance declined. Improved relative performance on total fertility has a stronger association with greater access to medical facilities and late female age of marriage, than with female literacy levels. In sum, while income growth is significant for lowering infant mortality and fertility, improved performance on non-income factors appears to be more important. Global knowledge improvements no doubt have played a major role. The excellent relative performance of low per capita income states like Kerala and (to a lesser extent) Tamil Nadu for IMR indicates that low incomes need not hinder improvement in social well-being. Kerala's success in having the lowest IMR and TFR in the country, levels comparable to some developed countries, is probably due largely to its universally literate population, better status of women, and more equitable distribution of health services—all of which have been due more to strong commitment to investments in the social sectors than to economic growth. This commitment has allowed Kerala's population to benefit from the rapid change globally in the means for improving health.

IV. CONCLUSION

The explanations of the various researchers on health performance in India and its determinants—economic as well as non-economic—provide important clues to our understanding of health services in India. The attempts to quantify the health-related deprivations and their significance in our development process indicate important failures of government policies to improve the quality of life of Indian population and the efficiency of public outlays in generating the desired objectives of policy. In the following chapter, we move on to macroeconomic trends of health outcomes in India and the states.

4

Health Sector in India—An Interstate Analysis

I. INTRODUCTION

The health status of a population is a reflection of the socioeconomic development of the country and is shaped by a variety of factors—the level of income and standard of living, housing, sanitation, water supply, education, employment, health consciousness, personal hygiene, and by the coverage, availability, accessibility, and affordability of health care delivery services. It is widely accepted that the poor health status of low-income countries is the product of inadequate nutrition, lack of a protected water supply, and overcrowded and insanitary housing conditions. Health is also an important aspect of human development—it is a dimension of human capital and healthier people are more productive. The relationship between health and income is bi-directional: the health status of a person influences his or her income status as well. Given the prevalence of mass poverty in India, the question is not only how to raise the incomes of the poor that will be instrumental in improving their health status, but also to identify policy intervention that can improve people's health status at existing income levels (and can be instrumental in raising incomes). Provision of public health services such as access to basic and preventive health care, sanitation, clean water and raising awareness about the causes of illness and their treatment are some of the ways in which the now industrialized countries view about levels of development.

On the eve of her independence, medical services in India were scattered and highly inadequate, not only in number but also in the kind of medical care they delivered. Rural populations, in particular, were starved of services. Some of India's most eminent medical professionals, such as Dr. B.C. Roy and Dr. A.R. Ansari, Dr. Khan Saheb, Hakim Ajmal Khan, Dr. Jeevraj Mehta, and Dr. N.M. Jaisoorya, occupied leadership positions in the national struggle. Inspired by the welfare state movement in the United Kingdom and the socialized health services in the Soviet Union, they demanded a more egalitarian health service system and made this demand an important plank in the anti-colonial struggle. Dr. B.C. Roy's presidential address at the All India Medical Conference at Lahore in 1929 presents many important facets of the health services during the movement (Roy, 1982). Another remarkable feature of the movement for health services was the initiative taken by prominent persons in different parts of this vast country to start a large variety of institutions on a voluntary basis.

An important feature of health policies, plans, and programs in India is that they originated during the national movement against colonial rule. The National Planning Committee (NPC) of the Indian National Congress was set-up in 1938. The then president of the Congress, Subhas Chandra Bose, nominated Jawaharlal Nehru as the chairman of the committee. This committee set-up a sub-committee on national health (Sokhey Committee) which made an incisive appraisal of the health situation and health services in the country and recommended measures for their improvement (NPC, 1948). Although the Health Survey and Development Committee, generally known as the Bhore Committee, was set-up by the British colonial authorities (1943), it was greatly influenced by the aspirations of the national movement (Government of India,

1946). The impact of the committee is clearly seen in the shaping of health services in independent India. The guiding principles adopted by the Bhore Committee were: (i) no individual should be denied adequate medical care because of inability to pay for it; (ii) the health services should provide when fully developed, all the consultant, laboratory, and institutional facilities necessary for proper diagnosis and treatment; (iii) the health program must, from the beginning, lay special emphasis on preventive work; (iv) medical relief and preventive health care must be urgently provided as soon as possible to the vast rural population of the country; (v) the health services should be located as close to the people as possible to ensure maximum benefit to the communities served; (vi) the active cooperation of the people must be secured in the development of the health programs. The idea must be inculcated that, ultimately, the health of the individual is his own responsibility; and (vii) health development must be entrusted to the ministers of health who enjoy the confidence of the people and are able to secure their cooperation.

II. HEALTH IN POST-INDEPENDENCE ERA

It is most essential to keep in mind the conditions prevailing at the time of the end of colonial rule in India in 1947. It was already densely populated and poverty-stricken, which meant a very heavy load of diseases of various kinds. This vicious cycle had been at the root of, and is reinforced by the rapid growth of the population. The population of India in the 1951 Census was 350 million; it is now one billion—an addition of 650 million. This is a colossal problem of human ecology, which gravely affects the health status of the people. Although the class interests of India's new rulers came to the fore after independence, yet they had to adopt an egalitarian stance given the democratic urges kindled among the masses and their own egalitarian convictions. This impelled them to take such actions in health and other fields, in the first two decades of independence, which placed the country very high among the newly sovereign countries. An example is that of ensuring protection and promotion of health and nutrition of the people by placing it in the Directive Principles for the State Policy in the

Constitution of India (Basu, 1970). The motive force generated by the leadership's commitment and the experience gained by the health administrators from their work in the IMS, enabled them to give concrete shape to the political vision of the rulers. This led to some far-reaching developments in the health services. Some of the landmarks requiring a mention are: vertical programs, primary health centers, social orientation of medical education, indigenous systems of medicine, Family Planning/Welfare Program, water supply and sanitation, nutrition, Minimum Needs Program, the Multi-Purpose Workers' Scheme, the Community Health Volunteers (Guide) Scheme, and the Statement of National Policy.

At the time of Independence, the health situation in India was extremely dismal. There have, indeed, been large gains in health status since Independence, reflected in the improvement in some health indicators presented in Table 4.1. Overall, mortality (in particular, infant mortality) has declined dramatically and life expectancy at birth has increased.

TABLE 4.1
Selected Health Indicators: India, 1947 and Current

Indicators	*At the time of Independence, 1947*	*Current level (2002)*
Birth rate	40.8	25.0 (SRS, 2002)
Death rate	27.4	8.1 (SRS, 2002)
Infant mortality rate	146	63 (SRS, 2002)
Life expectancy at birth	32.7	62

Source : SRS (Sample Registration System).

One of the major reasons for these gains has been the development of an impressively vast, three-tiered system of rural health infrastructure, namely, Sub-centres, Primary Health Centres (PHCs), and Community Health Centres (CHCs). The successful eradication of smallpox and elimination of guinea worm diseases are indisputably major public health achievements in India. Plague has remained in control since 1969. Yaws is near eradication and leprosy, near elimination. Cholera epidemics and deaths are comparatively infrequent and fewer. The incidence of measles, polio, whooping cough, and tetanus in children has been significantly lowered. Immunization has made a major contribution to these gains. Diagnostic laboratory services have developed considerably, and communication and transportation have improved immensely. Improvements in water supply and sanitation have also helped achieve these outcomes.

Despite these gains and achievements, there was a sharp decline in the quality of health services in the country, due mainly to the following reasons:

- Obsessive preoccupation with the Family Planning Program at the cost of serious neglect of the health service needs of the people, particularly the poor. Owing to the overriding priority given to the family planning program, plan allocations for it jumped a phenomenal 10,000 fold—from Rs. 6.5 million in the First Plan (1950-55) to Rs. 65,000 million in the Eighth Plan (1991-95) and further in the subsequent plans;
- The imposition of so-called "international initiatives in health," during the last two decades, by a formidable combination of "development aid" agencies of many Western countries and international organizations. The declaration of WHO in 1978 called for the introduction of selective primary health cares to implement WHO and *UNICEF* programmes of *universal immunization, oral rehydration and other child survival strategies, and social marketing of contraceptives.* Considerable damage was inflicted upon the provision of comprehensive health services by according overriding priority to a single vertical program over the former. Not only were the vertical programs technocentric, they were imposed on the people from above, their cost-effectiveness was not demonstrated; and worst of all, they made developing countries dependent upon the North for funds, supply of vaccines, and other logistic support;
- Initiation of the Structural Adjustment Program (SAP) from the late eighties onwards as per the Washington Consensus, outlining privatization of health services

and gradual withdrawal of state support towards comprehensive coverage of health services for all.

One of the best ways to judge the well being of the people of any nation is by examining the standards of health that ordinary people have attained. Healthy living conditions and access to good quality health care for all citizens are not only basic human rights, but also essential prerequisites for social and economic development. Hence, it is important that people's health is given priority in the national policy initiatives of the central government .

India's health sector is characterized by:

(a) A government sector that provides publicly financed and managed curative and preventive health services from primary to tertiary level, throughout the country and free of cost to the consumer (these account for about 18% of the overall health spending and 9% of the GDP), and

(b) A free levying private sector that plays a dominant role in the provision of individual curative care through ambulatory services accounts for about 82% of the overall health expenditure and 4.2% of the GDP. Nationwide health care utilization rates show that private health services are directed mainly at providing primary health care and financed from private resources, which could place a disproportionate burden on the poor.

The provision of health care by the public sector is a responsibility shared by state, central and local governments, although it is effectively a state responsibility in terms of service delivery. State and local governments incur about three-quarters and the center about one-quarter of public spending on health. The responsibility for health is at three levels.

First, health is primarily a state responsibility.

Second, the center is responsible for health services in union territories without a legislature and is also responsible for developing and monitoring national standards and regulations, linking the states with funding agencies, and sponsoring numerous schemes for implementation by state governments.

Third, both the center and the states have a joint responsibility for programmes listed under the concurrent list. Goals and strategies for the public sector in health care are established through a consultative process involving all levels of government through the Central Council for Health and Family Welfare.

The private and voluntary sectors have emerged as an important arm of the health sector. From 1 April 1996 a change has been effected in the family welfare services with targets for contraceptive methods being replaced by a target-free approach. A huge campaign to eradicate poliomyelitis through pulse polio immunization (PPI) was initiated in 1995. The traditional system of medicine is now playing a more significant role due to escalating costs of health care. State health systems/projects have formulated to improve efficiency in the allocation and use of health resources through policy and institutional development. Specific efforts have been made to consolidate and strengthen the PHC infrastructure, under the minimum needs programme, by providing enhanced assistance to regions with severe health problems, supporting voluntary organizations, improving IEC holistic approach to population control has also been promoted. In March 1995 a separate Department of Indian System of Medicine and Homeopathy (ISM & H) was created within the Ministry of Health and Family Welfare.

Health Status

We begin the analysis of health status outcomes in India by comparing India's disease burden with that of the world, and then examine India's trends in mortality, fertility, malnutrition, and illness. We also focus on disparities in health status within India, looking at differences between states, sexes, the poor, and Scheduled Tribes (STs) and Scheduled Castes (SCs). As Table 4.2 below demonstrates, India accounts for a fifth of the global disease burden, with a 17 per cent share of the world's population. Although India's share of the world's deaths (Table 4.3) is equal to its share of the world's population (17 per cent), the country's contribution to pre-health transition diseases affecting younger people is disproportionately high (Tables 4.3 and 4.4). Compared with its share of the world's population, India has high levels of deaths due to childhood infectious diseases such as acute lower respiratory infections (28.1 per cent), diarrhea (32.1 per cent), measles (21.4 per cent), and tetanus (40.3 per cent). These conditions, as well as tuberculosis (28.1 per cent), another disease with high death rate in India are common to low-income countries at an early stage of the epidemiological transition.

Table 4.2
India's Share of the World's Health Problems

	Percentage of World
Population	17
People living in poverty (less than US$ 1 per day)	36
Total deaths	17
Under five mortality (deaths per 1000 live births)	23
Maternal deaths	20
DALYs lost	20
Deaths preventable with childhood vaccinations	26
HIV cases	14
Tuberculosis cases	30
Leprosy cases	68

Source : World Bank (2000), WHO (2000).

A fuller measure of the burden of diseases counts not only deaths but also years of healthy life lost due to disability. A consolidated measure of losses from death and disability is disability-adjusted life years (DALY s) lost. India's share of world's total burden of DALYs lost was 19.5 per cent, moderately larger than its 16.7 per cent share of the worlds population (Table 4.5).

Except for depression (16.6 per cent), India's contributions to all leading causes of DALYs lost are greater than its proportion of world's population. However, other conditions are also significant. Injuries from falls, road traffic accidents,

TABLE 4.3
Distribution of Deaths in the World and India, 1998

	World		India		Number (thousands)
	Number (thousands)	Per cent	Number (thousands)	Per cent	
1. Distribution of population	5,884,576	100	982,223	100	16.7
Total deaths	53,929	100	9337	100	17.3
Communicable diseases, maternal and perinatal conditions					
and nutritional deficiencies	16,447	30.5	3944	42.2	24.0
(a) Infections and parasitic diseases	9802	18.2	2121	22.7	21.6
TB	1498	2.8	421	4.5	28.1
Diarrhoeal diseases	2219	4.1	711	7.6	32.1
Childhood diseases	1650	3.1	429	4.6	26.0
Pertusis	346	0.6	71	0 8	20.7
Measles	888	1.6	190	2.0	21.4
Tetanus	410	0.8	165	1.8	40.3
(b) Respiratory infections	3507	6.5	987	10.6	28.1
2. Non-communicable diseases	31,717	58.8	4470	47.9	14.1
3. Injuries	5765	10.7	923	9.9	16.0

Source : WHO (1999).

and fires; each account for relatively large portions of DALYs lost in India-and in comparison to the rest of the world.

The DALYs lost per 1000 population in India and the world are 274 and 234 respectively. Overall death rates and DALYs lost appear to have dropped somewhat in the last decade (Table 4.5).

At the same time, India continues to have a high burden of readily preventable and treatable conditions due to childhood communicable diseases, tuberculosis, malnutrition, and maternal illness. These illness are concentrated in the poorer

TABLE 4.4
Top 10 Specific Causes of Death in India, 1998

	India		India's share of worldwide cases
	Number (thousands)	*Per cent*	*per cent*
Ischemic heart disease	1471	15.8	19.9
Acute lower respiratory infections	969	10.4	28.1
Diarrhoeal diseases	711	7.6	32.1
Cerebrovascular disease	557	6.0	10.9
Tuberculosis	421	4.5	28.J
Road traffic injury	217	2.3	18.5
Measles	190	2.0	21.4
HIV/AIDS	179	1.9	7.8
Tetanus	165	1.8	40.3
Chronic obstructive pulmonary disease	153	1.6	6.8
Total deaths	9337	100.0	17.3
Total population	98,2223	100.0	16.7

Source : WHO (1999).

TABLE 4.5
Top 10 Specific Causes of DALYs Lost in India, 1998

Causes of DALYs lost	India		India's share of world
	Number of DALYs lost	*Percent*	*per cent*
Acute lower respiratory infections	24,806	9.2	30.1
Diarrhoeal diseases	22,005	8.2	30.1
Ischemic heart disease	11,697	4.3	22.5
Falls (injuries)	10,898	4.1	40.3
Unipolar major depression	9679	3.6	16.6
Tuberculosis	7577	2.8	26.9
Road traffic injuries	7204	2.7	18.5
Measles	6474	2.4	21.4
Anemia	6302	2.3	25.5
Fire-related injuries	5723	2.1	47.8
All causes	26,8953	100.0	19.5
Population (thousands)	98,2223	100.0	16.7

states and among the poor. Table 4.6 shows that the distribution of the burden of disease (BOD) in 1998 brings out the disproportionate share of communicable diseases in mortality, which accounts for 50.3 per cent of burden, followed by non-communicable diseases (33 per cent), and injuries (17 per cent).

There is no denying that health indicators have continued to improve over time in India. Infant mortality rates have shown a steady and secular decline in India and life expectancy too has continued its upward climb. Yet the state of affairs is far from satisfactory: health indicators in India are inferior not only compared to the rich countries of the West but also compared to the achievements of other developing countries like China and Brazil. For example, despite greater sources, life expectancy in some states of India is similar to those in some of the poorest sub-Saharan African countries. Only the state of Kerala records achievements in health that is better than not only the rest of India but also the rest of the developing world and often at par with the Western developed countries. In Table 4.7 below we present the selective health indicator in Indian states.

Infant mortality is a good indicator at how well nations are doing in protecting their most vulnerable members. Both infant and child mortality have continued their trend decline but remain at high levels in India. Table 4.7 lists infant and child mortality rates for 11 states in India for 1992-93 and 1997-98. Kerala stands out with its low infant and child mortality rates of 16.3 and 2.6 in 1997-98. In all the states, except Madhya Pradesh and Rajasthan, which actually register an increase in these two rates, infant mortality and child mortality rates have declined.

Sex ratio indicates both the absolute well being of women as well their relative well-being *vis-à-vis* men. Given adequate and equal nutrition and medical care, women live longer than men. In India, the overall sex ratio has always been unfavorable to women except in the states of the south. While sex ratios improve with income in general, in India, the relatively richer states of Punjab and Haryana have historically recorded the worst sex ratios in the country as a whole. Between 1991 and 2001, improvements in the sex ratio have had mixed results. In the traditionally adverse two states of Uttar Pradesh and Rajasthan sex ratios have improved and these increases are the highest overall, noting the fact that they start out at the lowest

TABLE 4.6

Cause of DALYs Lost in India

	Deaths per 1000 population			*Proportion of deaths (per cent)*			*DALYs lost per 1000 population*		*Proportion of DALYs lost (per cent)*	
	1990	*1998*	*Change Per cent*	*1990*	*1998*	*Change Per cent*	*1990*	*1998*	*1990*	*1998*
(1)	*(2)*	*(3)*	*(4)*	*(5)*	*(6)*	*(7)*	*(8)*	*(9)*	*(10)*	*(11)*
Communicable diseases maternal and perinatal condition, and nutritional deficiencies	5.6	4.0	-28.6	51.0	42.2	-17.3	191.0	J37.7	56.4	50.3
Non-communicable conditions	4.5	4.6	2.2	40.4	47.9	18.6	98.2	90.3	29.0	33.0
Injuries	1.0	0.9	-10.0	8.6	9.9	15.6	49.3	45.8	14.6	16.7
Total	11.0	9.5	-13.6	100.0	100.0	0	338.5	273.8	100.0	100.0

Source : Murray and Lopez (1996), WHO (2000).

TABLE 4.7

Selected Health Indicators in States of India

States	*Infant Mortality Rate*		*Child Mortality Rate*		*Total Fertility Rate*		*% of Children with Anemia*		*% of Women with Anemia*	
	1992-93	1997-98	1992-93	1997-98	1992-93	1997-98	1992-93	1997-98	1992-93	1997-98
(1)	(2)	(3)	(4)	(5)	(6)	(7)	(8)	(9)	(10)	(11)
Andhra Pradesh	70.4	65	22.4	21	2.59	2.25	NA	68	NA	50
Tamil Nadu	67.7	48.2	20.1	15.9	2.48	2.18	NA	66.1	NA	56.5
Bihar	89.2	73	42	34.6	3.98	3.47	NA	79.1	NA	63.6
Uttar Pradesh	99.9	86.7	46	39.2	4.75	3.96	NA	70.8	NA	48.7
Madhya Pradesh	85.2	86.1	49.3	56.4	3.85	3.27	NA	71.5	NA	54.4
Rajasthan	76.3	80.4	33.8	37.6	3.58	3.73	NA	76.4	NA	48.7
Karnataka	65.4	51.5	23.5	18.9	2.83	2.13	NA	65.8	NA	42.4
Kerala	23.8	16.3	8.4	2.6	2.0	1.96	NA	44.2	NA	22.6
Gujarat	73.5	62.2	32.7	24	2.97	2.7	NA	70	NA	46
Maharashtra	50.5	43.7	20.9	15	2.86	2.52	NA	72.2	NA	48.6
Orissa	112.1	82	21.3	25.5	2.92	2.45	NA	71.3	NA	63.1

Source : NFHS I and II.

levels across districts. On the other hand, in many districts of Maharashtra and Gujarat sex ratios have actually declined. Punjab and Haryana while recording some improvement, continue to have some of the lowest sex ratios.

The diversity in health status outcomes across the states of India is really enormous. Among the demographic and health indicators of 16 major states, Kerala compares favourably with most middle-income countries and even some high-income countries in West Asia. But Madhya Pradesh, Orissa, Rajasthan, and Uttar Pradesh are well below the average of low-income countries, and just above the levels of sub-Saharan Africa. Together the different states represent the whole range of health outcomes within these two extremes. The indicators conceal the wide disparities existing within the states—between urban and rural areas and between relatively developed areas, and remote areas inhabited by tribal and other marginalized groups. While metropolitan cities have what could be considered modern tertiary care facilities by international standards, people in many remote rural areas do not have access to even basic primary care. In Table 4.8 we present selected health status indicators in major Indian states compared to India as a whole.

Fertility rates also vary widely among the states. Only two of the 15 major states have reached the so-called replacement levels of fertility, that is, 2.1. Another five major states have total fertility rate of between 2.1 and 3. However, in eight major states, the rate is 3 or more—these states comprise about 44 per cent of India's population and include the poorest states with the highest rates of infant mortality. The differences among states stem largely from poverty, illiteracy, and inadequate access to health and family welfare services.

Gender disparity in health outcomes is also particularly significant in India. India has approximately 933 females to every 1000 males, the low ratio being prevalent for more than 40 years. The largest gender disparities in India are found in the northern states, notably Haryana and Punjab, despite their relative economic affluence. Among Indian states, only Kerala had more women than men in 2001. The low ratio of women to men is usually attributed to a preference for sons, discrimination against girls (which results in lower female

TABLE 4.8

Selected Health Status Outcomes in India and Major Indian States

Area	Life expectancy at birth, average for 1992-6 (years)	Neonatal mortality 1998-9 (per 1000 live births)	Infant mortality rate, 1998 (per 1000 live births)	Under-5 mortality rate, 1997	Total fertility rate, 1997	Underweight children (per cent)
(1)	(2)	(3)	(4)	(5)	(6)	(7)
India	61	43	72	95	3.3	47
Andhra Pradesh	62	44	66	86	2.5	48
Assam	56	45	78	90	3.2	36
Bihar	59	47	67	105	4.4	54
Gujarat	61	40	64	85	3.0	45
Haryana	64	35	69	77	3.4	35
Karnataka	63	37	58	70	2.5	44
Kerala	73	14	16	19	1.8	27
Madhya Pradesh	55	55	98	138	4.0	55
Maharashtra	65	32	49	58	2.7	50
Orissa	57	49	98	104	3.0	54
Punjab	67	34	54	72	2.7	29
Rajasthan	60	50	83	115	4.3	51
Tamil Nadu	64	35	53	63	2.0	37
Uttar Pradesh	57	54	85	123	4.8	52
West Bengal	62	32	53	68	2.6	49

Source : World Bank (2002).

literacy, among other things), female foeticide, and higher mortality levels among females.

Girls start out having lower mortality rates than do boys during the first month of life (the neonatal period), which accounts for their lower rates of infant mortality (that is, death in the first year of life) (Table 4.9). However, death rates in the post-neonatal period (age one month to one year), and in the whole period up to age five (under-five mortality), are higher for girls (lIPS, 2000). Girls have higher childhood mortality despite the fact that boys are reported to have a higher prevalence of ARI and similar levels of diarrhoea and anaemia, these being major causes of childhood death. This paradox may be explained by the fact that boys are more likely to receive health care: 66.5 per cent of boys with ARI are taken to a health provider, compared with 60.8 per cent of girls (IIPS, 2000). Girls also have marginally higher rates of malnutrition, which places them at higher risk of severe illness and death.

The relative neglect of women's health is also reflected in poor reproductive health indicator: maternal mortality is very high in India. A major reason for the poor maternal health outcomes are the high levels of malnutrition among women. In 1998-9, 52 per cent of all women in the reproductive ages were found to be anaemic, and 36 per cent were chronically malnourished (IIPS, 2000).

Although large-scale studies that assess specific causes of illness and death by level of poverty are not available in India, communicable diseases, malnutrition, and maternal conditions are concentrated among the poor. Compared with the poor, the rich are sick less, become sick at an older age, and suffer more from non-communicable diseases than from communicable diseases. A recent World Bank study (2001) in India has also shown the poorest quintile to be having almost double the exposure to lifestyle risk factors like tobacco use and smoking as compared to the richest 20% of the population. The poor are often concentrated in backward and remote areas having very weak infrastructure, degraded environment, poor sanitation, lack of access to safe drinking water, which combined with under-nutrition and poor hygiene makes them highly vulnerable to ill-health. Tables 4.10 and 4.11 bring out clearly the

TABLE 4.9

Comparison of Female and Male Health Outcomes in India, 1998-99

Sex and ratio	*Mortality per 1000 live births*				*Indicators for children under age 3*			*Tuberculosis under medical treatment (per 100,000 population)*
	Neo-natal	*Post-neo-natal*	*Infant*	*Under 5*	*Under weight (percent)*	*Acute respiratory infection in past 2 weeks (per cent)*	*Diarrhoea in past 2 weeks (per cent)*	
(1)	(2)	(3)	(4)	(5)	(6)	(7)	(8)	(9)
Females	44.6	26.6	71.1	105.2	48.9	17.9	18.9	357
Male	50.7	24.2	74.8	97.9	45.3	20.7	19.4	502
Female-Male ratio	0.88	1.10	0.95	1.07	1.08	0.86	0.97	0.71

Source : IIPS (2000).

striking disparities in health status among different income groups in India.

TABLE 4.10
Health Status Indicators—Comparison between the Poorest and Richest Quintiles of the Indian Population, 1992-93

Indicator	*Poorest quintile*	*Richest quintile*	*Risk ratio*
Infant mortality (per 1000 births)	109	44	2.5
Under-five mortality (per 1000 births)	155	54	2.8
Underweight children (per cent)	60	34	1.7
Total fertility rate	4.1	2.1	2.0

Source : Gwatkin *et. al.*, Socio-Economic Differences in Health, Nutrition, and Population in India, 2000. HNP Poverty Thematic Group of the World Bank, based on NFHS, 1992-93. Reproduced from India: Raising the Sights—Better Health System for India's Poor, World Bank, 2001.

The poor have much higher levels of mortality, malnutrition, and fertility than do the rich. Compared with the richest quintile, the poorest quintile generally had double the risks of infant and child death, malnutrition, and high fertility. The picture becomes more pronounced when we look at health status of Schedule Caste (SC) and Schedule Tribes (ST) which are socio economically the most backward sections of society eligible for affirmative action under the Indian Constitution. A comparison of the infant and child mortality levels in these groups with the general population brings out clearly the wide disparity in health status. Tables 4.12 and 4.13 provide these information.

Data on health outcomes among STs and SCs show consistently that these groups are at a disadvantage (Table 4.13). Of all disadvantaged groups in India, STs tend to have the highest rates of infant and child mortality, malnutrition, and morbidity, followed by SCs and then by other disadvantaged (or 'backward') classes.

The poor suffer much higher mortality and morbidity due to lack of access to both public health and medical services. A

TABLE 4.11
Health Outcomes According to Standard of Living, India : 1998-99

Standard of living index	*Infant Mortality (per 1000 births)*	*Under-Five Mortality (per 1000 births)*	*Total Fertility Rate*	*Children Underweight (% below 20 S.D)*	*Children with anemia (%)*	*Children with acute respiratory infection in past 2 weeks*	*Children with diarrhoea in past 2 weeks (%)*	*Anemia among women (%)*
(1)	*(2)*	*(3)*	*(4)*	*(5)*	*(6)*	*(7)*	*(8)*	*(9)*
Low	88.8	130	3.37	56.9	78.7	21	19.9	60.2
Medium	70.3	94.6	2.85	46.8	73.5	19.4	19.7	50.3
High	42.7	51.5	2.1	26.8	67.3	15.7	16.1	41.9
Low/High Ratio	2.08	2.52	1.6	2.12	1.17	1.34	1.24	1.44

Source : National Family Health Survey, 1998-99 (IIPS, 2000), Reproduced from India : Raising the Sights—Better Health Systems for India's Poor, World Bank, 2001. Also reproduced from: India Health Report, Oxford University Press, 2003.

TABLE 4.12
Health Indicators among SC/ST and Others (Rate per 1000)

Mortality Indicators	*SC*	*ST*	*Others*
Neo-Natal	53.2	53.3	40.7
Post-Neo-Natal	29.8	30.9	21.1
Infant < 1 year	83	84.2	61.8
Under 5 Years	119.3	126.6	82.6

Source : National Family Health Survey II. Reproduced from: India Health Report, Oxford University Press, 2003.

TABLE 4.13
Health among SCs, STs, and Rest of Population in India, 1998-99

Outcome	*SC*	*ST*	*Other disadvantaged classes*	*Rest of population*
Infant mortality (per 1000 births)	83.0	84.2	76.0	61.8
Under-five mortality (per 1000 births)	119.3	126.6	103.1	82.6
Total fertility rate	3.15	3.06	2.83	2.66
Children underweight (per cent)	53.5	55.9	47.3	41.1
Children with anaemia (per cent)	78.3	79.8	72.0	72.7
Children with acute respiratory infection during two-week Period (per cent)	19.6	22.4	19.1	18.7
Children with diarrhoea, during two-week period (per cent)	19.8	21.1	18.3	19.1
Anaemia among women (per cent)	56.0	64.9	50.7	47.6

Source : IIPS and ORC Macro (2000).

benefit incidence analysis done by the National Council of Applied Economic Research (NCAER) indicates that the rich have disproportionately utilized even public subsidies in health (Table 4.14).

TABLE 4.14
Share of Public Subsidy for Curative Care Benefiting Income Groups

Income Quintiles	*Share of public subsidy*
Poorest 20%	10.10%
2nd	13.40%
Middle 20%	17.80%
4th	25.60%
Richest 20%	33.10%

Source : Who Benefits From Public Health Spending in India, unpublished paper, NCAER, 2000. Reproduced from: India Health Report, Oxford University Press, 2003.

There are wide disparities in poverty and health outcomes across different sections of the population and across different regions of the country. Rural and urban India record large differentials in all social development indicators. Table 4.15 shows life expectancy and infant mortality rates for the rural and urban areas of India's 14 major states. Except Kerala, in all states there are large discrepancies in these two health outcomes across rural and urban populations. This is especially true of infant mortality rates.

Disparities in Health Status : A Sum Up

Health among Indian citizens has been improving over time but the large disparities across sections of the population are worrisome. In terms of health and from the view point of the framework of the epidemiological transition, different sections of Indian society seem to belong to different phases of the transition: the poor and the vulnerable sections of the population suffer from diseases of poverty and under-nutrition, largely infectious and gastro-enterical diseases; among the rising urban middle class, the diseases of affluence such as heart and non-communicable chronic degenerative diseases are more prevalent. Some of the glaring disparities are as follows:

- The Infant Mortality Rate in the poorest 20% of the population is 2.5 times higher than that in the richest

TABLE 4.15

Life Expectancy and Infant Mortality Rates for Major Indian States

States	*Life Expectancy at Birth, 1989-93*		*Infant Mortality rate, 1995*		*Total*
	Rural	*Urban*	*Rural*	*Urban*	
Andhra Pradesh	59.7	64.2	74	43	67
Bihar	57.7	65.2	74	57	73
Gujarat	59.1	62	68	47	62
Haryana	62.1	67	70	65	69
Karnataka	60.1	66.1	69	43	62
Kerala	71.8	72.8	16	13	15
Madhya Pradesh	52.3	61.9	104	61	99
Maharashtra	61.3	62	66	34	55
Orissa	54.9	63.6	107	65	103
Punjab	65.5	69.8	58	39	54
Rajasthan	55.6	63.2	90	62	86
Tamilnadu	60.5	66.3	61	39	54
Uttar Pradesh	55	60.4	89	66	86
West Bengal	60	66.8	61	45	58

Source : Sample Registration System.

20% of the population. In other words, an infant born in a poor family is two and half times more likely to die in infancy, than an infant in a better-off family;

- An Adivasi child is one and half times more likely to die before the fifth birthday than children of other groups;
- A girl is 1.5 times more likely to die before reaching her fifth birthday, compared to a boy. The female to male ratios for children are rapidly declining from 945 girls per 1000 boys in 1991, to just 927 girls per 1000 boys in 2001. This decline highlights an alarming trend of discrimination against girl children, which start well before birth (in the form of sex selective abortions) and continues into childhood and adolescence (in the form of worse treatment to girls);

- Dalit women are *one and half* times more likely to suffer the consequences of chronic malnutrition (stunted height) as compared to women from other castes. Children below 3 years of age in scheduled tribes and scheduled castes are twice as likely to be malnourished than children in other groups;
- A person from poorest quintile of the population, despite more health problems, is six times less likely to access hospitalization than a person from the richest quintile. This means that the poor are unable to afford and access hospitalization in a very large proportion of illness episode, even when it is required;
- The delivery of a mother from the poorest quintile of the population is over six times less likely to be attended by a medically trained person than the delivery of a well off mother, from the richest quintile of the population. An Adivasi mother is half as likely to be delivered by a medically trained person;
- The ratio of hospital beds to population in rural areas is fifteen times lower than that for urban areas;
- The ratio of doctors to population in rural areas is almost six times lower than the availability of doctors for the urban areas;
- Per person, Government spending on public health is seven times lower in rural areas, compared to Government health spending for urban areas;
- India's performance in improving the health of its population has been much inferior compared to educational development. Infant, child and maternal mortality rate remain at very high levels. Among the proximate causes of infant and child mortality is inadequate nutrition, among pregnant mothers and among small children. Rates of anemia among children are very high in India as can be seen from Table 4.1. Barring Kerala, where the percentage of children with anemia is 44%, all other states have more than 65% of children suffering from anemia. In Bihar, Rajasthan, Maharashtra and Orissa more than 70% children are anemic.

These health and health care inequalities are increasing and particularly after the onset of globalisation, because of relative neglect by the state on health care facilities, these inequalities and disparities are on the rise. This is despite the recognition by the World Bank on the centrality of the role of the state in the field of health and the setting of the Millennium Development Goals (MDGs) adopted by the Millennium Summit of the United Nations in September 2000. The WHO commission for Macroeconomics and Health (2001) represented a pioneering effort to understand the linkages between economic growth and poverty on the one hand, and health status on the other. It not only underscored the importance of investments in health for economic growth and alleviation of poverty, but also laid out a blueprint for both the developing countries and the donor community to move forward towards the achievement of the MDGs.

The poor in the developing countries like India ,are subjected to a disproportionate, and to a large extent avoidable, burden of disease (BOD) from pre-transition diseases (infectious diseases, pre-natal and maternal conditions and nutritional disorders). The BOD in low and middle-income countries on this account was estimated at 44% as against 7% in high-income countries (World Health Report, 1999). All these conditions are capable of being controlled very cost effectively with relatively simple and easily available technologies. Investment in the health of the poor could, therefore, not only yield quick results but also maximize the returns on such investments. If the world desires to move ahead rapidly towards the MDGs, the poor would be the best place to direct the efforts. Besides the pre-transition diseases, the new pandemic of HIV/AIDS is causing unimaginable consequences in the poorest regions of the world.

Whenever we consider development criterion of health sector, we have to take into account the health improvement under different government and private undertaking for children. When we see the number of immunized children since 1980-81, against the fatal diseases like diphtheria, tetanus, Pertussia, and polio etc., we see that throughout the periods from 1980-81 to 2001 the rate of immunized children has increased and also that at overall basis, the infant mortality rate also has decreased. But, again, the prevalence of complete immunization among children is heterogeneous across states and districts of India. In 1999, West Champaran in Bihar registered the abysmally low figure of 14% for children with complete immunization, which was a quarter of the mean of 60% for all districts. On the other hand, Madurai in Tamilnadu recorded near universal immunization with 99.5% of all children having received complete doses. District averages clustered around 45% in the other four poorly performing states of Uttar Pradesh, Madhya Pradesh, Rajasthan and Orissa. With less than half of all children immunized, high childhood

TABLE 4.16
Immunization of Children Against Specified Diseases in India

Year	*Diphtheria, Pertussia, Tetanus*	*Polio*
1980-81	7.15	1.61
1981-82	9.23	2.93
1982-83	10.34	4.55
1983-84	11.23	8.03
1984-85	12.43	9.89
1985-86	15.18	13.19
1986-87	12.99	11.14
1987-88	16.69	14.27
1988-89	16.81	15.9
1989-90	19.19	19.04
1990-91	22.5	22.68
1991-92	21.21	21.3
1992-93	22	22.12
1993-94	23.09	23.21
1994-95	23.4	23.58
1995-96	22.56	22.78
1996-97	23.25	23.55
1997-98	23.74	23.98
1998-99	23.55	23.93
1999-00	23.56	23.71
2000-01	24.13	23.61

causalities are not surprising. Table 4.16 summarises the information of the proportion of children given immunization, since 1980-81.

When we correlate the infant mortality rate with these immunization data, we can find that these two have a negative relation at a significant level, that is as long as immunization amongst children increases, infant mortality rate decreases. The Pearson Correlation Coefficient between IMR and DIPTET is found be significant at –0.98, and that between IMR and Polio vaccination is found to be significant at –0.973.

III. FAMILY WELFARE PROGRAMME IN INDIA AND ITS RELATION TO TOTAL FERTILITY RATE

The Family Welfare Programme is implemented through the State governments with full Central assistance. In rural areas, services are provided through the network of sub-centers, primary health centres and community health centres. Establishment of sub-centers has been made a hundred percent centrally sponsored scheme (except the salary of male health worker and construction of sub-centre building) since April 1981. Against the requirement of 1.34 lakh sub-centres, there are 1.37 lakh sub-centres functioning as on 30 June 1998.

Birth Control Methods

During 1998-99, 40.8 lakh sterilizations were performed in the country. The number of IUD insertions during the same period was 61.4 lakh. Besides, there were 140.2 lakh condom-users and 55.9 lakh OP users. It is estimated that 45.4 per cent of 16.59 crore eligible couples were protected by one or the other approved family planning methods as on 31 March 1998 averting 226.97 million births, since the inception of the programme.

Social Marketing of Contraceptives

Social Marketing of contraceptives aims at making contraceptives available to that segment of population, which can afford to buy the same from the market at a lower cost.

Under the scheme of Social Marketing of Contraceptives, condoms and Oral Pills are currently being sold at subsidized prices through the distribution network of private/public marketing companies and NGOs. The Government is providing subsidy ranging from 55-88 per cent on the procurement cost.

Maternal Health

The existing maternal health situation of the country is a cause of concern for all. India's maternal mortality rate at 437 per one-lakh live births is 50 times higher than the developed world. The causes of maternal deaths are known and treatable. However, it is not largely preventable or predictable. To tackle this enormous problem, a number of interventions have been provisioned for the current RCH programme. They are: provision of emergency obstetric care through establishment of First Referral Units; promotion of institutional delivery by providing round the clock delivery services in PHCs/CHCs; ensuring early ante-natal registration of pregnant women to provide regular check ups for taking preventive and promotive steps and to detect early complications to enable prompt action; at least three ante-natal check ups to monitor the progress of the pregnancy as well as three post-natal check ups to monitor the post-natal recovery have been provided for; linking the community with service delivery system through Panchayat by providing corpus fund for transportation costs of the pregnant women from poor families, improved mobility of ANMs for better outreach services, and community awareness through IEC as well as training.

Medical Termination of Pregnancy

It is estimated that about 12 per cent of the maternal mortality and a significant number of maternal morbidity are due to illegal abortions. In order to prevent these health hazards to women, the Medical Termination of Pregnancy Act, 1971 was promulgated. Under this Act, medical termination of pregnancy can be done in pregnant women up to 20 weeks, if pregnancy is likely to result in birth of a congenitally malformed child or continuation of pregnancy is likely to harm the mother in the existing circumstances and in cases of rape and contraceptive failures. Since the inception of the programme in April 1972, 115.8 lakh terminations up to December 1998 were conducted under the MTP Act.

Prevention of Pre-Natal Sex Determination

Any test to determine the sex of an unborn child has become illegal since the Pre-natal Diagnostic Techniques (Regulation and Prevention of Misuse) Act, 1994 came into effect from January 1996. Punishment is prescribed for illegal use of pre-natal diagnostic techniques like ultrasonography, amniocentesis, etc., to determine and communicate the sex of an unborn child (fetus) to prospective parents. These techniques can be utilized only for detecting certain abnormalities, subject to the fulfilment of specific conditions mentioned in the Act. These techniques can be conducted and genetic counseling can be offered only by genetic clinics, genetic laboratories and genetic counseling centres registered under the Act. The Department has launched a mass media campaign on this issue through press advertisements and video spots to raise awareness about the provisions of the Act.

Total Fertility Rate

Now we sec the relation between total fertility rate and different indicators of family welfare programme. In doing this what we lack is adequate time series data from NFHS-I and NFHS-II.

Total Fertility Rate is defined as the average number of children a woman would have if she were to pass through her reproductive years bearing children at the same rate as the women now in each age group. In 1998-99 the required total fertility rate in India was 2.13 but the actual is 3.12, indicating a large discrepancy. But the fertility rate has decreased over the years with the progress of the family welfare programmes, but still there is lot to be achieved. The total fertility rate among tribals is 3.06 which higher than the Indian TFR of 2.85. According to the Second National Family Health Survey (NFHS-II) which was carried out in 1998-99 on a sample of around 4000 households, on an average, women in the state of undivided Madhya Pradesh gave birth to only 2.25 children compared to over five children in the early 1970s. Such a decline in fertility rates had occurred in both rural and urban areas and in all the sections of the population almost at the same speed during the past three decades. Half of the women population in Andhra Pradesh was having their first child before their 19th birthday. The early start of childbearing is mainly due to the fact that women in the state tend to marry at an early age.

Now we present below (Tables 4.17 and 4.18) the data for percentage of couples effectively protected by various family planning methods in India as well as the data for family planning acceptors by method in India. Table 4.19 provides information about TFR in India during 1989-90 to 2002-03.

TABLE 4.17

Percentage of Couples Effectively Protected by Various Family Planning Methods in India

Year	*Eligible Couples*	*% of People Protected by all Methods*
1989-90	141990	48.6
1990-91	145140	49.6
1991-92	148430	48.6
1992-93	151720	48.7
1993-94	155020	51.3
1994-95	158310	51.6
1995-96	161593	52.2
1996-97	164749	51.0
1997-98	165868	45.4
1998-99	168558	44.0
1999-00	172700	46.2
2000-01	176647	50.3
2001-02	180056	47.6

TABLE 4.18
Family Planning Acceptors by Methods in India

Year	*Total Acceptors (in '000)*
1989-90	26082
1990-91	27356
1991-92	25717
1992-93	27031
1993-94	32099
1994-95	33862
1995-96	33668
1996-97	32015
1997-98	33603
1998-99	34682
1999-00	36678
2000-01	36368
2001-02	37385
2002-03	36763

TABLE 4.19
Total Fertility Rate Indicators in India

Year	*Total Fertility Rate*
1989-90	3.80
1990-91	3.60
1991-92	3.60
1992-93	3.50
1993-94	3.50
1994-95	3.50
1995-96	3.40
1996-97	3.30
1997-98	3.20
1998-99	3.20
1999-00	3.20
2000-01	3.10
2001-02	3.00
2002-03	3.00

When we find the relationship between TFR and Family Planning Acceptors by Method in India, it is found that the Pearson Correlation coefficient (significant at 2-tailed) is –0.885, which means that TFR and the increasing number of family planning acceptors are negatively related. As a result, as number of family planning acceptors are increased, the TFR decreases, indicating success of family planning programmes in controlling the population growth in India. Again when we view the relationship between TFR and Percentage of Couples protected by various Family Planning Method, the Pearson Correlation (Significant at 2-tailed) is found be positive at 0.404, indicating the scope for further improvement.

IV. ANAEMIA AMONG WOMEN AND CHILDREN IN INDIA

Acute anaemia among women and children is a serious health problem in India. The NFHS-3 data on anaemia among children (6-35 months) and also anaemia among women, especially pregnant women, is disturbing, not so much at the absolute values as in the adverse trend of increasing incidence of anaemia. The most astonishing aspect of the data shows that the comparatively prosperous states of Punjab and Gujarat, along with the backward tribal state of Chhattisgarh have a high percentage (over 80%) of children who are anaemic. The situation is quite depressing for women—high undernutrition and malnutrition among them increase the chance of getting infection. This hits the most vulnerable population of children and pregnant women and leads to high mortality levels, especially infant mortality, and maternal mortality. High incidence of maternal morbidity rate and child mortality rate along with anaemia among them is a serious curse on India's health sector. We present below in Tables 4.20, 4.21 and 4.22 the data on Anaemia affected persons specially women and children in India and the states.

From the above data, we can easily interpret that Bihar is the state with highest prevalence rate of Anemia among women and children and Rajasthan and Punjab are just behind it. The lowest anaemia affected state is Kerala. Table 4.21 provides information about the prevalence of anaemia among pregnant

Table 4.20
State-wise Prevalence of Anaemia Among Women and Children in India (1998-99)

States/Uts	*Percent of Women with*				
	Mild Anaemia	*Moderate Anaemia*	*Severe Anaemia*	*Percent of Women Age 15-49 with any Anaemia*	*Age 6-35 Months with any Anaemia*
Punjab	28.4	12.3	0.7	41.4	80.0
Rajasthan	32.3	14.1	2.1	48.5	82.3
Madhya Pradesh*	37.6	15.6	1.0	54.3	75.0
Uttar Pradesh*	33.5	13.7	1.5	48.7	73.9
Bihar*	42.9	19.0	1.5	63.4	81.3
Orissa	45.1	16.4	1.6	63.0	72.3
West Bengal	45.3	15.9	1.5	62.7	78.3
Assam	43.2	25.6	0.9	69.7	63.2
Gujarat	29.5	14.4	2.5	46.3	74.5
Maharashtra	31.5	14.1	2.9	48.5	76.0
Andhra Pradesh	32.5	14.9	2.4	49.8	72.3
Karnataka	26.7	13.4	2.3	42.4	70.6
Kerala	19.5	2.7	0.5	22.7	43.9
Tamil Nadu	36.7	15.9	3.9	56.5	69.0
India	35.0	14.8	1.9	51.8	74.3

Sources : (i) Lok Sabha Starred Question No. 421, dated on 26.04.2005.
(ii) Women and Men in India 2004, Ministry of Statistics and Programme Implementation, Govt. of India & India Yearbook, 2003, Manpower Profile.

women in India and the states. From the above Table 4.21, it is clear that the percentage of women affected by anaemia decreased between 1998 and 2002 in all states. And although the rate of decline is fast, but there is still more to achieve.

From Table 4.22, it is clear that when we consider the age group of children from 6-35 months, the rate of prevalence of anaemia is higher, but when we take the aggregate 0-72 months, we see that the percentage is lower. More serious is the fact that the rate of decline in Infant mortality, which was significant in

TABLE 4.21

State-wise Percentage of Anaemia among Pregnant Women, Currently Married (15-44 Years) and Ever Married Women in India (1998-1999 and 2002)

States	*Ever Married Women with Anaemia (%) 1998-99*	*Anaemia Among Pregnant Women, 2002*		
		Severe	*Moderate*	*Total*
India	51.8	3	36	39
Andhra Pradesh	49.8	3	34	37
Assam	69.7	—	—	—
Bihar	63.4	1	36	37
Gujarat	46.3	1	40	41
Karnataka	42.4	2	26	28
Kerala	22.7	1	4	5
Madhya Pradesh	54.3	2	0	42
Maharashtra	48.5	2	58	60
Orissa	63.0	4	34	38
Punjab	41.4	4	54	58
Rajasthan	48.5	3	39	42
Tamil Nadu	56.5	1	25	26
Uttar Pradesh	48.7	3	40	43
West Bengal	62.7	8	24	32

Source : National Institute of Public Cooperation and Child Development.

the 1970s and 1980s, has slowed down in the 1990s (Table 4.23).

Certain disquieting features are observed regarding mortality among children and mothers in India. They are : (a) Every year 130,000 mothers die during childbirth. Although the National Health Policy of 1983 had set a target for 2000 to reduce Maternal Mortality Rate to less than 200 per 100,000 live births, however, 407 mothers die due to pregnancy-related causes for every 100,000 live births, and as per the NFHS-II (1998-99) survey in the last decade, the Maternal Mortality Rate has increased from 424 maternal deaths per 100,000 live births to 540 maternal deaths per 100,000 live births; (b) Three completely avoidable child deaths occur in India, and the four

TABLE 4.22
State-wise Percentage of Anaemia among Children in Age Group 0-6 Years in India (2002)

States	*Percentage of Children Aged 6-35 Months with any Anaemia*	*Anaemia Among Children (0-72 Months)*		
		Moderate	*Severe*	*Total*
India	74.3	39	3	42
Andhra Pradesh	72.3	38	3	41
Assam	63.2	—	—	—
Bihar	81.3	41	2	43
Gujarat	74.5	43	1	44
Karnataka	70.6	35	4	39
Kerala	43.9	5	0	5
Madhya Pradesh	75.0	44	3	47
Maharashtra	76	53	3	56
Orissa	72.3	37	4	41
Punjab	80.0	48	6	54
Rajasthan	82.3	36	2	38
Tamil Nadu	69.0	27	4	31
Uttar Pradesh	73.9	41	2	43
West Bengal	78.3	24	4	28

Note : Union Territories were not covered.
Source : National Institute of Public Cooperation and Child Development.

TABLE 4.23
IMR Trends in India (Per 1000 live birth)

Year	*India Urban*	*India Rural*
1970	80	130
1980	65	120
1990	63	10
1995	60	95
2000	59	90

Source : Planning Commission, GOI, Tenth Five-Year Plan, 2002-07, Vol. II.

major killers (lower respiratory tract infection, diarrhoeal diseases, perinatal causes and vaccine preventable diseases) accounting for over 60% of deaths for children under five years of age are entirely preventable through better child health care and supplemental feeding programs. The most recent estimate of complete immunization coverage indicates that only 54% of all children under age three were fully protected; (c) India is experiencing a resurgence of various communicable diseases including Malaria, Encephalitis, Kala Azar, Dengue and Leptospirosis. The number of cases of Malaria has remained at a high level of around 2 million cases annually since the mid-eighties. By the year 2001, the worrying has emerged that nearly half of the cases are of Falciparum malaria, which can cause the deadly cerebral malaria. Environmental and social dislocations combined with weakening public health systems have contributed to this resurgence; (d) About 5 lakh people die from tuberculosis every year, and this number rises by about 20 lakh each year, and the incidence of this disease among mothers and children is quite high.

The National Family Health Survey–III (2005-06) brings out some revealing and disturbing facts on the health of women in the reproductive age group and also on children. Table 4.24 gives details about IMR, Neonatal mortality, post-neonatal mortality, Under-five mortality, and percentage of children in the age group of 12-13 months having all basic vaccinations, and percentage of children with no vaccination, for the 29 states including Delhi. It is seen that IMR varies from the high levels of 73 in Uttar Pradesh, 71 in Chhattishgarh, and 70 in Madhya Pradesh to low levels of 15 in Kerala and Goa. Andhra Pradesh has a fairly high IMR of 54 per 1000 live births compared to Himachal Pradesh's 36. It is shocking to note that despite much publicity, in India as a whole, only 43.5 percent of the children had all basic vaccinations, and the figures vary from 23% in Uttar Pradesh to 81% in Tamil Nadu. In Assam 15 per cent of children had no immunization at all, while in Orissa 12% of children did not have any immunization at all, and in the smaller states like Arunachal Pradesh, Tripura and Nagaland, the situation was still worse with respect to immunization.

It is really depressing to note the high prevalence of anaemia among women in the age-group of 15-49 years

TABLE 4.24
Early Childhood Mortality Rates (Deaths per '000 Children in Age Group)

Ranks	*States*	*Infant Mortality*	*Neonatal Mortality (NN)*	*Post-neonatal Mortality (PNN)*	*Under-five Mortality*	*% of children who had basic vaccination*	*% of children who had no vaccination*
(1)	(2)	(3)	(4)	(5)	(6)	(7)	(8)
	India	57	39	18	74	44	5
1	Uttar Pradesh	73	48	25	96	23	3
2	Chhattisgarh	71	51	20	90	49	3
3	Madhya Pradesh	70	45	25	94	40	5
4	Jharkhand	69	49	20	93	34	4
5	Assam	66	46	21	85	31	15
6	Rajasthan	65	44	21	85	27	6
7	Orissa	65	45	19	91	52	12
8	Bihar	62	40	22	85	33	7
9	Arunachal Pradesh	61	34	27	88	28	24
10	Andhra Pradesh	54	40	13	63	46	4
11	Tripura	52	33	18	59	50	15
12	Gujarat	50	34	16	61	45	5
13	West Bengal	48	38	10	60	64	6
14	Jammu & Kashmir	45	30	15	51	67	5
15	Meghalaya	45	24	21	71	33	17

(Contd.)

TABLE 4.24 (Contd.)

(1)	(2)	(3)	(4)	(5)	(6)	(7)	(8)
16	Karnataka	43	29	14	55	55	7
17	Uttaranchal	42	28	14	57	60	9
18	Haryana	42	24	18	52	65	8
19	Punjab	42	28	14	52	60	7
20	Delhi	40	29	11	47	63	9
21	Nagaland	38	20	19	65	21	18
22	Maharashtra	38	32	6	47	59	3
23	Himachal Pradesh	36	27	9	42	74	2
24	Mizoram	34	16	18	53	47	7
25	Sikkim	34	19	14	40	70	3
26	Tamil Nadu	30	19	11	36	81	0
27	Manipur	30	19	11	42	47	7
28	Goa	15	9	7	20	79	0
29	Kerala	15	12	4	16	75	2

Notes : (1) The states are in descending order of IMR.
(2) Neonatal Mortality: The probability of dying in the first month of life.
(3) Post-neonatal Mortality: The probability of dying after the first month of life before the first birthday.
(4) Infant Mortality: The probability of dying before first birthday.
(5) Child Mortality: The probability of dying between first and fifth birthdays.
(6) Under-five Mortality: The probability of dying before fifth birthday.

Source : NFHS-III, 2005-6.

TABLE 4.25
Percentage of Women (15-49) with Anaemia (Haemoglobin in g/dl = grams per declilitre)

Ranks	*States*	*Any Anaemia (<11.0 g/dl)*	*Mild (10.0-10.9 g/dl)*	*Moderate (7.0-9.9 g/dl)*	*Severe (<7.0 g/dl)*
	India	55.3	38.6	15	1.8
1	Jharkhand	69.5	49.6	18.6	1.3
2	Assam	69.5	44.8	21.2	3.4
3	Bihar	67.4	50.5	15.9	1
4	Tripura	65.1	49	14.8	1.3
5	West Bengal	63.2	45.8	16.4	1
6	Andhra Pradesh	62.9	39	20.6	3.3
7	Orissa	61.2	44.9	14.9	1.5
8	Sikkim	60	42.1	16.2	1.7
9	Chhattisgarh	57.5	39.9	15.7	1.9
10	Haryana	56.1	37.6	16.7	1.7
11	Madhya Pradesh	56	40.8	14.1	1
12	Gujarat	55.3	36.2	16.5	2.6
13	Uttaranchal	55.2	40.4	13.3	1.5
14	Tamil Nadu	53.2	37.4	13.6	2.2
15	Rajasthan	53.1	35.2	15.4	2.5
16	Jammu & Kashmir	52.1	37.3	13.1	1.6
17	Karnataka	51.5	34.4	15.1	2
18	Arunachal Pradesh	50.6	36.6	12.5	1.6
19	Uttar Pradesh	49.9	35.1	13.2	1.6
20	Maharashtra	48.4	32.8	13.9	1.7
21	Meghalaya	47.2	32.8	12.6	1.8
22	Delhi	44.3	35.2	8.8	0.2
23	Himachal Pradesh	43.3	31.6	10.5	1.2
24	Mizoram	38.6	29.1	8.8	0.7
25	Goa	38	29.6	7.8	0.6
26	Punjab	38	26.2	10.4	1.4
27	Manipur	35.7	30.1	5.1	0.5
28	Kerala	32.8	25.8	6.5	0.5

Notes : (1) The states are in ascending order of "any anaemia" and exclude Nagaland.

(2) Prevalence of anaemia, based on Haemoglobin levels, is adjusted for attitude using formula in CDC (1998).

Source : NFHS-III, 2005-06.

Table 4.26

Prevalence of Anaemia in Children 6-59 months (in %)

Rank	*States*	*Anaemia Status by Haemoglobin Level*			
		Any Anaemia (<11.0 g/dl)	*Mild (10.0-10.9 g/dl)*	*Moderate (7.0-9.9 g/dl)*	*Severe (<7.0 g/dl)*
	India	69.5	26.3	40.2	2.9
1	Bihar	78.0	29.6	46.8	1.6
2	Madhya Pradesh	74.1	27.1	43.6	3.4
3	Uttar Pradesh	73.9	25.4	45.0	3.6
4	Haryana	72.3	25.8	42.2	4.3
5	Chhattisgarh	71.2	24.0	45.2	2.0
6	Andhra Pradesh	70.8	23.7	43.5	3.6
7	Karnataka	70.4	28.6	38.6	3.2
8	Jharkhand	70.3	29.3	39.1	1.9
9	Rajasthan	69.7	22.8	40.2	6.7
10	Gujarat	69.7	25.0	41.1	3.6
11	Assam	69.6	28.7	38.7	2.2
12	Punjab	66.4	21.7	38.1	6.6
13	Orissa	65.0	28.9	34.5	1.6
14	Meghalaya	64.4	31.7	31.7	1.0
15	Tamil Nadu	64.2	27.1	34.6	2.6
16	Maharashtra	63.4	21.9	39.6	1.8
17	Tripura	62.9	27.5	34.6	0.7
18	Uttaranchal	61.4	28.5	30.6	2.3
19	West Bengal	61.0	30.0	29.4	1.5
20	Sikkim	59.2	28.9	29.5	0.8
21	Jammu & Kashmir	58.6	25.8	30.4	2.4
22	Delhi	57.0	26.3	30.0	0.7
23	Arunachal Pradesh	56.9	27.1	29.1	0.8
24	Himachal Pradesh	54.7	25.7	26.8	2.2
25	Kerala	44.5	23.5	20.5	0.5
26	Mizoram	44.2	23.5	20.2	0.6
27	Manipur	41.1	25.6	15.2	0.3
28	Goa	38.2	19.5	17.1	1.5

Notes : (1) The states are in ascending order of "any anaemia".
(2) This is based on children who stayed in the household the night before the interview. Prevalence of anaemia, based on Haemoglobin levels, is adjusted for altitude using formula in CDC (1998). Haemoglobin in g/dl = grams per declilitre. Excludes Nagaland.

Source : NFHS-III, 2005-06.

(Table 4.25), and among children in the age group of 6-59 months (Table 4.26). In majority of states of India, women suffer from anaemia: Jharkhand, Assam, Bihar, Tripura and West Bengal belong to high incidence states in so far as anaemia among women are concerned. Table 4.26 indicates that in India as a whole, 70% of the children suffer from some of anaemia, and even in demographically progressive states like Andhra Pradesh, Karnataka, and Tamil Nadu, the prevalence rate is alarmingly high as in states like Bihar, Jharkhand, Uttar Pradesh, Madhya Pradesh and Rajasthan. Table 4.27 also indicates that between NFHS-II and NFHS-III, i.e. in a span of about 7 years, the incidence of Children's Anaemia have gone up significantly in both rural and urban areas for India as a whole.

TABLE 4.27

Trends in Children's Anaemia

Anaemia Status by Haemoglobin Level	*NFHS-III (2005-06)*			*NFHS-II (1998-1999)*		
	Rural	*Urban*	*Total*	*Rural*	*Urban*	*Total*
Any Anaemia (<11.0 g/dl)	80.9	72.2	78.9	75.3	70.8	74.3
Mild (10.0-10.9 g/dl	25.7	25.8	25.7	22.7	23.7	22.9
Moderate (7.0-9.9 g/dl)	51.7	42.0	49.4	47.1	42.0	45.9
Severe (<7.0 g/dl	3.5	4.4	3.7	5.5	5.1	5.4

Notes : (1) This table includes only the last two children of 6-35 months of ever-married women who are interviewed.

(2) Prevalence of anaemia, based on Haemoglobin levels, is adjusted for altitude using formula in CDC (1998).

(3) Haemoglobin in g/dl = grams per declilitre. NFHS-III estimates of anaemia. Excludes Nagaland.

Source : NFHS-III, 2005-06.

V. HIV IN INDIA—A FAST SPREADING EPIDEMIC

An estimated 5.1 million Indians are currently living with HIV. Concentrated in seven states with over 1% antenatal prevalence in four of the industrialized western and southern states of India (specifically Andhra Pradesh, Karnataka, Maharashtra and Tamil Nadu) and in the northe-astern states of

Manipur and Nagaland, the epidemic is highly heterogeneous. Although data gathered by NACO in 2004 has revealed that HIV prevalence has stabilized in at least Tamil Nadu, Andhra Pradesh, Karnataka, and Maharashtra, it is increasing in at-risk populations in other states. As a result, overall HIV prevalence has continued to rise. A significant proportion of new infections is occurring in women who are married and who have been infected by husbands who either currently or in the past) frequented sex workers. Commercial sex (along with injecting drug use, in the cases of Nagaland and Tamil Nadu) serves as a major driver of the epidemic in most parts of India. Surveys in 2003 found 14% of commercial sex workers in Karnataka and 19% in Andhra Pradesh were infected with HIV. In Mysore, 26% of sex workers were HIV positive, according to a 2005 survey.

India has the highest number of people living with HIV/ AIDS and 70% of HIV infections in Asia. But only 7% of people infected with the virus have access to treatment, according to the 2006 AIDS Epidemic Update by UNAIDS/WHO (World Health Organization). According to the report, 5.2 million people in the (15-49) age group in India are affected, and among the affected 38% are women. The most distressing data is that only 7 in 100 patients have access to treatment, putting India in the company of sub-Saharan Africa (the epicenter of the HIV/ AIDS pandemic) and Russia, where treatment coverage is 3% and 5% respectively. This is way below the all-Asia average of 16% coverage, of which Thailand is said to have the most impressive coverage. Even China, where an epidemic has been recognized only recently, has better coverage than India. However, the HIV prevalence among women aged 15 to 24 years in the four southern Indian states of Andhra Pradesh, Tamil Nadu, Karnataka and Kerala declined from 1.7% in 2000 to 1.1% in 2004. In the northeast of India, HIV transmission is concentrated chiefly among drug injectors and their sexual partners (some of whom also buy or sell sex), especially in the states of Manipur, Mizoram and Nagaland, all of which lie adjacent to the drug-trafficking 'Golden Triangle' zone (Solomon *et. al.*, 2004). Some 20% of female sex workers said they injected drugs, according to behavioral surveillance. In

TABLE 4.28

State-wise Number of Deaths due to AIDS in India (1996 to June, 2006)

States/UTs	*1996*	*1997*	*1998*	*1999*	*2000*	*2001*	*2002*	*2003*	*2004*	*2005*	*2006 (June)*
(1)	*(2)*	*(3)*	*(4)*	*(5)*	*(6)*	*(7)*	*(8)*	*(9)*	*(10)*	*(11)*	*(12)*
Andhra Pradesh	4	—	6	—	—	53	36	185	237	229	22
Assam	—	—	1	—	1	0	2	0	1	0	0
Bihar	40	—	12	5	7	1	0	0	0	0	0
Gujarat	—	—	—	12	—	20	83	62	30	92	11
Haryana	—	1	—	—	5	0	0	0	0	0	0
Karnataka	7	17	12	20	19	27	40	27	28	172	0
Kerala	31	110	82	13	—	120	139	120	0	0	0
Madhya Pradesh	—	—	—	—	50	6	3	2	10	15	7
Maharashtra	—	—	—	80	77	354	404	415	338	194	63
Orissa	—	—	—	—	—	1	19	79	56		0
Punjab	8	5	4	—	—	12	2	0	0	13	5
Rajasthan	—	—	—	—	—	0	0	0	0	0	0
Tamil Nadu	—	—	2	—	119	249	285	351	297	187	0
Uttar Pradesh	—	—	—	—	4	15	4	23	7	0	0
West Bengal	—	—	—	—	—	27	48	62	0	0	0
India	174	300	185	229	378	1039	1265	1620	1170	1094	155

Source : Ministry of Health and Family Welfare, Govt. of India, Lok Sabha Unstarred Question No. 2295, dated 15.12.2002, Lok Sabha Unstarred Question No. 1987, dated 16.03.2005 and Lok Sabha Unstarred Question No. 3171, dated 23.08.2006.

TABLE 4.29

State-wise Allocation/Releases and Expenditure under National AIDS Control Programme in India (2000-01 to 2005-06)

(Rs. in Lakh)

State/UTs	2000-01		2001-02		2002-03		2003-04		2004-05	2005-06
	Allocation/ Releases	Expen- diture	Allocation/ Releases	Expen- diture	Allocation/ Releases	Expen- diture	Allocation/ Releases	Expen- diture	Allocation/ Releases	Expen- diture
Andhra Pradesh	1074.50	1097.80	1875.00	2171.84	2090.00	2004.00	2175.00	1794.86	3052.45	7511.66
Assam	375.00	346.27	653.80	561.90	614.50	643.77	475.00	226.27	1214.50	1395.18
Bihar	196.00	105.84	809.50	1017.85	600.50	573.56	700.00	218.43	1079.50	1757.78
Gujarat	681.78	528.96	1188.30	933.08	1295.19	1071.62	1477.62	730.31	1997.30	4163.1
Haryana	246.50	321.05	266.00	207.76	315.00	206.28	300.00	200.62	266.00	724.35
Karnataka	398.65	533.57	893.15	783.35	1025.00	916.51	1100.00	1316.67	1664.50	2071.35
Kerala	600.63	437.88	835.00	608.89	855.00	861.74	850.00	475.01	1104.00	2251.61
Madhya Pradesh	542.00	361.49	780.50	471.12	521.50	453.54	490.00	240.33	855.50	1779.61
Maharashtra	1296.58	1241.73	1598.65	858.47	2293.50	2345.07	2120.00	1641.23	3287.50	5202.27
Orissa	408.50	236.20	565.00	322.57	448.00	412.86	500.00	205.94	530.00	1563.29
Punjab	321.50	177.55	266.50	185.62	403.50	386.99	250.00	166.75	371.50	924.24
Rajasthan	380.00	232.68	409.50	297.01	368.50	370.94	250.00	77.27	867.50	1280.72
Tamil Nadu	1870.92	783.27	2072.32	2099.12	2221.95	2200.76	2588.38	2468.49	3893.34	4329.04
Uttar Pradesh	1175.00	448.53	1465.65	2367.17	1674.50	432.87	700.00	956.24	1070.80	1267.83
West Bengal	643.15	544.60	1059.50	1221.56	1503.50	1418.84	1200.00	1376.46	2393.00	4301.47
India	12346.45	9111.83	18843.37	17390.60	20482.14	17398.70	20163.00	14694.38	31052.72	54681.10

Source : Lok Sabha Unstarred Question No. 2236, dated 17.12.2003 and Rajya Sabha Unstarred Question No. 132, dated 09.07.2004 and Lok Sabha Unstarred Question No. 2535, dated 10.08.2005.

TABLE 4.30a
Descriptive Statistics for Deaths due to Aids and Fund Sanctioned

	N	*Minimum*	*Maximum*	*Mean*	*Std. Deviation*
Deaths	6	155.00	1620.00	1057.1667	487.5036
Funds	6	9111.83	54681.10	24054.8883	16652.7246
Valid N (list-wise)	6				

TABLE 4.30b
Correlations between Deaths due to Aids and Fund Sanctioned

		Deaths	*Funds*
Deaths	Pearson Correlation	1.000	-.820
	Sig. (2-tailed)		.046
	N	6	6
Funds	Pearson Correlation	-.820	1.000
	Sig. (2-tailed)	.046	
	N	6	6

Correlation is significant at the 0.05 level (2-tailed).

other north-eastern states, about half as many sex workers have reported injecting drugs harm reduction efforts (including needle and syringe exchange, as well as limited drug substitution programmes) were introduced in some states, such as Manipur. There, in 2003 the HIV prevalence among drug injectors was 24%—the lowest levels detected among injecting drug users in that state since 1998. Elsewhere the epidemics among drug injectors appear to be well established, with HIV prevalence having reached 14% in Nagaland in 2000–03, for example. But not only in the North-east, there has been a sharp rise in HIV infections among drug injectors in the southern state of Tamil Nadu, where 39% were HIV-infected in 2003, compared with 25% in 2001. In Chennai, Tamil Nadu, almost two-thirds (64%) of injectors were HIV-positive, according to sentinel surveillance done in 2003. Table 4.28 gives state-wise number of deaths due to AIDS in India (1996 to June, 2006).

From the Table 4.28, we can say that Kerala had the highest death rate due to AIDS in India till 2003, but after 2004, the data shown here is 0. The same can be seen from the data of West Bengal. And, from 2004 to 2006, Andhra Pradesh and Maharashtra show the highest value.

Now we want to analyze whether India Government with other collaborations can rectify Aids and how crude death rate due to Aids would decrease with availability of Funds. For this analysis, we take data from 2001 to 2006 from Tables 4.28 and 4.29 and present in Table 4.30a and b, the descriptive statistics and the correlation between funds and death due to aid. It is found that they are inversely-related suggesting that government expenditure on aids prevention and control has diminutive impact on the incidence of death due to aids.

VI. EFFECT OF CANCER IN INDIA

Among the Non-communicable diseases, Cancer is emerging as a major public health problem in India. In Cancer diseases, body's cells become abnormal and divide without control, and cancer cells may invade nearby tissues, and they may spread through the bloodstream and lymphatic system to other parts of the body. These diseases are lifestyle-related, have a long latent period and needs specialized infrastructure and human resources for treatment. The risk factors of the major non-communicable diseases in India (Diabetes Mellitus, Cardiovascular Diseases, Diabetes, and many types of Cancer are tobacco, dietary habits, inadequate physical activity and alcohol consumption. All these factors warrant the need for integrated primary prevention strategies.

Population-based registries within the National Cancer Registry Programme and outside the network has provided a picture of the cancer pattern in India. There are areas, which are largely un-represented, but the general pattern seems to hold good. Based on the registry data, it is estimated that there will be about 800,000 new cancers cases in India every year. At any given point there is likely to be 3 times this load that about 240,000 cases. Cancer sites associated with tobacco from 35 to 50% of all cancers in men and about 17% of cancers in women.

These cancers are amenable to primary prevention and can be controlled to a large extent.

Cancer is group of diseases with similar characteristics. It can occur in all living cells in the body and different cancer types have different natural history. Epidemiological studies have shown that 70-90% of all cancers are environmental. Lifestyle-related factors are the most important and preventable among the environmental exposures. Tobacco consumption either as chewing tobacco or smoking tobacco will account for 50% of all cancers in men. Dietary practices, reproductive and sexual practices, etc. will account for 20-30% of cancers. Appropriate changes in lifestyle can reduce the mortality and morbidity from a good proportion of Cancer, Diabetes Mellitus and Cardiovascular diseases. The States in India are in various levels of health care delivery and health infrastructure and it is possible that there are certain areas in which screening programmes could be initiated. The system for screening, with facilities for call back and proper referral are very important, irrespective of the screening strategy. The primary target should be to offer once a lifetime screening for all women at the age of 40 years. Mammography screening for breast cancer may not be cost-effective in India at present, but regular breast self-examination needs to be promoted for early detection of cancer in the breast. Breast self-examination can be propagated through print and electronic media as well as through health care personnel in various settings. Detecting a cancer when it is in the very early stage can improve the cure rate from breast cancer.

Prevention and Treatment Strategies in India

India is the one of the few developing countries that has formulated a National Cancer Control Programme. The programme envisages control of tobacco-related cancers; early diagnosis and treatment of uterine cervical cancer and distribution of therapy services, pain relief and palliative care through augmentation of health infrastructure. Suggested surrogate outcome measures include change in tobacco use, 'Knowledge, Attitude, Practice' (KAP) pattern, compliance to screening programmes, changes in referral practices and shift in age distribution.

Primary Prevention and Screening Programs

Primary prevention is the most cost effective prevention program as it aims to reduce the incidence of cancer by risk factor modification. Fifty percent of all cancers in males are tobacco-related and anti-tobacco programs can prevent a large proportion of them. This has to be publicized more widely. Teen-age students need to be targeted as most of them pick up habits at this time. The school curricula should involve messages for a healthy lifestyle and warn about the harmful effects of tobacco and alcohol. Legislation has to be enforced for prohibiting tobacco advertisement and sale of tobacco to youngsters. A proportion of cancers are considered to be related to the dietary practices and the importance of a healthy diet rich in green and yellow vegetables and fruits has to be highlighted. Cancer of the uterine cervix can be controlled to a certain extent by practicing genital hygiene and safe sexual practices. Cervical cytology (pap smear) screening programs were found to be successful in reducing cervical cancer incidence and women in the age group 35 to 64 years should undergo regular pap smear screening. Given the limitations in large-scale population-based screening programmes, India can consider primary prevention of cervical cancer by promoting genital hygiene and sexual behavior. States that have achieved a high level of health care delivery can consider starting organized screening programmes. Measures identified and propagated for cancer control in the developed countries may not be applicable for the Indian context. We have to find answers to our problems through methods, which are feasible and valuable in the Indian context. Cancer prevention needs to be considered as part of the No Communicable Diseases prevention programme as it will make it more effective and feasible. The risk factors, Alcohol, Tobacco, Bad Diet and Physical inactivity are risk factors for most of the Non-Communicable Diseases and have to be approached together as lifestyle modification.

Treatment Facilities

A multi-disciplinary approach to cancer treatment is essential and this has to be made available at all Regional Cancer Centres. The services of a trained surgeon and a Clinical Oncologist are needed to plan the most appropriate treatment. Radiotherapy services are still the mainstay of treatment given the large proportion of advanced epithelial cancers in India. Given the long waiting lists and the distance that patients have to travel to reach treatment facilities, optimal strategies have to be identified. Patients for palliative treatment and curative treatment need to be identified at the beginning of the treatment plan and palliation may be achieved with the minimum machine time and essential drug list has to be prepared for cancer chemotherapy, and chemotherapy services for common cancers have to be made available in all centres. Advanced facilities for high intensity chemotherapy for leukemia's and other cancers where chemotherapy is the mainstay of treatment, need be provided at the Regional Cancer centres. Surgical Oncology training has to be provided to General Surgeons during their training as well as to those in practice as majority of the cancers are likely to present themselves to a surgeon in the first instance.

More than 75% of cancers in India are in advanced stages and Palliative care and pain relief are essential to provide good quality life for these patients. Oral Morphine is the mainstay of cancer pain management and this has to be made available at all centres. The medical doctors as well as the administrators have to be sensitized and educated about the use of Oral Morphine and the regulations have to be made simple so that this essential drug is made available to those in pain. Half way homes and Hospices may be considered through Non-governmental Agencies as well as other sources, but they can work well when they are attached to a major cancer treatment centre. Cancer control programmes may be initiated in Registry areas so that effective monitoring the registry data can identify strategies. Table 4.31 presents information about the annual incidence of cancer in India, and Table 4.32 provide information about release of funds for cancer prevention.

TABLE 4.31

Group-wise Average Annual Crude Incident Rate of Cancer by Sex in India (1997-98)

Cancer Group with ICD-9 Code	*Rural*			*Urban*			*Total*		
	Male	*Female*	*Total*	*Male*	*Female*	*Total*	*Male*	*Female*	*Total*
(1)	*(2)*	*(3)*	*(4)*	*(5)*	*(6)*	*(7)*	*(8)*	*(9)*	*(10)*
140-190 (Malignant neoplasm of Lip, Oral Cavity and Pharynx)	7.75	2.51	10.26	13.37	6.14	19.51	10.56	4.32	14.88
150-159 (Malignant neoplasm of digestive organs and perioneum)	12.79	5.85	18.65	17.45	12.99	30.44	15.12	9.42	24.54
160-165 (Malignant neoplasm of respiratory and intrathoracic organs)	2.52	1.46	3.98	11.06	2.72	13.78	6.79	2.09	8.88
170-175 (Malignant neoplasm of Bone, Connective tissue, Skin and Breast)	1.55	7.94	9.49	3.17	21.33	24.49	2.36	14.63	16.99
179-189 (Malignant neoplasm of Genitourinary organs)	4.26	21.94	26.21	8.37	25.13	33.5	6.32	23.54	29.85
190-199 (Malignant neoplasm of other and Unspecified sites)	5.23	2.51	7.74	8.4	7.48	15.88	6.82	4.99	11.81
200-208 (Malignant neoplasm of Lymphatic and Haematopoietic tissue)	3.3	1.88	5.18	7.99	5.65	13.64	5.64	3.77	9.41
Total	37.41	44.1	81.51	69.8	81.44	151.24	53.61	62.77	116.38

Source : Ministry of Health and Family Welfare, Government of India.

TABLE 4.32

State-wise Fund Released Under National Cancer Control Programme in India (2001-02 to 2003-04)

(*Rs. in Lakh*)

States/UTs	*2001-02*	*2002-03*	*2003-04*
Andhra Pradesh	276.00	154.00	175.00
Assam	0.00	0.00	30.00
Bihar	299.00	77.50	0.00
Gujarat	375.00	75.00	75.00
Haryana	175.00	2.50	75.00
Karnataka	275.00	275.00	75.00
Kerala	75.00	78.00	75.00
Madhya Pradesh	75.00	157.00	75.00
Maharashtra	75.00	80.50	75.00
Orissa	78.00	77.00	0.00
Punjab	0.00	0.00	0.00
Rajasthan	82.50	185.00	75.00
Tamil Nadu	259.55	412.00	275.00
Uttar Pradesh	551.71	282.50	84.09
West Bengal	946.70	1077.00	767.00
India	6000.00	4713.95	2251.47

Source : Lok Sabha Starred Question No. 225, dated on 21.07.2004.

The investment in Cancer research and curement process is highest in West Bengal, and Uttar Pradesh is in very next position. But what we can see that the total investment has decreased over the period at the all India basis.

VII. HEART DISEASES AND CORONARY ATTACK

A heart attack occurs when the blood supply to part of the heart muscle is severely reduced or blocked due to a narrowing in one of the coronary arteries. This usually occurs as a result of arteriosclerosis. When platelets gather at the narrowing, they can form a clot that completely blocks the blood flow. If the blood supply is cut-off for more than a few minutes, the muscle cells of the heart may be permanently injured or die from lack of oxygen.

Coronary Heart Attack is the major killer disease in developed countries, and now it has spread rapidly in developing countries. Epidemiological studies of CHD show a lower prevalence of diseases in rural India than in urban India. Moreover, the disease is mostly shown in younger age group than old persons in India. There are risk factors associated with coronary heart disease (also called coronary artery disease), some of which can be treated or controlled and some cannot.

Based on an epidemiological study by Rajasthan Patrika Research Foundation and Monilek Hospital Research project on Coronary heart attack, a total of 3148 persons were surveyed of which there were 1982 males and 1166 females. The overall prevalence rate is 3.5%, and for males, it is 3.4% and for females it is found to be 3.7%. An increase in prevalence of coronary heart disease (CHD) with increasing age was found in both the sexes. Table 4.33 summarises the picture.

TABLE 4.33
Incidence of Heart Attacks—Sample Evidence

Age Group	*Male N= 1982*		*Female N=1166*		*Total N= 3148*	
	Total	*Patients*	*Total*	*Patients*	*Total*	*Patients*
20-29	571	10(1.8)	382	5(1.3)	953	15(1.6)
30-39	495	13(2.6)	342	9(2.6)	837	22(2.6)
40-49	366	12(3.3)	212	11(5.2)	578	23(4.0)
50-59	268	11(4.5)	127	11(8.7)	395	22(5.6)
60+	282	22(7.8)	103	7(6.8)	385	29(7.5)
Total	1982	68(3.4)	1166	43(3.7)	3148	111(3.5)

Source : Suresh Sarma (2001).

The number in parentheses will be in percentage. Table 4.34 presents the Standard risk factors, which causes Coronary heart attack.

These tables show that the significant associations of CHD, which increase the risk, are age, hypertension, and sedentary lifestyle, smoking in males and obesity in females. The lifestyle

TABLE 4.34

Risk Factors in Coronary Heart Attack

Risk Factor	*Sex*	*Total*	*CHD Present (M=68, F=43)*	*CHD Absent (M=1914, F=1123)*
Age	M	40	47	40
	F	37	45	37
Smoking	M	1006(51)	41(60)	965(50)
	F	54(5)	7(16)	84(7)
Physical Activity	M	386(19)	16(24)	370(19)
	F	91(8)	7(16)	84(7)
Hypertension	M	470(24)	19(2)	451(23)
	F	197(17)	13(30)	184(16)
High Cholesterol	M	45(22)		
	F	22(22)		
Obesity	M	104(5)	1(2)	103(5)
	F	74(6)	8(19)	66(6)
Alcohol Intake	M	377(19)	12(18)	365(19)
	F	26(2)	1(2)	25(2)

Source : Same as the previous table.

changes in urban areas and poor living conditions in rural areas are responsible for such effects, and in case of coronary heart diseases, the cost of treatment and of medicines are so high that the poor households cannot afford to carry out treatment.

VIII. HEALTH CARE EXPENDITURE IN INDIA

The Indian constitution charges the states with "the raising of the level of nutrition and standard of living of its people and the improvement of public health" (The Constitutional Framework, Ch.8). Central government's efforts at influencing public health have focused on the five-year plans, on coordinated planning with the states, and on sponsoring major national health programmes. For most national health programmes the central and state governments jointly share expenditures. Health care expenditure is a very necessary social expenditure for any country. Health care, like education, housing, old age security and other social provisions, has nowhere in the world been able to make an effective contribution without the active participation of the state. However, like any other social expenditure health expenditure also requires a significant contribution from the government. Even in the most advanced countries the role of the state has been extremely critical in assuming that health care become universally and more or less equitably available. Whether it is a developed country or a developing one, state's role in developing a good health infrastructure and assuring good heath to everybody becomes very critical and important. Investment in health care is necessary social investment without which the large mass of working classes cannot realize good health and contribute to the economy.

In India, though the state has a large stake in the health sector, investment has not been effectively utilized. Part of the reason is a misdistribution of investment and parts other factors such as the growth of the private sector, which makes for an unhealthy competition for manpower resources, etc. The unchecked growth of private heath care and its absolutely unregulated functioning in India, unlike in most other countries where a large private sector exists, has made profiting from human misery a big business. The consequence of this is underdeveloped health services, public and private, and the poor health of the people in the country. At 0.9% of GDP and 4.2% of GDP respectively, few countries display such a wide gap between government and private spending on health.

In terms of public spending on health, India ranks an abysmal 171st out of 175 countries for which data is available, in stark contrast to an impressive 18th rank in private spending on health, according to the UNDP's Human Development Report 2004. Only four countries—Nigeria, Indonesia, Sudan and Myanmar—rank behind India in terms of public expenditure on health sector.

Public spending on health in India is a mere 0.9% of the country's Gross Domestic Product (GDP). In China, with which India is often compared, the government spends 2% of its GDP on health, even Nepal (1.5%), and Bangladesh (1.6%) spend more than India on their citizens' health. In South Asia, only Pakistan (1%) does almost as badly as India. The Planning

Commission's latest review of the country's health sector also reveals that there is just one doctor for 1800 people, and one bed per 1123 of the population. Government hospitals are in desperate need of doctors and paramedics—there is a shortage of more than 42,000 doctors only in government-run hospitals. Given these figures, it's hardly surprising that the argument that reform is about taking public money out of unproductive investments and deploying it in the social sector does not seem convincing.

Compare this gloomy picture with India's private spending on health. According to the UNDP report, only 17 countries exceed India's 4.2% figure for private expenditure as a percentage of the country's GDP. Countries that spend more than India include the United States, Switzerland, South Africa, Brazil, Kenya, Cambodia, EI Salvador, Armenia, Bosnia and Cyprus. Only in few countries does such a wide gap exist between government and private spending on health. In India, the gap has seen medical entrepreneurs step in to fill the breach, but only for some sections of the population. Private expenditure on health includes the money spent by entrepreneurs in setting up private hospitals and fees paid by patients treated there. The private sector is expectedly concentrated in more developed areas, which offer better commercial prospects. The poor thus have very limited access to the qualified private sector due both to locational disadvantages and financial constraints. A large number in India have no alternative but to depend on unqualified providers—often with disastrous results. The low literacy levels, poor health information and often persistence of traditional beliefs and superstitions compounds the problem by making the poor ill-equipped to make rational choices in health-related matters. In its Common Minimum Programme, the United Progressive Alliance Government has promised to spend 2% of GDP on health. But this has remained a promise, perhaps with additional emphasis on health during the XIth Five Year Plan formulation, this figure may go up.

In India, the spending on health has major contributions coming from private households (75%). State governments contribute 15.2 percent, the central government 5.2%, third party insurance and employers 3.3% and municipal government and foreign donors about 1.3% (World Bank, 1995). Of these proportions, 58.7% goes toward primary health care (curative, preventive and promotive) and 38.8 percent is spent on secondary and tertiary in-patient care. The rest goes for non-service costs. Table 4.35 below provides comparison of public expenditure on health of various countries.

TABLE 4.35
Public Expenditure on Health as % of Total Expenditure on Health

Country	*Percentage*
Bhutan	90.6
Maldives	83.5
Democratic People's Republic of Korea	73.4
Timor-Lesti	59.5
Thailand	57.1
Sri Lanka	48.9
Bangladesh	44.2
Nepal	29.7
Indonesia	25.1
India	17.9
Myanmar	17.8

The comparison of health expenditure with other countries suggests that India's public health expenditure is only 17.9% of total expenditure on health care while it is close to 90 per cent for smaller countries like Bhutan and Maldives.

Centre and State's Roles in Public Healthcare Expenditure

The total public health care expenditure is composed of state level allocations and allocations from central government. The central sponsored programmes have been the result of policy initiative by the Government of India to support the health sector programmes directly. The center provides direct and partial (matching grant) support to the states in meeting both recurring and non-recurring expenditure of programmes under the policy initiative. The state's share in the total revenue expenditure has been declining. This is also a reflection of the fact that state governments are going through serious fiscal problems, and this trend has developed during the post-reform period. As compared to these allocations, the private expenditure on health care is increasing. In fact in the past five six years it has grown exponentially. From just 195 billion in 1994 it rose by more than five times to Rs. 1283 billion in 2003.

Private Health Care Sector Dominates in India

As the public health infrastructure in the country is very small and grossly inadequate to meet the health care demands, the private health care sector has taken a dominant position. Private general practice is the most commonly used health care service in both rural and urban areas. It may be noted that the dominance of the private health sector is not something that has emerged recently or out of specific policies favoring privatization under the new economic regime of liberalization and globalization. It has always been there, including the state's support for it to grow and flourish. In the eighties, data from small micro-studies as well as national level studies by the National Sample Survey and the NCAER, provided necessary evidence to show the overwhelming dominance of the private health sector in India. These studies show that 60-70% of health care is sought in the private sector of which households contribute 4% to 6% of their incomes. This means a whopping Rs. 400 to 600 billion private health care markets in the country at today's market prices. This includes the hospital sector where the private sector has about 50% of the market share.

While some policies of the state governments have actively promoted the private health sector's growth, others have done this through sheer inaction and lack of concern. Some examples are given below :

- Medical education is almost wholly state-financed and its major beneficiaries are the doctors who set-up private practice after their training. More than three-fourths of medical college graduates from state institutions work in the private sector or migrate abroad. Though they are trained using public funds, their contribution to social development is very little because they engage in health care as a business activity.

- The government provides concessions and subsidies to private medical professionals and hospitals to set-up private practice and hospitals. It provides incentives, tax holidays, and subsidies to private pharmaceutical and medical equipment industry. It manufactures and supplies raw materials (bulk drugs) to private formulation units at subsidies rate/low cost. It allows exemptions in taxes and duties in importing medical equipment and drugs, especially the highly expensive new medical technologies.
- The government has allowed the highly profitable private hospital sector to function as trusts, which are exempt from taxes. Hence they don't contribute to the state exchequer even when they charge patients exorbitantly.
- The government has been contracting out of its programs and health services selectively to NGOs in rural areas where its own services are ineffective. This will further discredit public health services and pave the way for further privatization.
- Construction of public hospitals and health centres are generally contracted out to the private sector. The latter makes a lot of money but a larger part of the infrastructure thus created, especially in rural areas is inadequately provided and hence cannot meet the health care demands of the people.
- Medical and pharmaceutical research and development is largely carried out in public institutions but the major beneficiary is the private sector. Development of drugs and medical and surgical techniques are pioneered in public institutions, but commercialization, marketing and profit appropriation is left with the private sector.
- The government has allowed the private health sector to proliferate uncontrolled. Neither the government nor the Medical Council of India has any control over medical practice, its ethics, its rationale, its

profiteering, etc. There is no regulation of quality of practice and standards in hospital care of any kind whatsoever.

- Forty percent of hospitalized people are forced to borrow money or sell assets to cover expenses. Over 2 crores of Indians are pushed below the poverty line every year because of the catastrophic effect of out of pocket spending on health care.
- Irrational medical procedures are on the rise—according to just one study in a community Chennai, 45% of all deliveries were performed by Cesarean operations, whereas the WHO has recommended that not more than 10-15% of deliveries would require Cesarean operations. Due to irrational prescribing, an average of 63 per cent of the money spent on prescriptions is a waste. This means that nearly two-thirds of the money that we spend on drugs may be for unnecessary or irrational drugs.
- The pharmaceutical industry is rapidly growing. Yet only 20% of the population can access all essential drugs that they require. There is a proliferation of brand names with over 70,000 brands marketed in India, but the 2002 Drug Policy recommends that only 25 drugs be kept under price control. As a result, many drugs are being sold at 200 to 500 percent profit margin, and essential drugs have become unaffordable for the majority of the Indian population.

In today's liberalized scenario, and with World Bank's advice of limiting state's role to selective health care for a selective population, the private health sector is ready for another leap in its growth. And this will mean further appreciation in the rates of people's treatment and a worsening health care scenario for the majority of our population. Private health care and essential drugs are becoming increasingly unaffordable to the majority of poor families suffering from illness. A growing proportion of Indians cannot afford health care when they fall ill. National sample surveys on Morbidity show that the number of people who could not seek medical care because of lack of money increased significantly between

1986 and 1995. The proportion of such persons unable to afford health care almost doubled, increasing from 10 to 21% in urban areas, and growing from 15 to 24 % in rural areas in this decade. The dominance of the private sector not only denies access to poorer sections of society, but also skews the balance towards urban biased, tertiary level health services with profitability overriding equity, and rationality of care often taking a back seat.

Table 4.36 portrays expenditure of Central and state governments on health.

TABLE 4.36
Expenditure of Central and State Governments on Health

Years	*Percentage to GDP at current market prices*
1993-94	1.25
1994-95	1.22
1995-96	1.02
1996-97	0.95
1997-98	1.00
1998-99	1.11
1999-2000	0.90

Source : Centre for Monitoring of Indian Economy (CMIE), Public Finance.

Public health investment is among the lowest in the world for India. As a percentage of GDP, it declined from 1.3% in 1990 to 0.9% in 1999. In the states, which have the major responsibility for public health expenditures declined from 7% to 5.5%. The draft of the proposed National Health Policy, 2001 of the Government of India admits, "Economic liberalization has resulted in the declining percent of state resources allocated to the health sector".

Trend of Public Health-Care Expenditure at State Level

Per capita public healthcare expenditure in different states in India does not show any trend, except in two states: Punjab and Kerala. State government revenue expenditure for medical and health care increased from just around Rs. 50 billion in 1992 to more than 150 billion in 2001, an increase of more than three times in a decade. Around 1996, there was a sharp dip in public healthcare expenditure (PHCE) across all states, which tended to rise thereafter. The large states like Bihar and UP experience about the lowest PHCE among all states consistently, compared to even smaller states like Kerala and Assam. States like Tamilnadu, Rajasthan and Maharashtra does not show much fluctuation in PHCE. So we do not find much interstate variations in PHCE. If we divide the period being studied into two parts, from 1990 to 1996 and from 1996 to 2002, then we can compare variations in PHCE across states of India between these sub-periods and as a whole. This is presented in Table 4.37 below.

TABLE 4.37
Growth of Public Healthcare Expenditure (PHCE) Per Capita (in real terms)

	*Change**			*Percentage Change*		
	1990-96	*1996-2002*	*1990-2002*	*1990-96*	*1996-2002*	*1990-2002*
Andhra Pradesh	- 211.1	263.4	52.3	-28.16%	48.92%	6.98%
Assam	3.4	- 15.5	- 12.1	0.56%	-2.56%	-2.01%
Bihar	- 111.7	160	48.2	-26.25%	50.96%	11.33%
Gujarat	-156.6	110.3	-46.3	-17.48%	14.91%	-5.17%
Karnataka	-103.6	270.3	166.7	-13.23%	39.79%	21.30%
Kerala	-73.2	172.2	99.1	-7.99%	20.43%	10.81%
Madhya Pradesh	-103.6	161.1	57.5	-18.54%	35.41%	10.30%
Maharashtra	-144.2	278.3	134.1	-16.80%	38.97%	15.62%
Orissa	-186.9	154.3	- 32.6	-30.32%	35.92%	-5.29%
Punjab	-414.9	583.8	168.9	-33.29%	70.20%	13.55%
Rajasthan	-86.7	152.1	65.5	-10.95%	21.60%	8.28%
Tamil Nadu	-44.6	134.5	89.9	-5.07%	16.09%	10.2%
Uttar Pradesh	-160	- 5.3	-165.2	-26.40%	-1.18%	-27.27%
West Bengal	-35.5	251.8	216.3	-5.69%	42.76%	34.64%
All India (States)	-107.8	160.8	53.1	-14.9%	26.14%	7.34%

Source : CMIE.; *Figures are in million.

From the above table few interesting points emerges. First, the public health care expenditure (PHCE) in real terms of all the states except Assam declined in the period 1990-96, but it increased during the period 1996–2002 for all states except Uttar Pradesh and Assam. Overall in this period PHCE increased for most of the states except Assam, Gujarat, Orissa and Uttar Pradesh. Secondly, when we observe per capita heath expenditure as a percentage of per capita gross state domestic product (GSDP) for the same period of time, we find a declining trend of this percentage spending of state governments. But states like Bihar, Assam, Andhra Pradesh and Punjab shows very high fluctuation in PHCE to GSDP ratio while some states like Maharashtra and Gujarat does not show much fluctuations. But, one thing that clearly emerges from the above table is that when we observe PHCE as a percentage of GSDP, we notice that Bihar and Uttar Pradesh does not fare very badly here. In fact Bihar comes across as one of the state with highest ratio. Here big states like Maharashtra, Madhya Pradesh, and Gujarat have not done well. One thing which comes out from the above figure is that in almost all the states PHCE as a percentage of GSDP has not increased much during past decade, and in fact during the period 1994 to 2002, health care expenditure as a percentage of Gross SDP had shown a decline. Table 4.38 summarises the percentage change in PHCE/GSDP ratio in the states of India.

From the Table 4.38 we can see that for all the states PHCE as a percentage of GSDP went down significantly in the period 1990-96, and for the period 1996-2002 again it went down except for Andhra Pradesh, Madhya Pradesh, Maharashtra, Orissa, Punjab and West Bengal. But on the whole, for entire period it went down for all the states. From this a very important point emerges that government priority for health care expenditure is decreasing over the years in all the states which means that less and less money per capita is being spent by the government on health care as a percentage of income. Table 4.39 summarises the percentage decreases in the ratio between 1990-2002 in different states.

From the Table 4.39 it is evident that Gujarat has maximum decrease in HCE as a percentage of income, followed by most of

TABLE 4.38

Percent Change in PHCE/GSDP Ratio

	1990-96	*1996-2002*	*1990-2002*
Andhra Pradesh	-40.51%	16.46%	-30.72%
Assam	-5.79%	-6.55%	-11.96%
Bihar	-19.21%	-5.14%	-23.36%
Gujarat	-38.11%	-7.95%	-43.03%
Karnataka	-31.08%	-0.33%	-31.31%
Kerala	-31.20%	-5.61%	-35.07%
Madhya Pradesh	-31.14%	18.24%	-18.58%
Maharashtra	-37.15%	21.36%	-23.72%
Orissa	-31.53%	16.30%	-20.37%
Punjab	-40.24%	44.05%	-13.91%
Rajasthan	-26.81%	-0.74%	-27.35%
Tamil Nadu	-30.40%	-11.56%	-38.45%
Uttar Pradesh	-28.96%	-12.90%	-38.12%
West Bengal	-25.90%	3.49%	-23.31%

Source : CMIE.

TABLE 4.39

The Percentage Decreases in PHCE as a Ratio of GSDP

% Decrease (1990-2002)	*States*
More than 40%	Gujarat
Between 30-40%	Andhra Pradesh, Karnataka, Kerala, Uttar Pradesh, Tamilnadu
Between 20-30%	Orissa, West Bengal, Bihar, Maharashtra, Rajasthan
Less than 20%	Madhya Pradesh, Punjab, Assam

the southern states and Uttar Pradesh, followed by the eastern states and western states of India. Since 1991, economic reforms were initiated in India, and during the early years, fiscal compression put a slowdown on public expenditure on health, but since 1996, the situation somewhat eased.

5

Efficiency of Health Outcomes in Rural India : Interstate Variations

The current health situation in India is a sad story of deprivation. The blatantly paradoxical spectacle of buying and selling of health improvements as a consumer goods by the well-off minority in the metros on the one hand, and the denial of basic health facilities to the vast majority of the population along the length and breadth of the country on the other, is a cause for serious concern among policy-makers and managers of the economy. Besides, the fact that the morbidity and mortality levels in the country are still very high and that the health indices are still unsatisfactory, in turn, is an indication of the limited success of the public health system in meeting the preventive and curative requirements of the general population, and the data released by the government often fail to indicate the nature and extent of neglect and deprivation of health of the vast majority of the population.

In the era of reform system in the health sector and with the role of Government in health provision diminishing, emphasis is shifting to making the sector efficient. Health systems deserve the highest priority in any endeavor to improve people's health, since they provide in the critical interface between life saving interventions and the people who need them. The primary goal of a health system should be to provide better health in a responsive manner and with a fair financial distribution. However, how well the health system accomplishes this goal is reflected in actual health outcomes (attainments) in relation to potential, given the endowments/health investments (performance).

The present chapter is organized as follows. Section I describes the health status in India and its interstate variations. Section II describes the efficiency of health system in rural India and their interstate variations in terms of non-parametric econometric method of Data Envelopment Analysis. Section III summarises the main conclusions of this chapter.

I. HEALTH STATUS IN INDIA

Health status in Indian states are as diverse as the states are, and available statistics shows very uneven levels of attainment of health across the rural-urban divide as also across the geographical divide between the better performing and the poorly-performing (BIMARU) states (Table 5.1). It cannot be a matter of pure coincidence that all the better-performing states (Kerala, Maharashtra, Tamil Nadu) are known to have better preserved public health systems right down to the PHC level as opposed to the poorly performing ones, where even the physical infrastructure and the manpower resources are grossly inadequate and frequently non-existent.

In states like Uttar Pradesh, the State Health Service is basically engaged in administering the Pulse Polio Programme, whereas in states like Bihar and Jharkhand, the doctor or the compounder/pharmacist posted with the designated rural health centers, usually visit the village market weekly or fortnightly and run some sort of an out-patients' department service. This is because either the physical infrastructure (building etc.) is non-existent or is too dilapidated or has been acquired for some other purpose. In still more remote areas, even such service is unheard of. In fact, the State Health Service simply does not exist for large parts of the population of many

Table 5.1
Differentials in Health Status Across Indian States

Sector	Populations BPL (%)	IMR/1000 Live Births (1999-SRS)	<5 Mortality 1000 (NFHS-II)	Wt. forage % of children < 3 yrs (<2SD)	MMR/lakh (Annual Report 2000)	Leprosy Cases/10000 Population	Malaria+Ve cases in year 2000 (in '000s)
(1)	(2)	(3)	(4)	(5)	(6)	(7)	(8)
India	26.1	70	94.9	47	408	3.7	2200
Rural	27.09	75	103.7	49.6	—	—	—
Urban	23.62	44	63.1	38.4	—	—	—
Better Performing States							
Kerala	12.72	14	18.8	27	87	0.9	5.1
Maharashtra	25.02	48	58.1	50	135	3.1	138
TN	21.12	52	63.3	37	79	4.7	56
Low Performing States							
Orissa	47.15	97	104.4	54	498	7.05	483
Bihar	42.60	63	105.1	54	707	11.83	132
Rajasthan	15.28	81	114.9	51	607	0.8	53
UP	31.15	84	122.5	52	707	4.3	99
MP	37.43	90	137.6	55	498	3.88	528

Note : BPL – Below Poverty Line; IMR – Infant Mortality Rate; NFHS-2 – 2nd National Family Health Survey; SD – Standard Deviation; MMR – Maternal Mortality Rate; TN – Tamil Nadu; UP – Uttar Pradesh; MP – Madhya Pradesh.

Source : NFHS-II.

of these states, and the poor health service seeking population virtually remain at the mercy of private operators in the market.

TABLE 5.2

Differentials in Health Status among Socio-economic Groups

Indicator	*Infant Mortality/ 1000*	*Under 5 Mortality/1000*	*% Children Underweight*
India	70	94.9	47
Social Inequity			
Schedule Tribes	84.2	126.6	55.9
Other Disadvantaged	76	103.1	47.3
Others	61.8	82.6	41.1

Source : NHP-2002.

Now, it is evident from Tables 5.1 and 5.2 above that the national averages of health indices do not reflect the wide disparities in public health facilities and health standards in different parts of the country. Given a situation in which national values of most health indices are themselves at

FIG. 5.1

Differentials in Health Status among Socio-economic Groups

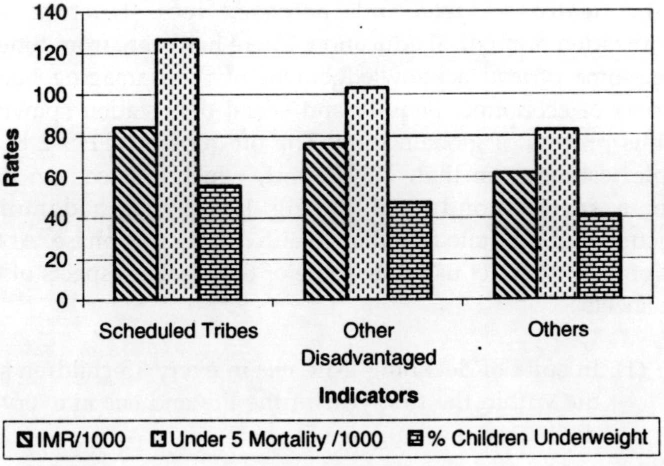

unacceptably low levels (often comparable to the least developed nations like those in the Sub-Saharan Africa, vide Human Development Reports), the wide disparity implies that, for vulnerable sections of society in several states, access to health services is nominal and health standards, at the very best, are grossly inadequate. If the current norms are applied to the population projected for the year 2000, it is estimated that the shortfall in the number of SCs/PHCs/CHCs would be of the order of 16 percent, and when disaggregated for CHCs (rural hospitals), the shortage turns out to be as high as 58 percent. It may be noted that classifying 'women, children and the socially disadvantaged sections of the society' as being part of the 'other disadvantaged' group in Table 5.2 basically hides the pathetic health conditions of these groups as are revealed through successive rounds of National Family Health Surveys. Though the National Health Policy (NHP)-2002 is an official acknowledgement of the policy imperatives inspired by the process of globalization as applied to the field of health, the policy shifts were in force much earlier, from the 1990s itself, or even earlier than that. The policy shifts in the health sector, like other sectors, have been, *inter alia,* an increasing stress on private health care recognizing healthcare as an industry, application of industrial standards of operation and discipline upon healthcare workers including doctors, 'liberalization' of patent laws, increasing stress on user fees, further contraction of public health services and increased fees structure and privatization of medical education. There has been, from time to time, some official acknowledgement of the damaging health impacts of economic inequity and social deprivation spawned by this process of globalization. The oft-quoted NFHS–2 bears ample testimony to that. The Report, which is based on data from a survey conducted during 1998-99, is a damning indictment of the state of Indian health during this phase. At the risk of repetition, let us quote some of the bleaker aspects of the fact sheets:

(1) In spite of declining IMR, *one* in every 15 children still die within the first year of the life and *one* in every 11 die before reaching age 5;

(2) 19% of total fertility is contributed by very young mothers (age 15-19);
(3) Continuing low levels of education among women contribute to the high IMR and MMR. The IMR for illiterate mothers is more than 2.5 times the rate for mothers who have completed at least high school;
(4) Mothers giving 20% of births receive all of the various types of antenatal care. Less than half of all deliveries are attended by health professional and only 1/3rd of births take place in a medical institution.;
(5) More than 1/3rd of women aged 15-49 years are undernourished (according to the body mass index) and almost half the children under the age of 3 years are underweight or stunted. By the age of 6 to 11 months, almost 1/3rd of children are malnourished;
(6) More than ½ women of age 15-49 years and almost ¾ of children of age 6-35 months are anaemic;
(7) Only 2/5 of all children of age 12-23 months receive all of the recommended childhood vaccinations; and
(8) Lastly (this would seem obvious to many of us), the NFHS-2 found that the households that have a low standard of living perform distinctly worse on most demographic and health outcome indicators than households that have a relatively high standard of living.

The National Human Development Report, 2001 (NHDR-2001), brought out by the Planning Commission, also indicates the continuation of the trends of disparities reported by the NFHS–2. For example, while the expectation of life at birth in urban India has been 66.3 years during 1992–96, the same for rural India has been 59.4 years. Similarly, the expectation of life at the age of 1 year in rural India is 63.9 years, whereas it is 68.9 years in the urban areas. Among persons not expected to survive beyond the age of 40 years in 1991, 16.9% were male while 19.1% were females. The rural-urban dichotomy continues in the IMR figures: 84 *vs.* 51. More eye-catching is the disparity in the age specific mortality rate for the age group 0-4 years (1991): 40.8 and 16. Similar is the case for the crude death rate—9.6 and 6.5 in 1997 and so on.

II. EFFICIENCY IN HEALTH OUTCOMES— AN INTERSTATE ANALYSIS

In the era of reform system in the health sector and with the role of Government in health provision diminishing, emphasis is shifting to making the sector efficient. Since health care system in India, being mostly a combination of public and private goods, shows persistent gaps in manpower and infrastructure with wide inter-state disparities, especially at the primary health care level, with detrimental impacts on less developed, backward and rural areas, it is important to focus on relative efficiency of public health systems in improving the health outcomes in the rural areas of different areas in India, given the resource base. Taking into account the level of investments (in health infrastructure) the process of attaining the outcomes (the efficiency of the system) and the actual outcomes such as analysis should assist the states in devising an appropriate health investment strategy.

(i) To achieve a higher level of overall goal attainment without increasing its resource inputs,
(ii) To address the question of adequacy of the health infrastructure, and
(iii) To address the exogenous determinants of its efficiency.

It is widely felt that a better understanding of the factors underlying the variations in performance at the state level is needed for reform strategies and better management of the health sector. It is also acknowledged that the differences in efficiency are related to the differences in the way the health infrastructure and facilities are provided and managed. This may require identifying factors outside the health sector that explain differences in efficiency.

The present study focuses on rural areas, public health, Government provision and state level performances on the basis of following considerations:

(i) The majority of the Indian population live in rural areas, and so the variations in performances of rural health systems are reflected in the overall health outcomes of different states (and the country as a whole).

(ii) Public health, comprising mostly preventive and promotive care and family and community welfare activities, and representing a merit good offering both community and private benefits, is the key to maintaining healthy society.

Concept of Efficiency

An efficient health services is one that achieves its objectives with the least cost. The idea of an 'efficient' health facility is derived from the neo-classical production model in which agents choose inputs to minimize costs. However, in health care, outcomes are the most important aspect and efficiency would essentially mean improving the health of people, either by utilizing current level of inputs to the maximum or, if that is achieved increasing the inputs to reach a higher level of outcomes. One way to achieve this is to identify those systems that are performing better than others and to look into the factors that have induced these systems to perform better.

Farrell (1957)'s definition of technical efficiency, i.e. the availability to produce the maximum possible output from a given set of inputs, is similar to the definition of health system efficiency in overall health system performance. This is because both tend to measure the relationship between observed output and the maximum attainable output for the observed inputs, i.e. what the system achieves compared to its potential.

Here we have used expenditure on health care infrastructure as the input into the health sector to achieve the two outputs: Infant Survival Rate and Life Expectancy. Efficiency then reflects not only within health programmes and the interventions are produced at the lowest possible costs (technical efficiency), but also whether the health system achieves most within the given level of expenditure (sometimes called the allocative efficiency in the health economics literature). The combination of technical efficiency and allocative efficiency gives the economic efficiency in health system. Here we only focus on the technical efficiency aspect using output-oriented DEA (Data Envelopment Analysis) approach under VRS. Here we have taken 11 states in India for the year 2001-04. The data are taken from "indiastat.com".

Methodology of Efficiency Measurement

The performance of productive units is typically described in terms of productive efficiency which implies a comparison of actual output/input to optimal output/input. In what follows, we make efficiency comparison in terms of technical efficiency. Technical efficiency refers to the ability to avoid waste by producing as much output as input usage allows, or by using as little input as output production allows. There are, however, two major alternative approaches towards defining technical efficiency: the Pareto-Koopmans approach and the Debreu-Farrell approach.

(a) *The Pareto-Koopmans Approach: Koopmans (1951)* gave a formal definition of technical efficiency: a producer is technically efficient if an increase in any output requires a reduction in at least one other output or a increase in at least one input, and if a reduction in any input requires an increase in at least one other input or a reduction in at least one output. Because of its Paretian implication, this approach is known as the Pareto-Koopmans approach.

(b) *The Debreu-Farrell Approach*: Another popular measure of technical efficiency is by *Debreu (1951)* and *Farrell (1957)*. Debreu defined the coefficient of resource utilization as a measure of technical efficiency for the economy as a whole. Farrell constructed a linear programming model using actual input-output data of a sample of firms. The solution of the linear programming model gave a numerical measure of the technical efficiency.

The Debreu-Farrell approach yields a radial measure of technical efficiency. As efficiency is measured along a ray from the origin to the observed production point. Consequently, the efficiency measure hold the relative proportions of inputs (or outputs) constant. In case of output-oriented models, their measure is defined as one minus the maximum equi-proportionate expansion in all outputs with given input. In case of input-oriented models, it is one minus the maximum equi-proportionate reduction in all inputs that still allows continued production of given output. A score less than unity implies that the firm is technically inefficient. In the present paper, we have followed the Debreu-Farrell approach.

A comparison of the two approaches show that the Pareto-Koopmans approach is stricter than the Debreu-Farrell approach. In the radial approach, radial expansion (contraction) of output (input) can give rise to output (input) slacks. The Pareto-Koopmans does not allow the existence of any such slack if a firm is to be declared technically efficient. The two definitions of efficiency are same only when the underlying production technology which comprises only properly enveloped units is efficient for each output.

Computation

Computation of technical efficiency can be done by using either the parametric (econometric) or the non-parametric (mathematical programming) approach.

The econometric approach seeks to measure efficiency by accommodating a non-positive error term in the production function that captures technical inefficiency. The presence of a disturbance term and the non-positive error term make the production frontier stochastic. The degree of technical efficiency of a producer is given by the ratio of observed to maximum feasible output, where maximum feasible output is given by the stochastic production frontier. The stochastic production frontier is in turn determined by the structure of production technology—the deterministic production frontier—and by external events, favourable and unfavorable, beyond the control of the producer.

The non-parametric methods as compared to their parametric counterparts, enjoy a number of inherent advantages;

(a) The simple Ordinary Least Squares Technique provide us 'average' rather than best practice' points. In contrast to this, mathematical programming techniques are essentially bounding techniques and consequently require little or no modification to be employed in the analysis of production frontiers.

(b) The parametric approach is stochastic in nature and consequently attempts to distinguish the effects of noise from the effects of inefficiency. In so doing, it often misspecifies the functional form with inefficiency. The non-parametric approach consolidates noise and inefficiency together and calls the combination inefficiency. It is therefore less prone to specifications errors.

(c) Non-parametric methods can easily handle multiple outputs. In contrast, in the parametric approach, one needs to adopt multiple equation models which are much more cumbersome.

In this study we have chosen the data envelopment approach (a non-parametric method) primarily because of two reasons:

(i) It does not require the assumption of any particular functional form regarding the input-output relationship with reference to the banking industry.

(ii) It can handle multiple outputs quite easily which is difficult in the case of the parametric approach.

(iii) The radial approach to the measurement of technical efficiency used in this paper is invariant to the units of measurement.

The Data Envelopment Approach

Data Envelopment Analysis is a non-parametric mathematical programming technique used for assessing/evaluating and comparing the relative performances of economic units with minimal prior assumption on input-output relation. The DEA method is a generalisation of Farrell's Single input single output technical efficiency measure to the multiple output-multiple input case. The methodology was originally developed by Charnes, Cooper and Rhodes (1978) and was later further extended by Banker, Charnes and Cooper (1984).

The DEA approach forms the efficiency frontier out of piecewise linear stretches thereby forming a convex production possibility set. In DEA frontier, efficient observations are those for which no other decision-making unit or linear combination of units has as much or more of every output (given inputs) or as little or less of every input (given outputs). The DEA approach is now described in brief.

Let us consider a productive unit producing a scalar output Y from bundles of m inputs $x=(x_1, x_2, ..., x_m)$

Let (x^j, y^j) be the observed input-output bundle of firm j (j=1, 2, ..., n). The technology is defined by the production possibility set.

$P_s = \{(x,y) : y \text{ can be produced from } x\}$

An input-output combination (x^0, y^0) is feasible if and only if $(x^0, y^0) \in Ps$.

The underlying assumptions are as follows:

(i) All observed input-output combinations are feasible. Thus $(x^j, y^j) \in Ps$ (j=1, 2, ..., n)

(ii) The production possibility set Ps is convex. Hence, if $(x^1, y^1) \in Ps$ and $(x^2, y^2) \in Ps$ then $\{ùx^1 + (1-\omega) x^2, \omega y^1 + (1-\omega) y^2\} \in Ps$ i.e. weighted averages of feasible input-output combinations are also feasible

(iii) Inputs are freely disposable. Hence, if $(x^0, y^0) \in Ps$ and $x^1 \geq x^0$ then $(x^1, y^0) \in Ps$

(iv) Output is freely disposable. Hence if $(x^0, y^0) \in Ps$ and $y^1 \leq y^0$ then $(x^0, y^1) \in Ps$

Computation of Technical Efficiency

The production possibility set of a productive organisation can be represented by two alternative but equivalent ways in terms of the input and output set. For any output bundle y^0 the input requirement set is

$$V(y^0) = \{x: (x, y^0) \in Ps\}$$

Similarly for any input bundle x^0, the producible output set is :

$$P(x^0) = \{ y : (x^0, y) \in Ps \}$$

There are accordingly three alternative ways of computing technical efficiency: the revenue maximization approach, the output maximisation approach and the cost minimisation approach. In this paper the output maximization approach has been followed.

In the output maximisation approach, the firm seeks to maximise output given the input bundle. As per the Banker, Charnes, Cooper (1984) orientation (under the assumption of variable returns to scale) the problem is,

$$\begin{aligned} & \text{Max } \phi \\ & \text{s.t. } \phi Y^o \leq \lambda Y \\ & X^o \geq lX \\ & \Sigma\lambda j = 1\lambda j \geq 0 \end{aligned}$$

$1 \leq \phi < \infty$ and $\phi - 1$ is the proportional increase in outputs that could be achieved by the ith bank, with input quantities kept constant. $1/\phi$ defines a technical efficiency score which varies between zero and one.

Results from the Data Envelopment Analysis

Tables 5.3, 5.4, 5.5 and 5.6 below present the state-wise technical efficiency scores relating to eleven observed states for the year 2001-04.

The results presented in Tables 5.3 to 5.6 show that for all the observed years Kerala and Punjab were found to be technically efficient. Madhya Pradesh was found to be efficient for 2003. All the other states were found to be technically inefficient for the observed years. Table 5.7 sums up the year-wise efficiency ranking of the states of India.

Efficiencies differ across states, due to the differences not only in health sector endowment, but also in its efficient use. This demonstrates that states should not only increase their investment in the health sector, but should also manage it more efficiently in order to achieve better health outcomes. In an era

TABLE 5.3
Technical Efficiency and Ranking of States for 2001

State	*Score*	*Rank*	*1/Score*
Andhra Pradesh	0.944388	9	1.058887
Assam	0.975769	3	1.024833
Gujarat	0.950455	8	1.052128
Karnataka	0.952477	7	1.049894
Kerala	1	1	1
Madhya Pradesh	0.924166	11	1.082057
Maharashtra	0.965622	4	1.035602
Punjab	1	1	1
Rajasthan	0.930233	10	1.075
Tamil Nadu	0.961577	5	1.039958
West Bengal	**0.959555**	**6**	**1.04215**

Source : Calculated.

TABLE 5.4
Technical Efficiency and Ranking of States for 2002

State	*Score*	*Rank*	*1/Score*
Andhra Pradesh	0.947475	8	1.055437
Assam	0.940336	9	1.06345
Gujarat	0.96968	3	1.031268
Karnataka	0.954545	7	1.047619
Kerala	1	1	1
Madhya Pradesh	0.932018	11	1.072941
Maharashtra	0.964646	5	1.036649
Punjab	1	1	1
Rajasthan	0.935295	10	1.069181
Tamil Nadu	0.965657	4	1.035565
West Bengal	**0.960606**	**6**	**1.041009**

Source : Calculated.

TABLE 5.5
Technical Efficiency and Ranking of States for 2003

State	*Score*	*Rank*	*1/Score*
Andhra Pradesh	0.970193	7	1.030722
Assam	0.965205	10	1.03605
Gujarat	0.971776	6	1.029044
Karnataka	0.979213	5	1.021228
Kerala	1	1	1
Madhya Pradesh	1	1	1
Maharashtra	0.961672	11	1.039855
Punjab	1	1	1
Rajasthan	0.98666	4	1.01352
Tamil Nadu	0.967993	8	1.033066
West Bengal	**0.96544**	**9**	**1.035797**

Source : Calculated.

TABLE 5.6
Technical Efficiency and Ranking of States for 2004

State	*Score*	*Rank*	*1/Score*
Andhra Pradesh	0.974187	5	1.026497
Assam	0.94754	10	1.055364
Gujarat	0.979877	3	1.020536
Karnataka	0.962551	8	1.038906
Kerala	1	1	1
Madhya Pradesh	0.932186	11	1.072747
Maharashtra	0.975709	4	1.024896
Punjab	1	1	1
Rajasthan	0.948041	9	1.054806
Tamil Nadu	0.970648	7	1.03024
West Bengal	**0.97166**	**6**	**1.029167**

Source : Calculated.

TABLE 5.7
Year-wise Ranking of States

State	2001	2002	2003	2004
Andhra Pradesh	9	8	7	5
Assam	3	9	10	10
Gujarat	8	3	6	3
Karnataka	7	7	5	8
Kerala	1	1	1	1
Madhya Pradesh	11	11	1	11
Maharashtra	4	5	11	4
Punjab	1	1	1	1
Rajasthan	10	10	4	9
Tamil Nadu	5	4	8	7
West Bengal	6	6	9	6

Source : Calculated.

of liberalization of the health sector and diminishing role of government in health provision, the emphasis should definitely be on improving performance.

FIG. 5.2
Efficiency Scores of Observed States (2001)

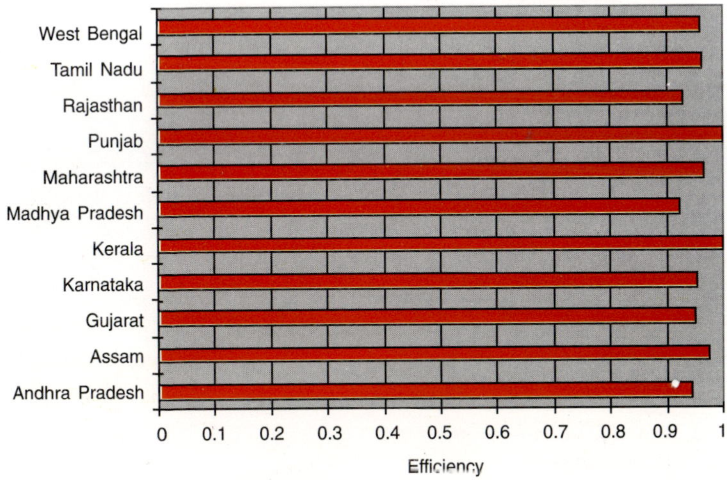

Fig. 5.3
Efficiency Scores of Observed States (2002)

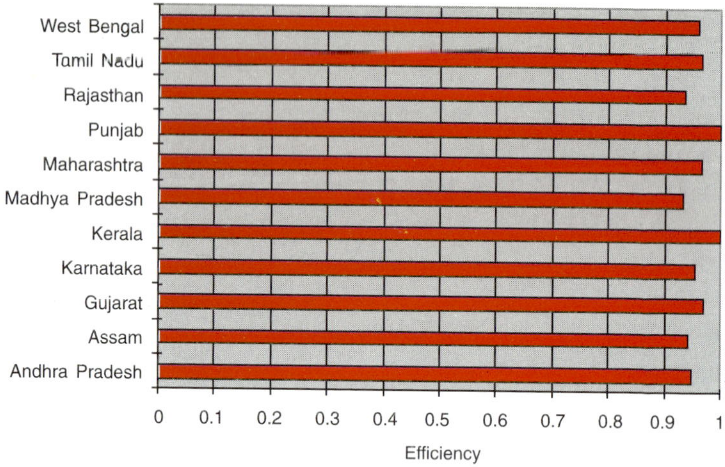

Fig. 5.4
Efficiency Scores of Observed States (2003)

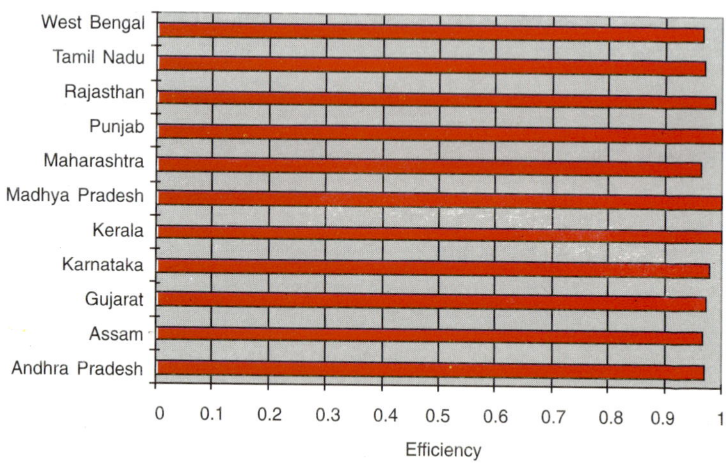

FIG. 5.5
Efficiency Scores of Observed States (2004)

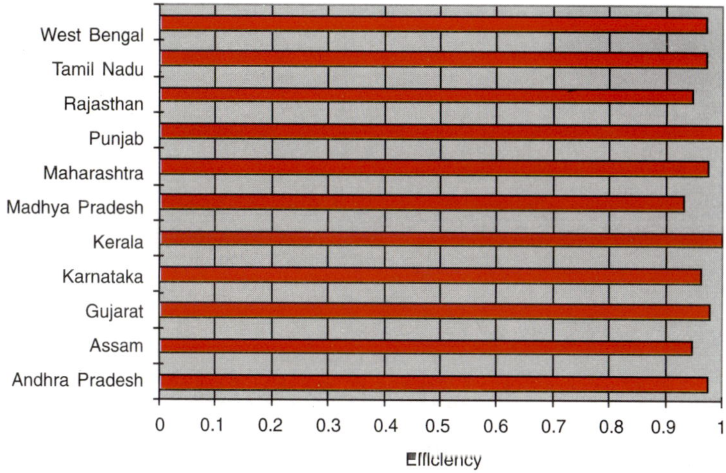

6

Poverty, Under-nutrition and Morbidity in India

One of the most important reasons for high levels of mortality and morbidity in India is under-nutrition. Food security continues to elude many, despite the country having large food stocks per capita. Endemic undernourishment claims many more lives than large scale famines. The former has less political visibility, which leads to its neglect in public discussion and the political agenda of political parties. As a result a huge proportion of the Indian population continues to suffer from chronic under-nutrition and the burden of avoidable illness and morbidity.

I. HEALTH, POVERTY AND HUMAN DEPRIVATION

Human development is a process of enlarging people's choices. The most critical ones are to lead a *long and healthy life,* to be educated and to enjoy a decent standard of living. The concept of human development looks beyond per capita income, human resource development and basic needs as a measure of human progress and also assesses such factors as human freedom, dignity and human agency, that is, the role of people in development. Progress in human development has two perspectives: one is attainment, and another one is shortfall from the development targets. The various indicators of these attainments and composite indices that they support could capture the process of development and well-being of people from two perspectives. The "conglomerate perspective" capture advances made by the society as a whole—and the 'deprivational perspective' assesses status of the deprived society.

If human development is about enlarging choices, poverty means that opportunities and choices most basic to human development are denied—to lead a long, healthy creative life and to enjoy a decent standard of living, freedom, dignity, self-respect and the respect of others. Poverty is viewed not only in terms of lack of adequate income, but as a state of deprivation in socio-economical and political aspects. These deprivations prevent people from participating in the development process and utilize the available resources to day's world has greater resources and know-how than ever before to tackle the challenges of infectious disease, low productivity, lack of clean energy and transport and lack of basic services such as clean water, sanitation, schools and health care. Deprivation in human society therefore takes different forms, of which health and nutritional deprivations constitute important ones

In a more general term, the concept of poverty is basically a state of deprivation. In absolute terms it reflects the inability of an individual to satisfy certain basic minimum needs for a sustained healthy and a reasonably productive living. The proportion of population not able to attain the specified level of expenditure is then designated as poor. Poverty is reflected in hunger, lack of shelter, being sick and not being able to see a doctor, and not being able to school and not knowing how to read.

The relationship between health and poverty or health and development, is complex multifaceted and multidirectional. Poverty in its various dimensions could be a manifestation, as well as a determinant of an individual's health. In its most basic form—as a state of food deprivation and nutritional inadequacy

– poverty has a direct bearing of the morbidity and longevity of people. How does health relate to development? The first point is that the enhancement of health is a constitute part of development; second given other things, good health and economic prosperity tend to support each other. Better health, also contributes one of the key ultimate goals of development and increasingly seen as a dimension of poverty in its own right.

Human Deprivation in Indian States

The status of human deprivation in India and the states can be gauged when we look at the deprivation in human development in the sense of denial of decent standard of living absence of education and health, measured by poverty ratio, illiteracy and infant mortality rate (IMR). Literacy is a person's first step in learning and knowledge building and therefore literacy indicators are essential for any measurement of human welfare related to economic growth as it reduces production losses on account of illness of workers or potentially, also in terms of higher work productivity for healthy workers. Improvements in educational attainments have invariably been accompanied by improvement in health and longevity of the population and in their economic well-being. Educated people are likely to be more productive and hence better off. They are also likely to contribute more to a country's economic growth. Lack of education robs an individual of a full life. It also robs society of a foundation for sustainable development because education is critical to improving health, nutrition and productivity. Income poverty may pull children from out of the school system, thus denying them the opportunity of participating in school education, even at the basic level as evidenced in the third world country situations. It is a known fact that illiteracy, one of the key factors contributing to poverty is a fall out of the poor participation of children in elementary education.

Some of the main issues of human deprivation are hunger, illiteracy, epidemics and the lack of health services or safe water. Improving health outcomes not only improves well-being but also increases income earning potential. Increasing education not only improves well-being it also leads to better health outcomes and to higher incomes. Health along with education is seen as human development. Illiteracy rate,which is calculated as 100 minus the literacy rate, is taken as an indicator of educational deprivation.

A complex set of biological, socio-economic, demographic and cultural factors underlie infant mortality. Infant mortality rate is a sensitive index of socio-economic condition of a population. It is an excellent indicator of the level and quality of health care and other social infrastructure available to a population. Infant and child mortality rates provide a good approximation of a community's current health status and by implications, of the welfare of a population and the quality of life itself. Infant mortality rate is the number of infants who die before reaching one year of age, expressed per 1000 live births in a given year.

Based on poverty ratio (1999-2000) {which is percentage of population whose income or consumption per capitalies below the official poverty line}, illiteracy rate (2001) and infant mortality rate (2001), state-wise "human deprivational index" are constructed. The three indicators are given equal weight age to measure "Human Deprivational Index" of Indian states:

> Human Deprivational Index: 1/3(PR) + 1/3 (IR) + 1/3 (IMR), where PR = Poverty Ratio, IR = Illiteracy Rate, IMR = Infant Mortality Rate.

After arriving at deprivation indices, the states are ranked according to their deprivational index point. The state ranking first in deprivation is clearly the worst in terms of human development. According to the rank, the number one state is first in deprivation and worst in human development.

From the above analysis presented in Table 6.1 below, it is evident that Orissa is first in human deprivation with 60.50 points in the human deprivation index followed by Madhya Pradesh with 56.77 points, Bihar with 54.02, Uttar Pradesh with 52.92 points, Assam with 49.93 points and Rajasthan with 45.74 points. These six states are most deprived states and their deprivation indices are above the national deprivation index point (43.96). Except Dadra and Nagar Haveli, other Union Territories are least deprived.

Table 6.1
Human Deprivational Index for Indian States

Sl. No.	States/UT	Poverty Ratio	Illiteracy Rate, 2001	IMR, 2001	Deprivation Index	Rank
	(1)	(2)	(3)	(4)	(5)	(6)
1.	Andhra Pradesh	15.77	38.89	66	40.21	9
2.	Arunachal Pradesh	33.47	45.26	44	40.89	7
3.	Assam	36.09	35.72	78	49.93	5
4.	Bihar	42.60	52.47	67	54.02	3
5.	Goa	4.40	17.68	36	19.35	27
6.	Gujarat	14.07	33.57	64	37.21	12
7.	Haryana	8.74	31.41	69	36.38	16
8.	Himachal Pradesh	7.63	24.09	64	31.90	18
9.	Jammu & Kashmir	3.48	45.54	45	31.34	19
10.	Karnataka	20.04	32.96	58	36.99	13
11.	Kerala	12.72	9.08	16	12.59	30
12.	Madhya Pradesh	37.43	35.92	97	56.77	2
13.	Maharshtra	25.02	28.73	49	34.24	17
14.	Manipur	28.54	31.13	25	28.21	21
15.	Meghalaya	33.87	36.69	52	40.85	8
16.	Mizoram	19.47	11.51	23	17.98	29

17.	Nagaland	32.67	32.89	NA		
18.	Orissa	47.15	36.39	98	60.50	1
19.	Punjab	6.16	30.05	54	30.06	20
20.	Rajasthan	15.28	38.97	83	45.74	6
21.	Sikkim	36.55	30.32	52	39.61	10
22.	Tamilnadu	21.12	26.58	53	23.54	23
23.	Tripura	34.44	29.36	49	36.59	15
24.	Uttar Pradesh	31.15	42.64	85	52.92	4
25.	West Bengal	27.02	30.78	53	36.92	14
26.	Anandaman & Nicobar Islands	20.99	18.81	30	23.06	24
27.	Chandigarh	5.75	18.24	32	18.65	28
28.	Dadra & Nagar Haveli	17.14	39.97	61	39.36	11
29.	Daman & Diu	4.44	18.91	NA		
30.	Delhi	8.23	18.18	51	25.80	22
31.	Lakshadweep	15.60	12.48	30	19.36	26
32.	Pondicherry	21.67	18.51	21	20.39	25
	India	26.1	34.80	71	43.96	

Sources : Own Calculations based on data from the following sources:
1. National Human Development Report, 2001, India.
2. Based on NHDR, 2001, Literacy rate
3. Economic and Political Weekly Report, May 10, 2003.

Among the states, Kerala is least deprived with only 12.59 deprived points. That means it is developing very well in human development aspects. Mizoram also is less deprived with 17.98 points. Tamil Nadu is also notable state because with more than 60 million people, its deprivational index is only 23.54 point. This shows that among bigger states Tamil Nadu is placed well in human development aspects, and comparing with all the bigger states in India, it stood first in least deprivation. Goa is also among the least deprived states, as it gets only 19.35 points.

The most deprived states need to take necessary steps to improve the human development. To achieve human development, deprivation should be eliminated. For this overall economic growth is necessary, which can alleviate poverty and its evil consequences. With economic enrichment, good health and education can make an enormous difference in the lives of poor people and these are the main goals of development.

II. UNDERNUTRITION

Undernutrition has remained one of the leading global causes of loss of health and life of the children around the world. Estimates indicate that 6.6 million out of 12.2 million, that is, 54 percent of deaths among children under five in developing countries is associated with malnutrition. The health of future population depends on the nutritional and health status of the children who are being considered as the backbone of the economy, especially in developing countries. Thus, in recent times, improving child health has emerged as a challenging task of the Governments.

India is one of the most undernourished countries in the world. The World Bank (1995) suggests that the cost of undernutrition in India is at least US $ 10 billion annually in terms of lost productivity, morbidity and mortality. A close look at the NSSO 1993-94 survey data reveals that the lowest 20 percent of Indian population get just about 1500 calories of energy per capita per day, much lower than the average recommended level of 2400 kcal. The National Family Health Survey (1992-93) indicated that, in India more than half of the children, that is, 54 percent of children under age four are low weight for age, and 52% are low height for age and 29 percent are low weight for height. The proportion severely malnourished is 21 percent, 29 percent and 3 percent for low weight for age, low height for age and low weighty for height respectively. The state-wise data shows the highest prevalence of under-nutrition in Bihar and lowest in Kerala.

For India as a whole, just a slight improvement is observed in the nutritional status of children in NFHS-II when compared to NFHS-I. It shows that almost half of the children under three years of age that is, 47 percent are low weight for age, 46 percent are low height for age and 16 percent are low weight for height. In case of severity, low weight for age is 18 percent, low height for age is 23 percent and low weight for height is 3.0 percent. The average child low weight for age rate of 47 percent conceal considerable inequity between states that vary from a low of 24 percent in the North-Eastern states and Kerala, 37 percent in Tamil Nadu to 51-55 percent in the states of Bihar, Rajasthan, Uttar Pradesh, Madhya Pradesh and Orissa.

The second important point of fact is that India is a country with very high burden of diseases. The three major disease burdens among children arise due to Acute Respiratory Infection or Pneumonia (that is, cough with fast, rapid breathing), Diarrhoea beside Anaemia. The National Family Health Survey, 1998-99 shows that acute respiratory Infection (ARI) is a major illness among infants and children and the leading cause of childhood mortality throughout the developing countries in the world (Murray and Lopez, 1996); Diarrhoea is the most important killer of children under age five next to ARI. Anaemia, which is marked low hemoglobin level, is another serious problem impacting young children's health. The prevalence of ARI in India is around 19 percent, any diarrhoea is almost around 19 percent and any anaemic is around 74 percent among the children who had suffered during the two weeks preceding the survey. These percentages refer to the surviving children in age 1-35 months.

Under-nutrition, morbidity and poverty are very closely interrelated phenomena. These three factors are interlinked in such a way that each contributes to the presence and permanence of the others. A large share of population in many developing countries suffers from chronic under-nutrition, which is the outcome of deficiency of the energy components in food over a long period. As a result, under-nutrition increases the incidence, severity and duration of common childhood diseases, such as diarrhoea, acute respiratory infections, and measles (Davidson, 2004). Under-nutrition is the cumulative effect of factors like poverty, inadequate access to food, illiteracy, large size families, poor environmental sanitation, lack of basic minimal health care, lack of personal hygiene, lack of easy access to adequate safe drinking water and lack of awareness. The manifestations of under-nutrition could be seen in the prevalence of specific nutrient—deficiency disorders such as protein-energy malnutrition, anaemia, night blindness, goiter, susceptibility to a number of infectious diseases, low birth weight of children, high IMR and MMR, lack of resistance to illness among mothers and children, growth retardation (both physical and mental) and stunting among toddlers.

The nutritional status among children may be explained in terms of indices viz. weight for age, height for age and weight for height. The National Family Health Survey II (1998-99) shows that in Tamil Nadu nearly 37 percent of the children under three years of age are underweight and 29 % children are stunted according to height for age. Similar estimates at the National level are 47% and 46% respectively. It has been found that the proportion of children who are under-nourished increases with age. The proportion of children with three years of age who are underweight decreases from 46% in NFHS-I (1992-93) to 37% in NFHS-II, the proportion of severely underweight decreased from 13% to 11%. Between 24-35 month, 17% of the children are known to be severely stunted and 14% severely underweight. Girls are found to be slightly more malnourished than boys.

A comparison of children under-nourished according to the three nutritional indices of some of the major states along with All India reveals that among the Southern States, Tamil Nadu has a moderately high percentage of underweight according to each of the three indices used by NFHS-II (1998-99).

Iron deficiency anaemia is the most widespread form of malnutrition. It may have detrimental effects on the health of women and children and may become an underlying cause of

TABLE 6.2
Nutritional Status of Children

State	*Weight for Age **		*Height for Age $*		*Weight for Height #*	
	% Below 3 SD	*% Below 2 SD*	*% Below 3 SD*	*% Below 2 SD*	*% Below 3 SD*	*% Below 2 SD*
(1)	*(2)*	*(3)*	*(4)*	*(5)*	*(6)*	*(7)*
Andhra Pradesh	10.3	37.7	14.2	38.6	1.6	9.1
Bihar	25.1	54.4	33.6	53.7	5.5	21.0
Gujarat	16.2	45.1	23.3	43.6	2.4	16.2
Karnataka	16.5	43.9	15.9	36.6	3.9	20.0
Kerala	4.7	26.9	7.3	21.9	0.7	11.1
Maharashtra	17.6	49.6	14.1	39.9	2.5	21.2
Punjab	8.8	28.7	17.2	39.2	0.8	7.1
Tamil Nadu	10.6	36.7	12.0	29.4	3.8	19.9
India	18.0	47.0	23.0	45.5	20.8	15.5

Notes : * Under weight for age, 'percentage below –3 SD (Standard Deviation)' indicates severely underweight and 'percentage –2 SD' indicates underweight.
$ Under height for age, 'percentage below –3 SD' indicates severely stunted and 'percentage – 2 SD' indicates stunted.
# Weight for height indicates thin or wasted children.

Source : National Family Health Survey (NFHS-II), 1998-99.

maternal mortality and perinatal mortality. Early detection of anaemia can help to prevent complications related to delivery as well as child development problems. In Tamil Nadu 57% of women have some degree of anaemia i.e., 37% of women are mildly anaemic, 16% are moderately anaemic and 4% are severely anaemic. Prevalence of anaemia is slightly higher for young women less than age 25 than for older women. It is higher for rural women (59%) than for urban women (52%). The anaemic levels of children age 3 to 35 months are 69% including 25% mild anaemic, 40% moderately anaemic and 7% severely anaemic. Children aged 12 to 23 months, children of higher order births, children in rural areas, children of working women and children with low standard of living have high levels of anaemia. The morbidity—mortality pattern and related malnutrition among children and pregnant women necessitated launching of nutrition intervention programmes by the Government.

Among the low-income countries, the route of waiting for growth to address the problem of malnutrition has been found to be unacceptably long. The consequences of such delays are costly in terms of not only productivity but also the direct well being of the population, which is ultimately the objective of all development efforts. Direct interventions could shorten the time taken for improved nutritional status. Nutrition is the outcome of interactions between a variety of factors and processes, including health care, environmental hygiene, etc.

Under-nutrition, Morbidity and Poverty

Nutritional status is one of the indicators of the overall well being of population and human resources development. Malnutrition is the cumulative effect of factors like poverty, inadequate access to food, illiteracy, large size families, poor lack of easy access to adequate safe drinking water and lack of awareness.

Under-nutrition in young children is conventionally determined through measurement of height, weight, skin fold thickness (or subcutaneous fat) and age. The most commonly used indices derived from these measurements are stunting (low height for age), wasting (low weight for height) and underweight (low weight for age). Stunting is an indicator of chronic under-nutrition, the result of prolonged food deprivation and/or disease or illness; wasting is an indicator of acute under-nutrition, the result of more recent food deprivation or illness; underweight is used as a composite indicator, to reflect both acute and chronic under-nutrition, although it can not distinguish between them. These indices are compared against an international reference population, developed from anthropometric data collected and standards set in the USA by the National Center for Health Statistics (NCHS). Children whose measurements fall below –2z-scores from the reference population median are considered undernourished, i.e., stunted, wasted and underweight. Those children with measurement below –3z scores are considered severely undernourished.

These indices reflect distinct biological processes, and are necessary for determining appropriate interventions. However, due to an overlap between them, none is able to provide a comprehensive estimate of the number of undernourished children in a population; some children who are stunted will also be wasted and or underweight, some children who are underweight will also be wasted and stunted and some children who are wasted will also be stunted and underweight.

Under-nutrition, morbidity and poverty are very closely interrelated phenomena. These three factors are interlinked in such a way that each contributes to the presence and continuance of the others. A large share of population in many developing countries suffers from chronic under-nutrition, which is the outcome of deficiency of the energy components in food over a long period. As a result, under-nutrition increases the incidence, severity, and duration of common childhood diseases, such as diarrhoea, acute respiratory infections, and measles. Under-nutrition is more an economic issue related to food entitlements, poverty and the socio-economic structure of societies throughout the developing countries.

In what follows we present the results of a study on comparing the prevalence of child under-nutrition in Tamil Nadu and Bihar based on revised anthropometric indicators. Tamil Nadu is one of the Southern States with moderately high incidence of under-nutrition and Bihar tops the ranking in whole India in terms of under-nutrition in the results of successive rounds of NFHS and NSSO Surveys. The present study tries to relate the linkages between child under-nutrition, morbidity and poverty in measuring under-nutrition; and tries to assess prevalence of children in cumulative risks of under-nutrition, morbidity and poverty. The data on nutritional indicators, morbidity and standard of living from NFHS-2 are used here. Under-nutrition is assessed based on anthropometric indicators. Newly developed composite measures of under-nutrition, morbidity and poverty are used. Standardised percent of children who suffered different morbidities by revised indicators of anthropometry are calculated.

A CASE STUDY

Indicators of Under-nutrition

Anthropometry is used as a tool to estimate the nutritional status of population and monitor the growth and health of individuals. This part discusses the measurement of under-nutrition with a new approach beyond the conventionally used standard indices.

In NFHS, three common "Anthropometric Indices" that have used to assesss the nutritional status of children are :

- Stunting (Low height for age);
- Wasting (Low weight for height); and
- Underweight (Low weight for age)

Of these, stunting is the result of chronic undernutrition. For instance, when a child does not receive adequate nutrition of the required diet for a considerable period and also because of disease/illness, it has a high chance of being undernourished. On a population basis, high levels of stunting are associated with poor socio-economic conditions and increased risk of frequent and early exposure to adverse conditions such as illness and/or inappropriate feeding practices. As per the annual report of UNICEF 2001, India is one among the 23 countries where stunting in under-five children is 40 percent or more, that is, 46 percent. Similarly, wasting is the result of acute under-nutrition, which is a current status phenomenon due to the environmental factors such as poor quality water, poor sanitation, and other-related causes. Prevalence of wasting between 10-14 percent is regarded as serious, and when it is above or equal to 15 percent, it is considered as critical.

When a child has both low heights for age and low weight for height or when a child suffers both from chronic and acute under-nutrition, it is considered low weight for age, which is used as a proxy indicator of measuring under-nutrition by WHO. These indices are compared to an international reference population developed from anthropometric data collected in the United States by the National Center for Health Statistics (NCHS).

Peter Svedberg (2000) has mentioned some of the flaws in these basic indices that it does not capture the true extent of under-nutrition. According to him, the conventional index of anthropometric groups (stunting, wasting and low weight for age) which is a more aggregated classification, may fail to give the risk of various types of anthropometric failures and the exact number of undernourished population because the children who are low height for age are also likely to have under weight and wasting, and similarly in the case of under-weight and wasting with the rest. He has suggested a composite index of anthropometric failure, which disaggregates the conventional indices into six following categories.

Composite indicators of anthropometric failure are :

(a) *No failure*: The children having acceptable weights and heights for the age as well as weight for height.
(b) *Wasting only* : The children having acceptable weights and heights for age but having subnormal weights for their heights.
(c) *Stunting only*: The children having acceptable weights for height and weight for age, but having low heights for age.
(d) *Stunting and underweight*: The children having acceptable weight for height but having low height and weight for age.
(e) *Wasting and underweight*: The children having

acceptable heights for age, but having low weight for height and age.

(f) *Wasting, stunting and underweight*: The children suffer from all the three anthropometric measures.

(g) *Underweight only*: The children having acceptable heights for age and weight for height.

In the present study these seven newly developed categories of measuring under-nutrition is used to provide a more clear extent of the under-nutrition problem among children in the states of Tamil Nadu and Bihar. Table 6.3 below provides the disaggregated figure of anthropometric failure sub-groups. This when compared to Table 6.2 with the standard indices, the disaggregated categories provide the percentage of each anthropometric failures separately. The common feature in both the states is the high prevalence of stunting and underweight but Bihar is showing extremely high rate of anthropometric failure compared to Tamil Nadu. The no failure cases are high, that is nearly half (49%) in Tamil Nadu showing difference of 20 percent when compared to Bihar. This difference demonstrates the worst situation of under-nutrition in Bihar when compared to Tamil Nadu.

TABLE 6.3

Anthropometric Failure Sub-groups Number and Percentage

Disaggregated anthropometric sub-groups	*Tamil Nadu – 2 SD*		*Bihar – 2 SD*	
	Number	*Percentage*	*Number*	*Percentage*
(a) No failure	586	49.0	620	29.8
(b) Wasting only	76	6.4	89	4.3
(c) Stunting only	89	7.5	232	11.1
(d) Underweight only	80	6.7	96	4.6
(e) Stunting and underweight	199	16.7	691	33.2
(f) Wasting and underweight	101	8.5	159	7.6
(g) Wasting, stunting and underweight	63	5.2	196	9.4
Number of children	1194	100.0	2083	100.0

From the sub-groups categorization in Table 6.3, the Composite index of anthropometric failure (CIAF) is estimated as follows:

CIAF = (1–a)/(a+b+c+d+e+f+g+h)
= (1–a)/1
= 1–a

The **'a, b, c, d, e, f and g'** being the sub-groups of anthropometric failure in the groups and the index is obtained by taking their sum as the proportion and deducting the no failure category from the sum.

The strength of this index is that the standard indices do not capture the true extent of undernourished children in a child population. In Table 6.4 below, the percentage of stunted, wasted, and under-weight is given. But according to CIAF, more than two-thirds of children in Bihar have anthropometric failure compared to half in Tamil Nadu. However, it is important to note in Table 6.3, that the children with stunted and underweight who are acute conditions of under-nutrition are 33 percent in Bihar. This is almost twice than the 17 percent in Tamil Nadu.

TABLE 6.4
Standard Indices and Composite Index of Under-nutrition

Index of Under-nutrition	*Number*	*Percentage*	*Number*	*Percentage*
Stunted*	351	29.4	1120	53.7
Underweight*	443	37.1	1143	54.9
Wasted*	240	20.1	444	21.2
CIAF**	608	51.0	1463	70.2

Note : * as in NFHS-2, ** calculated from Table 6.3.

Indicators of Child Morbidity

The purpose of anthropometric index is to provide the measure of risk of various anthropometric failures, which have more impact on morbidity and result in poor health. However, there may be genetic reasons for being low height. Thus when height for age and weight for height is obtained, due to the mentioned genetic reasons, they may fail to provide the estimate of actual risk, and thus conclusions can be erroneous. So it is necessary to give a clear percentage of child population and their likeness to the various morbidities. To understand this linkage, a bivariate analysis of under-nutrition and morbidity prevalence is first shown.

Table 6.5 provides the unadjusted and adjusted percentage of children reported with morbidity by anthropometric sub-groups of children. The adjusted percentage from the bivariate analysis is useful to compare and understand the linkage between under-nutrition and morbidity. The adjustment is made with respect to certain variables such as household standard of living, place of residence, sex of the children, age of the children, religion and caste so as to control the impact of those factors, which is expected to affect the levels in morbidity. Say, a woman living in urban area will be in good standard of living or better education. Thus she will be aware of nutritional requirement or trained assistants would have attended her delivery and this residential difference is expected to have impact on morbidity prevalence. Similarly, several other variables are also expected to have impact on morbidity, are adjusted.

The unadjusted percentage shows, in ARI, the categories A, B, E, and F show high variation between the states. Only in the no failure anthropometric category, 'A', this variation is very high. Though there is no high variation in case of Diarrhoea, the overall difference is showing the better-off position in Tamil Nadu and Bihar. Also, the adjusted percentage did not differ with respect to diarrhoea with blood. But the severity is concentrated among underweight children in both the states. The overall failure shows that the morbidity level is high in Bihar when compared to Tamil Nadu in case of unadjusted percentage.

The adjusted percentage of children in morbidity by anthropometric sub-group provides an estimate, controlled for interrelated factors. In Tamil Nadu, adjusted percentage for ARI decrease by 3 percent for children in stunting and underweight, but in Bihar, the prevalence indicates very little difference. In Bihar, in stunting and underweight category, significant change is found for diarrhoea prevalence, but in Tamil Nadu, the

Table 6.5
Unadjusted and Adjusted Percentage of Prevalence of Morbidity by CIAF in Tamil Nadu and Bihar

CIAF Subgroups	Tamil Nadu						Bihar					
	ARI		Any Diarrhoea		With Blood		ARI		Any Diarrhoea		With Blood	
	Unadj%	Adj%	Unadj%	Adj%	Unadj%	Adj%	Unadj%	Adj%	Unadj%	Adj%	Unadj%	Adj%
(1)	(2)	(3)	(4)	(5)	(6)	(7)	(8)	(9)	(10)	(11)	(12)	(13)
(A) No Failure	7.3	7.7	14.5	14.6	1.9	1.4	22.5	22.4	15.7	14.1	2.1	2.2
(B) Wasting	17.1	17.4[a]	12.0	11.1	—	—	17.0	17.2	14.4	12.5	1.2	1.2
(C) Stunting only	11.1	10.5	11.2	13.0	2.2	1.7[b]	22.9	23.3	19.3	18.3[b]	2.6	2.5
(D) Underweight only	13.8	12.2	15.0	15.8	3.8	4.3	18.8	18.1	17.7	17.2	6.3	6.1[b]
(E) Stunting and Underweight	15.6	12.9[a]	14.6	15.2	2.0	1.7	24.5	24.9	20.7	21.3[a]	3.9	3.5
(F) Wasting and Underweight	12.9	12.1	17.8	18.0	2.0	1.8	22.6	22.6	17.6	16.9	1.9	1.8
(G) Stunting, Wasting and Underweight	12.7	11.1	19.0	19.7	—	—	16.6	16.6	17.3	17.7	4.6	4.1

A 99%, B 95%

Note : Adjusted percentage of prevalence of morbidity for CIAF estimated by logistic regression controlling variables such as age of the children, sex of the children, standard of living, and place of residence, caste, mother's education and religion. When calculating adjusted percentage for categories of CIAF, other variables are held constant at their mean value.

change is negligible. In most other categories, the unadjusted and adjusted percentage differed very little. Thus, in overall, the adjusted percentage indicates only small difference in prevalence of morbidity. However, both the bivariate analysis and adjusted percentages improve our understanding of the extent of linkage between the two but cannot provide an estimate of cumulative risk of undernutrition and morbidity.

An independent anthropometric index fails to provide true prevalence of undernutrition, for the reason that nutrition failure can occur or reoccur if the child has illness or in economic poverty. The risk of reoccurrence of nutrition failure is almost certain if the child has both risks of illness and economic poverty, given that the cycle of poverty, morbidity and undernutrition are well demonstrated. Within this, if children suffer multiple illnesses, they are in more acute risk. So there is a need to focus on the extent of morbidity and poverty risks.

The disaggregated morbidity index in Table 6.6 below provides the individual morbidity failures and the group of failures among the children. Accordingly, no health failure category is 77 percent in Tamil Nadu and 67 percent in Bihar. The children in ARI are 15 percent in Bihar when compared to 8 percent in Tamil Nadu. However, percentage of children in morbidity risk of any diarrhoea is 11 percent in Tamil Nadu, which is slightly high when compared to 9 percent in Bihar. The

TABLE 6.6
Morbidity Failure Sub-groups—Number and Percentage, 1998-99

Disaggregated morbidity categories	*Tamil Nadu*		*Bihar*	
	Number	*Percentage*	*Number*	*Percentage*
No Failure	992	77.3	1809	67.4
ARI only	107	8.3	398	14.8
Any Diarrhoea only	139	10.8	248	9.2
Diarrhoea with Blood only	21	1.6	42	1.6
ARI and any Diarrhoea	24	1.9	151	5.6
ARI, any Diarrhoea and Blood	1	0.1	36	1.3
Number of children	1284	100.0	2684	100.0

sub-indices of morbidity risks again indicate greater difference of children in multiple morbidity risks (ARI and any diarrohea) between Tamil Nadu and Bihar.

In Table 6.7, similar to the composite index of anthropometric failure, a 'Composite index for Morbidity Risk' is used to assess the extent of morbidity prevailing among children in Tamil Nadu and Bihar.

TABLE 6.7

Sub-Indices and Composite Index for Morbidity Risk—Percentage of Children by Categories

Disaggregated morbidity categories	*Tamil Nadu*		*Bihar*	
	Number	*Percentage*	*Number*	*Percentage*
ARI*	132	10.3	585	21.8
Any Diarrhoea*	185	14.4	477	17.7
Diarrhoea with Blood*	22	1.6	78	2.4
No Health Failure	992	77.3	1809	67.4
CIMR	292	22.7	875	32.6

**Source* : NFHS-2.

The logic of using this index is similar to the CIAF because, there is a chance for not capturing the gross prevalence of morbidity among the children. In this index, ARI and any diarrhoea are included and diarrhoea with blood is excluded because any diarrhoea considers this category. This index shows the extent of morbidity and the aggregated percentage of disease prevalence among children. Also it captures the children who had ARI and any diarrhoea together. In Table 6.7, the CIMR shows the cumulated morbidity categories in which Tamil Nadu is 23 percent and Bihar is 33 percent. The CIMR shows the extent of morbidity risk is 22.4 percent in Tamil Nadu and 32.1 percent in Bihar.

Indicator of Child Poverty Risk

The risk of children in poverty is also similarly assessed. The index for poverty is generated where the children in the risk of poverty are measured. The children from low standard of living category are determined as children in poverty. The standard of living is a permanent income measure and the households at the lower end of distribution indicate households (and children) in relative poverty. That is the percent of household in low standard of living is an approximating criteria of poverty measurement. These percentages show children in relative poverty risks and provide an approximation for assessing children in poverty risks. However this provides only gross estimates of children in poverty. The importance here is to focus on differentiating the extent of children with poverty and also the risk of illness, which can lead to Undernutrition of children. This indicator based on households in low standard of living index is named as 'poverty index'.

TABLE 6.8
Percentage Distribution of Children by Standard of Living in Tamil Nadu and Bihar, NFHS-2

SLI	*Tamil Nadu*	*Bihar*
Low (Children in poverty risks)	39.5	57.0
Medium	46.6	34.9
High	13.8	8.1

Table 6.8 shows the percent of children in risk of household poverty, that is, children in households' low standard of living. The children who are in poverty, is 40 percent in Tamil Nadu and 57 percent in Bihar.

Linkages between Under-nutrition, Morbidity and Poverty

In order to further understand the interlink ages and multiple risks, Table 6.9 provides trivariate classification where the household economic condition is included to find the prevalence of morbidity among the various anthropometric groups. This table shows the percentage of children who are undernourished by prevalence of morbidity and according to their economic status. The overall prevalence shows that in Tamil Nadu, the prevalence of morbidity is low when compared

TABLE 6.9
Prevalence of Morbidity by Nutrition and Economic Status using Composite Index for Anthropometrics Failure

Standard of living	*CIAF*	*ARI*	*Any Diarrhoea*	*Diarrhoea with blood*	*ARI*	*Any Diarrhoea*	*Diarrhoea with blood*
(1)	*(2)*	*(3)*	*(4)*	*(5)*	*(6)*	*(7)*	*(8)*
Low	No failure	11.1	15.4	1.9	25.6	15.4	2.0
	Wasting only	19.2	23.1	—	14.9	12.8	—
	Stunting only	16.2	13.5	5.4	21.1	17.4	0.9
	Underweight only	16.2	16.2	2.7	15.2	19.6	4.3
	Stunting and Underweight	16.3	13.5	2.9	24.6	21.4	4.9
	Wasting and Underweight	11.4	31.1	2.2	28.4	18.9	3.2
	Stunting, Wasting and Underweight	17.1	22.9	—	17.1	18.5	3.8
	Total	13.8	17.3	2.2	23.2	18.4	3.2
	No failure	7.1	13.9	2.0	17.6	16.3	2.0
Medium	Wasting only	18.6	4.7	—	16.3	14.0	2.3
	Stunting only	9.1	9.1	—	25.3	20.8	4.2
	Underweight only	11.6	14.3	4.8	21.4	16.7	7.1
	Stunting and Underweight	12.8	16.1	1.2	25.5	20.0	2.9
	Wasting and Underweight	13.7	9.6	2.0	15.8	15.5	—

(*Contd.*)

TABLE 6.9 (Contd.)

(1)	(2)	(3)	(4)	(5)	(6)	(7)	(8)
	Stunting, Wasting and Underweight	9.5	18.2	—	16.4	14.8	4.9
	Total	9.9	13.0	1.7	20.9	17.7	2.9
High	No failure	3.2	12.0	0.8	19.4	10.8	2.1
	Wasting only	14.3	7.1	—	14.3	—	—
	Stunting only	—	11.1	—	25.0	20.0	5.0
	Underweight only	—	—	—	14.3	14.3	14.3
	Stunting and Underweight	—	—	—	15.4	17.9	—
	Wasting and Underweight	—	—	—	—	12.5	—
	Stunting Wasting and Underweight	—	—	—	20.0	20.0	20.0
	Total	3.6	10.3	0.6	17.9	13.4	2.8

— cases not available.
Tamil Nadu (N) = Low – 491; Medium – 584; High – 167
Bihar (N) = Low – 1143; Medium – 786; High – 179

to Bihar. The ARI percentage in low standard of living is 14.0 percent for all children, medium standard of living is 10 percent and high standard of living is 4 percent in Tamil Nadu and 23 percent for low standard of living, 21 percent for medium standard of living and 18 percent for high standard of living children in Bihar.

Also the patterns of variation can be seen within the state and by the nutritional status, that is, the children from 'high standard of living' are having lowest prevalence and 'medium standard' are having lower prevalence when compared to the children from low economic status. Another notable outcome from the table is the prevalence of inequalities within states in morbidity. The table shows high inequality between economic groups and the prevalence of disease is also low in Tamil Nadu when compared to Bihar (ARI – 14 percent, 10 percent and 4 percent; and Any Diarrhoea – 17 percent, 13 percent and 10 percent and 2.2 percent, 1.7 percent and 0.6 percent in the case of Diarrhoea with blood for low, medium and high standard of living respectively).

In Bihar the inequality between the economic groups is not so high as the prevalence of disease is high in all groups when compared to Tamil Nadu (ARI – 21.5 percent, 21.8 percent and 18.1 percent, Any Diarrhoea – 18.7 percent, 18.5 percent and 13.6 percent, and Diarrhoea with blood – 3.3 percent, 3.0 percent and 2.8 percent for low, medium and high standard of living respectively). In this case, Tamil Nadu is showing high inequality within various standards of living shows better performance, while Bihar is showing noticeable inequality and high prevalence of morbidity in all the standards of living is comparatively poor in performance.

Cumulative Risks of Children in Undernutrition, Morbidity and Poverty

The three separate indices of Under-nutrition, morbidity and poverty again provide an estimate of independent risks, which does not consider risks arising from interrelated failures. In order to address this issue, a composite index is generated comprising of all children with nutrition failure, morbidity risk and poverty risk. This index is named as 'Composite Index for

Under-nutrition, Morbidity and Poverty Risks' (CINMPR). This index shows the percentage of children with risk of any one of the failures and/or multiple risks/failures.

The need for this cumulative risk index arises due to the fact that there would be some children from poorer background who are well nourished and have good health. Also some children from richer household may be suffering from bad health and/or are undernourished. In some cases, children will be from any one failure/risk, and they will not be suffering in other deficiencies. Thus the logic behind this index is to provide the children who are in extreme condition of suffering, and risk from all Undernutrition, morbidity risk, and of all, they come from poor socio-economic status. In other words, this CINMPR provides both disaggregated and aggregated estimates of children with multiple and individual risks. It also provides greater refinements in the way in which children in various risks are estimated. The main feature of this index is that the children from poverty risk may not have good health condition and from poor environmental condition as their expenditure on nutritional intake will also be low and thus have a high chance of getting various diseases (Sukatme, 1978). The children who are having the risk of morbidity and nutritional failure but are from comparably better socio-economic status may have sufficient resources to recover and they are not so vulnerable.

Table 6.10 shows, according to this index, the children who are at risk of any one of the three failures, is 72 percent in Tamil Nadu and 89 percent in Bihar. It provides comparatively higher prevalence of risks as it indicates gross rate of children in any one of the risks but indicates very little about children in multiple risks or more intensive forms of risk.

As mentioned earlier, the children who are having multiple risk categories such as nutrition failure, morbidity and poverty risks, poverty-associated multiple failure, nutrition-associated multiple failure and two and more multiple risks/failures are more vulnerable compared to single failures. According to this index, nutrition failure only is high in Tamil Nadu and is around 21 percent as compared to 20 percent in Bihar. But the children in poverty risk are low in Tamil Nadu when compared to Bihar

TABLE 6.10
Percentage Distribution of Children by Composite Risk Index of Undernutrition, Morbidity and Poverty

Undernutrition, Morbidity and Poverty indicators	*Tamil Nadu*	*Bihar*
(a) No failure	28.1	10.7
(b) Nutrition failure only (all the anthropometric indices)	21.3	20.2
(c) Morbidity risk only (health failure)	6.1	4.6
(d) Poverty risk only (economic security failure)	9.3	11.5
(e) Nutrition failure and morbidity risk	5.9	9.7
(f) Poverty risk and nutrition failure	15.9	26.2
(g) Poverty risk and morbidity risk	3.7	4.9
(h) Nutrition failure, morbidity and poverty risks	7.5	14.2
(x) Poverty-associated multiple failure	27.1	45.3
(y) Nutrition-associated multiple failure	29.3	50.1
(z) Two and more multiple failure/risks	33.0	55.0
CINMPR	71.9	89.2

From the above categories, CINMPR **is derived as**
CINMPR = (1–a)/(a+b+c+d+e+f+g+h) = (1–a)/1
CINMPR = 1–a

showing that these children have the chance of recovery. The children from poverty-associated multiple failure categories is 27 percent in Tamil Nadu and 45 percent in Bihar, nutrition-associated multiple failure is 29 percent in Tamil Nadu and 50 percent in Bihar, and two and more multiple risks is 33 percent in Tamil Nadu and 55 percent in Bihar. Thus in Bihar, multiple failure factors are very high when compared to Tamil Nadu showing the high-risk rate and poor performance in Bihar. Thus this index shows the cumulative risk in children who are in the risk of Undernutrition, morbidity and poverty, which is more realistic than other individual indices. Clearly the percent of children in multiple risks that is, with two and more interrelated risks indicate stark differences between the better performing state of Tamil Nadu and poor performing state of Bihar. The differences suggest the need for concentrated policy on these children with multiple risks.

Child Malnutrition: Behind the Numbers

The *UNICEF* report card for world children shows that India accounts for one-third of the low-weight births in developing countries and has the largest number of underweight children in the world. The report also reiterates the fact that younger children in India still display some of the worst nutrition indicators in the developing world—one of every four children is underweight. From the National Family Health Survey II conducted in 1998-99, we know that over 47 per cent of children under the age of three in India display severe to moderate undernutrition (weight for age), with serious consequences for proper mental and physical development. If the millennium development goal of halving undernutrition by 2015 is to be achieved, the average rate of reduction of undernutrition needs to make rapid strides; the present rate of 1.7 per cent per year is simply too slow. In India, researchers have found that in the period between the previous two National Family Health Surveys (1992-93 and 1998-99) the percentage of underweight children below three years of age came down by only 0.8 per cent annually. Achieving target reductions in under-nutrition means little when the specificities of the situations that create and perpetuate malnutrition are ignored

The reasons for the slow progress in reducing the prevalence of under-nutrition in children have been analyzed mostly in terms of proximate causes: weaknesses in delivery services, faulty feeding practices and poor maternal health. Though the Integrated Child Development Services (ICDS) programme was intended to incorporate a multi-pronged approach to under-nutrition, its central thrust remains supplementary nutrition, to the neglect of other aspects such as immunization, antenatal services, advice on feeding practices, and health monitoring and referrals, which have a significant impact on overall health. The reach and distribution of the ICDS has also been criticized: states with the highest prevalence of under-nutrition among children below six years of age, namely, Uttar Pradesh, Bihar, Rajasthan, Orissa and Madhya Pradesh, tend to be the most sparsely covered by the programme. In addition, it is precisely the age bracket that has the highest levels of undernourishment (0-3 years) that is not adequately targeted through ICDS. The malnutrition that sets in at this critical time of development becomes difficult to reverse later on. Accompanied by low birth weights, faulty feeding practices and the fact that 36 per cent of women between the ages of 15 and 49 years who are ever married suffer from chronic energy deficiency like anaemia, the cycle of under-nutrition is perpetuated.

III. UNDERNOURISHMENT AND GOVERNMENT INTERVENTIONS

1. Undernourishment of Children and Adolescent Girls

The question of food security or rather of food insecurity should necessarily engage one and all intrinsically, as it is the most fundamental violation of all human rights. Yet, in this country, shamefully, as grain stocks pile up, millions migrate, undergo conditions akin to slavery, and suffer untold misery due to lack of food. Over the years, as the Government projects figures of increasing food production, and urges farming communities to shift from subsistence to cash crops, we find that malnutrition levels are increasing, and the most vulnerable sections of the population, the women and children are undernourished.

Undernourishment of children in millions implies that one generation of people are not being allowed to reach their full active potential. On the other hand, the centralized systems of welfare including PDS, and other programmes of food and nutrition safety nets that the Government has set-up have hardly worked, as people in the rural and tribal areas, where much of the underdevelopment still occurs, have little control over the management and running of these systems. Thus enormous subsidies given to run these systems in terms of Government of India finances, international finances and direct food resources are rendered to nought, as misappropriation, and poor management result in distress and hunger and hunger conditions continuing the same as ever before. The poorest communities in this country, do not derive any benefit from these institutions for all the good that they do to these communities through their supports for nutrition and feeding.

2. Nutrition Programme for Adolescent Girls (NPAG)

Government of India has approved the implementation of the scheme Nutritional Programme for Adolescent Girls (NPAG) in the year 2005-06 on a pilot basis, through the Department of Women and Child Development, Ministry of Human Resource Development. Funds for implementation of this scheme would be released as Additional Central Assistance (ACA) on a 100% grant basis to the States. The scheme would be implemented in the same 51 districts as were identified by the Planning Commission earlier. The scheme was to be implemented as per the Guidelines issued by the Planning Commission earlier, with two major modifications as under:

(i) The scheme was to be restricted only to adolescent girls, as pregnant women and lactating mothers are covered under ICDS; and

(ii) The list of the beneficiaries was to be approved in the Gram Sabha. The revised guidelines were circulated to all States with a request to ensure that steps for implementation of the scheme be taken immediately. Steps for implementation of this scheme must be taken up by the State Governments/UT Administrations by coordinating with the Food and Civil Supplies Department of the State to ensure the availability of food grains under this scheme. State Governments may apprise of the position on the implementation of the scheme.

A healthy and well-balanced diet is essential for good health. When there is not enough food, or if the diet does not contain the right balance of foodstuffs, people become more prone to illness and may become undernourished or malnourished. Children, in particular, are vulnerable to poor nutrition. Undernourishment and malnourishment can lower their resistance and make them more likely to suffer from infectious diseases. Often, children will eat only small amounts of food if it is spicy, even if it is nutritious, and it is important to make children's food less spicy than adult food. Also, because their stomachs are small, children can eat only small portions and need to be fed more frequently than healthy adults. It is also important that children are fed not just foods high in starch or carbohydrate (for instance rice). Although these foods can quickly make a child feel full, he or she may become malnourished if other key foodstuffs are not eaten.

- A well-balanced diet usually has a mixture of food.
- Proteins (for example beans, peas, meat, fish or eggs).
- Carbohydrates (such as maize, potatoes, cassava, rice and many other staple foods).

Now let us look at the effect of nutrition on Infant Mortality Rate and how they are related. We have taken all the major Indian states into consideration for the year 2004, as are presented in Table 6.11 below.

TABLE 6.11

Undernourishment in Major Indian States

States	*Severe Undernourished*	*Undernourished (total)*
Andhra Pradesh	10.3	37.7
Assam	13.3	36.0
Bihar	25.5	54.4
Gujarat	16.2	45.1
Haryana	10.1	34.6
Karnataka	16.5	43.9
Kerala	4.7	26.9
Madhya Pradesh	24.3	55.1
Maharashtra	17.6	49.6
Orissa	20.7	54.4
Punjab	8.8	28.7
Rajasthan	20.8	50.6
Tamil Nadu	10.6	36.7
Uttar Pradesh	21.9	51.7
West Bengal	16.3	48.7

Source : Lok Sabha Unstarred Question No. 1188, dated on 30.11.2004.

The Pearson Correlation Ceffient between IMR and undernutrition is found to be 0.042, which is insignificant. The positive sign suggests a link between between nourishment deprivation and infant mortality rates, despite increase in nutritional intakes over time, which is rather slow in nature. When the nutrition levels among children and mothers shall be high enough among all the income classes, we may expect that nutrition would help to lower infant mortality. The National Human Development Report, 2001 (NHDR-2001), brought out by the Planning Commission, indicates that while the expectation of life at birth in urban India was 66.3 years during 1992-96, the same for rural India was 59.4 years. Similarly, the expectation of life at the age of 1 year in rural India is 63.9 years, whereas it is 68.9 years in the urban areas. Among persons not expected to survive beyond the age of 40 years in 1991, 16.9% were male while 19.1% were females. The rural-urban dichotomy continues in the IMR figures: 84 *vs.* 51. More eye-catching is the disparity in the age specific mortality rate for the age group 0 – 4 years (1991): 40.8 and 16. Similar is the case for the crude death rate – 9.6 and 6.5 in 1997 and so on.

IV. INFANT AND CHILD MORTALITY IN INDIA—CASE STUDY OF THREE STATES

Infant mortality rate is of special interest because infant deaths account for a major share of all losses of life, especially in developing countries like India where conditions of health are poor. In case of India, it shows great regional or inter-state variations in infant and child mortality levels as compared to most of the developing countries of the world. The level of IMR was remarkably high in early eighties (more than 100 deaths per 1000 live births) in most of the states in India including Orissa and Rajasthan. So there is a need to study the high levels and trends of IMR and also CMR of these two underdeveloped states (Orissa and Rajasthan) in comparison with relatively developed state (West Bengal) during the last two decades. Also we need to examine what are the socio-economic, demographic and maternal factors that effect infant and child mortality in these three states.

Objective of the Study

The main objectives of this study are as follows:

- To study the levels and trends of infant and child mortality in three Indian states namely Orissa, Rajasthan and West Bengal during the period 1982-2000.
- To analyze the relationship between infant and child mortality and socio-economic, demographic and maternal health care characteristics in the above states.

Data and Methodology

The data for the present study has been extracted from various publications of Sample Registration System (SRS) and National Family Health Survey-2, 1998-99. The levels, trends and regional differentials in IMR and CMR have been analyzed from the SRS. This source has also helped to draw the variations by sex and urban-rural differentials by place of residence.

National Family Health Survey-2 was carried out by IIPS, Mumbai as a nodal agency during 1998-99 in all the 26 states of the country. In this survey in Orissa, a number of 4425 ever-married women of 15-49 age group from 4689 households, in Rajasthan 6813 from 6311 households and in West Bengal 4408 women from 4725 households were interviewed. Kids file data have been used to examine the effect of demographic, socio-economic and maternal health care covariates on child survival.

In this study, the births three years preceding the survey has been taken, though NFHS provides data for 10-year period preceding the survey. Because during the period not only the scenario of infant and child mortality get changed significantly, but also at the same time there could also change in socio-economic, demographic and maternal health care characteristics. Thus in this present study those variables are selected for which there were sufficient number of births in these three years period as mentioned above.

Methodology of Logistic Regression

In order to discuss the logistic regression model, we have to first consider logistic distribution function. To explain the basic ideas underlying the logit model we can consider the following LPM:

$$P_i = E\ (Y=1/\ X_i) = \beta_1+\beta_2X_i \qquad \ldots\ldots (i)$$

where X_i s income and Y=1 means the family owns a house.

Now consider the following representation of home ownership.

$$P_i = E\ (Y=1/X_i) = 1/(1+e\text{-}\ (\beta_1+\beta_2X_i) \qquad \ldots\ldots ii)$$

For case of exposition, we write (ii) as

$$P_i = 1/(1+e^{-z}{}_i) \qquad \ldots\ldots (iii)$$

where $Z_i = \beta_1+\beta_2X_i$

Equation (iii) represents what is known as the (cumulative) logistic distribution function.

Here as Z_i rages from $-\infty$ to $+\infty$, P_i ranges between 0 and 1 and that P_i is non-linearly related to Z_i (i.e. X_i). So, there is an estimation problem because P is non-linear not only in X but also in the β's. This means that we can not use the familiar OLS procedure to estimate the parameters. But this problem is more apparent than the real because (ii) is intrinsically linear, which can be shown as follows:

If P_i, the profitability of owning a house, is given by 6 (iii), then $(1\text{-}P_i)$, the probability of not owning a house is

$$1\text{-}P_i = 1/(1+e^{-z}{}_i) \qquad \ldots\ldots (iv)$$

Therefore, we can write

$$P_i/1\text{-}P_i = (1+e^{z}{}_i\ /1+e^{z}{}_i)^*\ e^{-z}{}_i \qquad \ldots\ldots (v)$$

Now $P_i/1\text{-}P_i$ is simply the odds ratio in favor of owning a house—the ratio of the probability that a family will own a house to the probability that it will not own a house. Thus if $P_i = 0.8$, it means that odds are 4 to 1 in favor of the family owning a house.

Now if we take the natural log of (v), we obtain a very interesting result, namely

$$L = \ln (P_i/1\text{-}P_i) = \beta_1+\beta_2X_i \qquad \ldots\ldots \text{(vi)}$$

That is, L, the log of the odds ratio, is not only linear to X, but also (from the estimation viewpoint) linear in the parameters. L is called the logit and hence the name logit model for the 4 models like (vi).

For estimation purpose, we write (vi) as follows:

$$L_i = \ln (P_i/1\text{-}P_i) = \beta_1+\beta_2X_i + U_i \qquad \ldots\ldots \text{(vii)}$$

To estimate the model, we need, apart from X_i, the values of the logit L_i.

For our study, we have considered the dependent variables as infant mortality, and early childhood mortality. The independent variables included are: Demographic variables, socio-economic variables, and maternal health care variables. Under demographic characteristics, we have considered the following variables:

- Age of mother at birth
- Birth order of the child
- Birth interval
- Sex of the child

Under socio-economic characteristics, we have considered the following variables:

- Rural-urban differentials in input and child mortality
- Standard of living

- Mother's education
- Mother's occupation

Under "maternal healthcare", we have considered the following variables:

- Prenatal care
- Place of delivery
- Birth attendant

Here we have run two regressions. In the first regression equation infant mortality is considered as dependent variable and in the second regression equation early childhood mortality is considered as dependent variable. Here we have used SPSS package for running regression.

Selection of Variables for Logistic Regression

Some of the variables are taken to analyze the relationship between infant and child mortality and socio-economic demographic and mother's health care factors. The dependent variables are infant mortality, early childhood mortality. The independent variables included are: demographic variables, socio-economic variables, and maternal health care variables.

Demographic Characteristics

Age of Mother at Birth

The age of mother affects the risk of death for a child. Mother's age affects the probability of her child dying during pregnancy. Children born to mothers under age 20 are more likely to die before their first birthday. Babies born to young mothers are more likely to be premature, have low birth weights and suffer from complication of delivery. Children born to mothers over age 40 years, about one-fourth of their children born are also likely to die. Older mothers are more likely to give birth to children with congenital abnormalities who may be less likely to survive childhood. The relationship between neonatal and infant and age of mothers is U-shaped. The child mortality increases with the increase age of the mothers. Infant mortality among the children born to mothers below age 20 years is higher than those born to mothers of ages 20-29 years.

Birth Order of the Child

The association between the birth order and neonatal, infant and child mortality risks shows upward trend with the increase of birth order from 1 to more than four, the infant mortality also increases. Mortality risks are high among first births, which are predominantly too younger mothers. Similarly, higher order births belong to mothers of higher ages. Infant mortality is higher for mothers with age 35 years and above than mothers aged below 35 years.

Birth Interval

Birth interval is one of the intermediate variables defined by Mosley (1983) on the determinants of infant and child mortality. The interval between births is the most consistent reproductive factors associated with high infant and child mortality. The effect of birth interval may relate either to the previous child referred as subsequent birth interval or to the next child referred as previous birth interval. Both the subsequent and previous birth interval has been found to have an effect on survivorship of the reference child, both in infancy and childhood. Children born after short intervals (less than two years) are more likely to die than children born after relatively long birth intervals (two or three years). The association (birth interval between two births) prevails in all the age groups of the children but it is most pronounced in case of neonatal mortality.

Sex of the Child

Sex of the children has influence on infant and child mortality. There are sex differentials in childhood mortality, especially in situations where the usual male disadvantage is not evident. Males have higher mortality rates during the first six months of life for genetic reasons (primarily because of higher vulnerability to infectious diseases). Excess male mortality risk declines after six months. However in situations where girl children are considered more of a financial burden to the family than boys, health care pattern tend to favour boys.

Socio-Economic Characteristics

Rural-Urban Differentials in Infant and Child Mortality

The place of residence—usually in the rural- urban dichotomy has generally been regarded as an important area where meaningful differentials in infant and child mortality can be observed. The infant and child mortality rates vary substantially among states for rural as well as urban areas. For each state, the infant and child mortality rate in urban areas is much lower than that in rural areas. This is not surprising as because urban residents are relatively better-off than their rural counterparts in terms of their economic conditions as well as their access to medical and educational facilities.

Standard of Living

Standard of living index (SLI) depicts the economic condition of the household, which is based on the availability of various modern objectives owned by household such as bicycle, clock, watch, sewing machine, radio, transistor, television, refrigerator, motorcycles, car etc. SLI includes type of amenities available to the household like type of structure of the house, electric power supply, source of drinking water, type of sanitation facilities and average monthly consumer expenditure on food, clothing, fuel, education, housing, medical care and entertainment, etc.

Mother's Education

Education is considered to be one of the most important variables of personal advancement. It provides an opportunity to acquire new knowledge, new outlook and creates a desire to be free from traditional beliefs, thinking and superstition. Education helps women overcome the barriers set by low autonomy, low social and low economic status. Maternal education is an important determinant of child survival and child mortality. Educated women might be more likely to receive appropriate and timely care, when they do reach a health facility, either because they are in a better position to pay for the acre or because, by virtue of their status, they are more likely to be well treated.

Mother's Occupation

Occupation of women is another important variable, which determines the extent of care that a woman can provide for the newborn infant. If the occupation of mother is outside the household (workers), there will be less care for the new born, to take special care in the rearing of children. It is also considered as a source of income and thereby influence on the standard of living.

Maternal Health Care Variables

Prenatal Care

Medical care taken during the delivery of the child constitutes another important dimension of childcare, on which its survival depends. From the point of view of the survival of the child it is very essential that the mother get proper care right from the conception. Proper medical care at delivery can reduce the risk of death from birth injury and tetanus. The period of 21 months from conception to first year after birth is very crucial for understanding the determinants of infant mortality. As it is known that anti-tetanus administered to the pregnant mother can eliminate deaths of child due to neonatal tetanus. Also proper medical care at the time of delivery can reduce the rates of deaths due to birth injury or due to tetanus.

Place of Delivery

Place of delivery is an important determinant of child survival. Traditional birth attendants attend most of the deliveries with the risk to both mother and the newborn baby. Neonatal, infant and child mortality rates are higher if the children born in unhealthy place and attended by professional doctor/nurse.

Birth Attendant

If live births are classified into two groups according to the person who attended the births it is of two types. One carried out by trained personnel, which included trained mid-wives, auxiliary nurse mid-wives, doctors and other hospital staffs. Another one attended by untrained personnel like Dai and aged females. The medical attendant doctor or nurse at the time of delivery is expected to significantly reduce the risk of the newborn. If deliveries taken by relatives, traditional dais or untrained dais which leads to higher mortality during infancy.

Infant Morality Differentials in Selected States

The overall pictures of infant and child mortality of these three states based on SRS data during the last two decades are given here.

Orissa

Infant mortality in Orissa has been significantly the highest in comparison with the country as a whole. The IMR of Orissa shows a fluctuating tendency: from 132 in 1982 it declines to 126 in 1983 rises to 132 in 1985, declined to 121 in 1989, increased to 122 in 1990 and until 1991 it showed fluctuating tendency. Since 1991, the trend indicates a declining trend (except 98 in 1998) upto 2001 (from 124 in 1991 to 91 in 2001). The rural IMR was high as compared to Urban and also total in 1982. Among all the IMR male rural mortality was quite high as compared to all deaths. The rural male IMR was consistently high as compared to their female counterpart. During 1985-86 the urban male mortality dramatically declined from 106 to 66 whereas in the same year female urban deaths increased from 41 to 84. During 1995-96 the female mortality raised from 59 to 79 when urban male deaths showed a downward trend from 70 to 52 in 2000, the total mortality rate decreased to 95 with 99 in rural areas and 66 in urban areas.

Rajasthan

The IMR of Rajasthan was 97 in 1982 and increased upto 107 in 1983. The IMR was almost same total male and female but differed significantly with respect to urban-rural residence (105 and 62). In 1983, urban male mortality raised from 64 to 88 and female deaths from 56 to 75. During 1983-84 rural mortality drastically increased from 115 to 133 at the same time the urban mortality decreased from 82-69. In 1992-93, and 1996-97 dramatically urban male mortality increased from 58-62 and 54 to 76, and the urban female mortality decreased from 75 to 46 and 74-42 respectively. Then suddenly urban male deaths decreased upto 58 in 1997 and urban female deaths increased to 64. In 1997 there was a significant rural-urban differential in female mortality (101 and 64). Since 1995, the total infant mortality rate is showing a continuous declining trend upto 2001.

West Bengal

The IMR of West Bengal was not so high as compared to other eastern states of India. In 1982 it was 86 and it came down upto 51 in 2001. There are large variation in urban rural as well as male female mortality in these state. The male mortality remained high as compared to female mortality except a little exception. During 1984-85 the rural male mortality decreased from 99 to 79 whereas rural female mortality was increased from 65 to 72. Also during the same period the urban female deaths decreased from 77 to 46 as compared to their male counterpart, which is increased from 33 to 64. The rural-urban differentials are also high from 1982-93. Since 1994, the gaps between rural and urban areas are lessening as compared to other states. Also deaths in rural areas are not so high as compared to the total IMR of the state. During 1994-95 the urban female deaths reduced from 63 to 47. And since 1994 upto 2000, IMR shows downward trend with slight variation.

Differnentials in Child Mortality in Selected States

Orissa

The child mortality rate (0-4) reduced from 42 in 1981 to 25 in 2000. It reduced significantly from 1991 to 1996 (39 to 32), but at the same time the urban male mortality remained same. The rural male death was more than 200 percent than that from the urban deaths. And the gap was widened in 1991 (41 in rural and 17 in urban). In 1996 the urban male and female mortality were 17 and 23 respectively, but rural-urban gap was double in case of male mortality. Male and female childhood mortality rates are fluctuating over the years in both urban and rural areas. In 2000 the urban-rural female mortality was high 15 and 26.

Rajasthan

In 1981, the child mortality rate was 50 as compared to 54

in case of female death rates. During the same period, the rural-urban variation was high 57 and 19 respectively. The child mortality was halved during the period 1981-2000. The female death rate was quite high as 54 and 34 in 1981 and 1991 as compared to males, 47 and 28 respectively. In 1991, the urban female death rate was high as compared to urban male deaths (25 and 17). In 1996 as compared to urban rural male mortality the difference was high (21 and 31) and in 2000 the gap became wider (11 and 24).

West Bengal

The child mortality rate is showing a declining trend from 1981-2000. The rural-urban differential was quite high in 1981; rural 39 and urban 16. Over the years there are not so difference in urban male and female mortality rates, but in rural male mortality rates it showed variation, 39 in 1981 and 15 in 2000 and rural female mortality from 36 to 14 at the same time period. It remained almost same in urban female mortality rate during period 1981-96. The rural-urban difference was quite high in 1981 and 2000 in case of female deaths (36 and 11) and (14 and 7) respectively.

Table 6.12 presents that IMR of India in 2001 was reduced by 40% during 1982-02. In early eighties, the male infant mortality was slightly higher than the female infants (106 as against 104). The rural-urban differentials were wider during 1982-84 that was 104 and 66 respectively. Over the years the level of male infant mortality was higher in urban areas than their female counterparts whereas it is reverse in case of rural areas, i.e., mortality level was higher during the period 1982-2002.

In Table 6.12a it is shown that in India in early 1981 the early childhood mortality of urban areas was 50 percent of rural areas. The same trend continued up to 1986, it was 200 percent more than the urban areas. The female mortality does not have positive association with the place of residence. Throughout the years (from 1981-2000) it remained high as compared to the total child deaths. The child mortality shows no variation by place of residence throughout the last two decades.

Table 6.13 indicates that during the period (1982-2001) the reduction in rural male mortality was less (22 points in West

TABLE 6.12

Infant Morality Rate for India by Sex and Place of Residence

Years	*Total*			*Rural*			*Urban*		
	Total	*Male*	*Female*	*Total*	*Male*	*Female*	*Total*	*Male*	*Female*
(1)	(2)	(3)	(4)	(5)	(6)	(7)	(8)	(9)	(10)
1982-84	105	105	104	114	114	114	66	69	63
1985-86	96	96	97	105	106	106	61	61	60
1988-90	88	89	88	95	96	96	57	58	55
1991-93	78	78	78	85	86	86	50	51	49
1994-96	73	73	73	79	80	80	49	48	45
1997-99	71	70	72	76	78	78	45	45	44
2000-02	66	64	67	72	74	74	42	42	42

Source : Office of the Registrar General, India, Compendium of Fertility and Mortality Indicators, 1971-97 and SRS Statistical Report, 1998, 1999, 2000 and SRS Bulletin April, 2004.

TABLE 6.12a

Child Mortality Rate of India By Sex and Place of Residence, 1981-2000

Years	Total			Rural			Urban		
	Total	*Male*	*Female*	*Total*	*Male*	*Female*	*Total*	*Male*	*Female*
(1)	(2)	(3)	(4)	(5)	(6)	(7)	(8)	(9)	(10)
1981	41	39	43	46	43	48	20	20	21
1986	37	35	39	41	39	43	21	20	22
1991	27	26	28	29	28	30	16	15	17
1996	24	22	26	26	24	28	14	14	15
2000	20	19	21	22	21	23	12	11	12

Source : Office of the Registrar General, India, Compendium of Fertility and Mortality Indicators, 1971-97 and SRS Statistical Report, 1998, 1999, 2000.

TABLE 6.13

Infant Mortality Rates of Orissa, Rajasthan, West Bengal by Sex and Place of Residence, 1982-2001 by 5 year Average

States and place of residence	*Male*				*Female*			
	1982-86	*1987-91*	*1992-96*	*1997-2001*	*1982-86*	*1987-91*	*1992-96*	*1997-2001*
(1)	(2)	(3)	(4)	(5)	(6)	(7)	(8)	(9)
Rural								
Orissa	139	129	112	100	128	127	106	99
Rajasthan	115	96	88	81	118	101	92	90
West Bengal	91	80	65	59	81	72	62	51
Urban								
Orissa	83	74	70	61	69	69	67	65
Rajasthan	74	56	62	59	68	65	60	58
West Bengal	55	45	40	48	51	46	45	31

Source : Office of the Registrar General, India, Compendium of Fertility and Mortality Indicators, 1971-97 and SRS Statistical Report, 1998, 1999, 2000 and SRS Bulletin, April, 2004.

Bengal as compared to 39 and 34 points in Orissa and Rajasthan respectively). During 1992-96 and 1997-2001 the rural female infant mortality reduction level was only 2 points in comparison with 13 and 11 in Orissa and West Bengal respectively. With reference to urban male mortality, it came down significantly by 23 points in Orissa and by 15 and 8 points in Rajasthan and West Bengal. In West Bengal the urban female mortality was decreased significantly (from 51 to 31) during the period 1982-2001, whereas it was only by 4 points in Orissa and by 10 points in Rajasthan. A rural-urban comparison over the years 1982-2001 in West Bengal, reveals that male infant deaths came down significantly in rural areas in the state by 22 points, but in urban areas it was only by 7 points.

In Table 6.14, it is seen that in 1981 the total child mortality was more than 200 percent high as compared to urban mortality. From 1981-2000, the total child mortality reduced notably from 44 to 16 in Orissa. In 1981, in total child mortality rate, the difference between rural and urban was little, but it differed greatly in case of rural-urban and male-female child mortality in West Bengal. There was also difference between male-female mortality in Orissa and Rajasthan. Rural male mortality was high in all the three states during the time period 1982-2000. In 1986 and 1991 urban female mortality was more than the other two states. In comparison to Orissa and West Bengal, rural female mortality was high in Rajasthan.

Table 6.15 shows that Rajasthan experienced a less percentage decadal change in total IMR reduction compared to India as a whole and other states during the time period 1982-2001. The percentage change in infant mortality in rural West Bengal was the highest (26 percent) compared to 20 and 18 in Orissa and Rajasthan respectively. In contrast, the urban areas experienced stagnation in the reduction in Infant mortality during this period with respect to all states. In urban area the percent change in Rajasthan was less compared to India and other two states.

From Table 6.16, it is depicted that in male mortality, Rajasthan (-17.89) has experienced less decadal change as compared to Orissa and West Bengal (–21.87 and –24.80) respectively. At the same time, in Female infant mortality rate Orissa has shown less change (–18.24) in that decade in

TABLE 6.14

Child Mortality Rates of Orissa, Rajasthan and West Bengal by Sex and Place of Residence, 1981-2000

States and place of residence	*Male*					*Female*				
	1981	*1986*	*1991*	*1996*	*2000*	*1981*	*1986*	*1991*	*1996*	*2000*
(1)	*(2)*	*(3)*	*(4)*	*(5)*	*(6)*	*(7)*	*(8)*	*(9)*	*(10)*	*(11)*
Rural										
Orissa	49	45	41	34	26	44	48	41	30	26
Rajasthan	53	43	30	31	24	62	46	36	37	29
West Bengal	39	28	22	20	15	36	28	22	19	14
Urban										
Orissa	20	26	17	17	19	23	12	16	23	15
Rajasthan	18	25	17	21	11	20	26	25	19	21
West Bengal	16	19	13	13	14	11	15	14	12	7

Source : Office of the Registrar General, India, Compendium of Fertility and Mortality Indicators, 1971-97 and SRS Statistical Report, 1998, 1999, 2000.

TABLE 6.15

Decadal Percent Change in Infant Mortality Rates in India and Selected States by Place of Residence between 1982-1991 and 1992-2001

India and States	*Total*			*Rural*			*Urban*		
	1982-91	*1992-01*	%	*1982-91*	*1992-01*	%	*1982-91*	*1992-01*	%
(1)	(2)	(3)	(4)	(5)	(6)	(7)	(8)	(9)	(10)
India	94.7	72.0	-23.97	103.0	77.9	-24.37	60.2	46.4	-22.92
Orissa	125.9	100.4	-20.25	130.7	104.5	-20.04	74.1	65.7	-11.33
Rajasthan	100.7	83.5	-17.08	107.2	87.6	-18.28	66.0	59.8	-9.39
West Bengal	74.8	56.0	-25.10	80.9	59.5	-26.45	48.3	41.1	-14.9

Source : Office of the Registrar General, India, Compendium of Fertility and Mortality Indicators, 1971-97 and SRS Statistical Report, 1998, 1999, 2000 and SRS Bulletin, April, 2004.

TABLE 6.16

Decadal Percent Change in Infant Mortality Rates of India and Selected States by Sex between 1982-91 and 1992-2001

India and States	Total			Male			Female		
	1982-91	1992-01	%	1982-91	1992-01	%	1982-91	1992-01	%
(1)	(2)	(3)	(4)	(5)	(6)	(7)	(8)	(9)	(10)
India	94.7	72.0	-23.97	95.0	71.2	-25.05	94.9	73.0	-23.07
Orissa	125.9	100.4	-20.25	130.3	101.8	-21.87	121.1	99.0	-18.24
Rajasthan	100.7	83.5	-17.08	98.9	81.2	-17.89	102.6	86.0	-16.17
West Bengal	74.8	56.0	-25.13	78.2	58.8	-24.80	71.2	53.2	-25.28

Source : Office of the Registrar General, India, Compendium of Fertility and Mortality Indicators, 1971-97 and SRS Statistical Report, 1998, 1999, 2000 and SRS Bulletin, April, 2004.

comparison with India and West Bengal (-23.07 and -25.28) respectively. Whereas West Bengal is almost same in all the cases of both male and female infant mortality rates as compared to national decadal change.

Figure 6.1 presents the IMR of India and Orissa, Rajasthan and West Bengal from 1990-2002. India has a continuous decline over the years. Assam has the highest level of IMR in 1995. Rajasthan was 65 in 1990 but suddenly increased upto 115 in 1995, and in early nineties it came down since then it is showing somewhat constant level. While West Bengal is showing a declining trend over the period 1990-2002, except the year 1992.

FIG. 6.1
Infant Mortality Rate

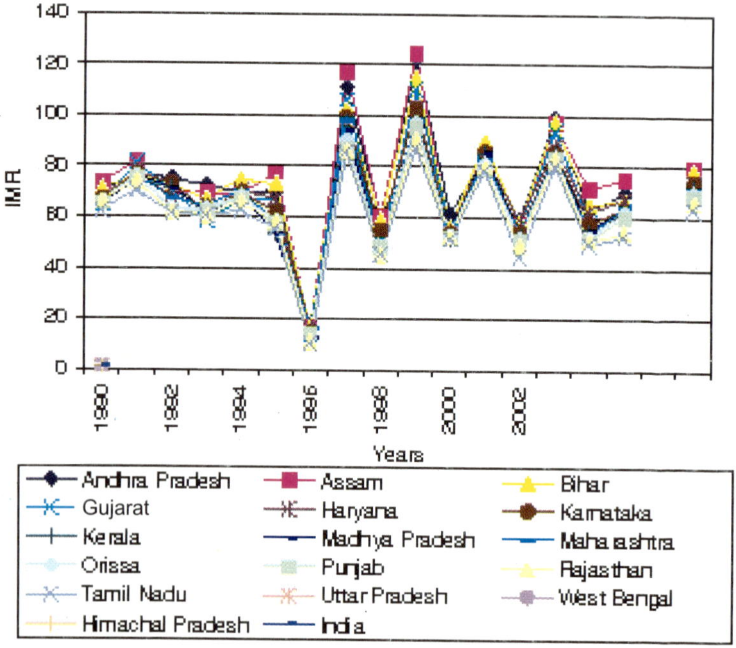

Figure 6.2 depicts about the child mortality rate over the last 20 years in India and Orissa, Rajasthan and West Bengal. India and West Bengal are showing declining trend. However,

FIG. 6.2
Child Mortality Rate

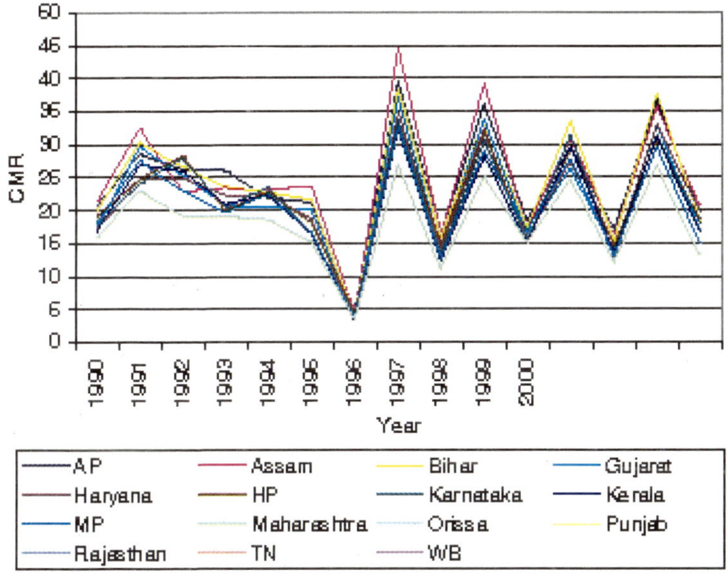

in Orissa it is increasing trend from 1981-86, then it is reduced and in 1996 and 2000 Orissa and Rajasthan had the same IMR and both overlapped at one point.

In Figure 6.3, it is presented that in 1982-86 there was not much difference in urban male IMR of Orissa and Rajasthan and in 1997-2001 it was same for both the states. In case of rural IMR, Orissa was found to be highest and West Bengal was lowest over the years. Rural-urban differential was clearly seen in the figure, as rural mortality was high as compared to urban in all the states over the years.

Figure 6.4 presents that in West Bengal, urban IMR remained almost constant during the period 1987-91 and 1992-96 and in 1982-86 Orissa and Rajasthan were same. In case of rural infant mortality rate, the difference between Orissa and Rajasthan in 1987-91 was higher but the gap was lessening during 1997-2001. However in case of urban IMR, Rajasthan was found to be almost stagnant during these years.

In Figure 6.5, it is shown that in 1982 and 1996, the rural and urban child mortality rates were higher in the state of Rajasthan as compared to Orissa and West Bengal. But in

FIG. 6.3
IMR (Male) of Three States by Residence, 1982-2001 (Five Year Average)

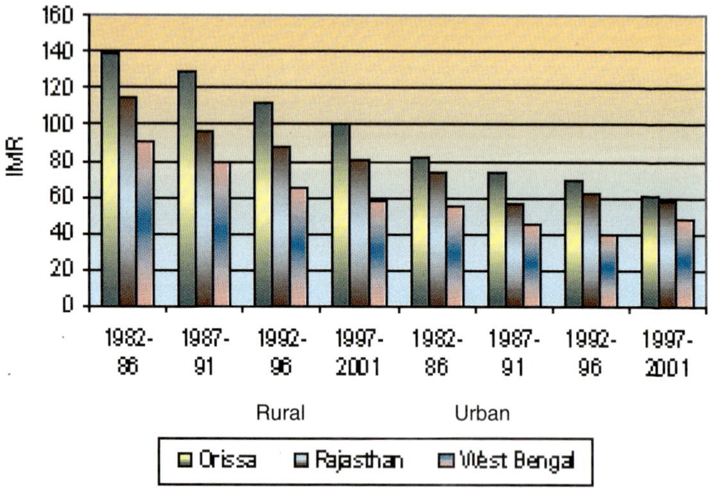

FIG. 6.4
IMR (Female) of Three States by Residence, 1982-2001 (Five Year Average)

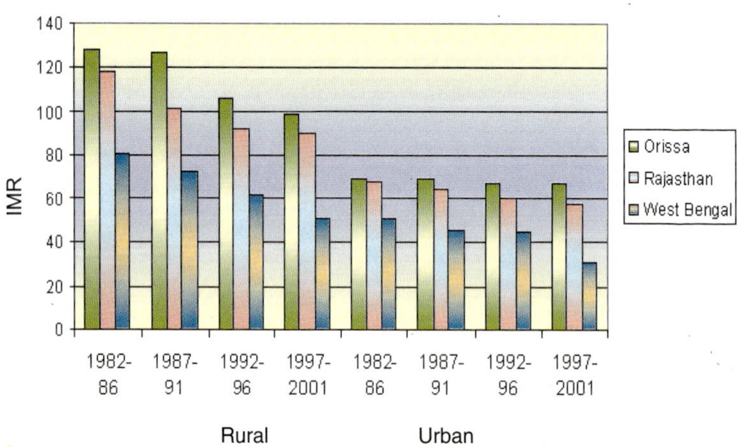

2000, it reduced drastically. The rural child deaths were higher compared the urban, among all the states over the year. In 1991, the urban mortality rate was same in both Orissa and Rajasthan

FIG. 6.5
Child Mortality Rate (Male) of Three States by Residence,1981-2000

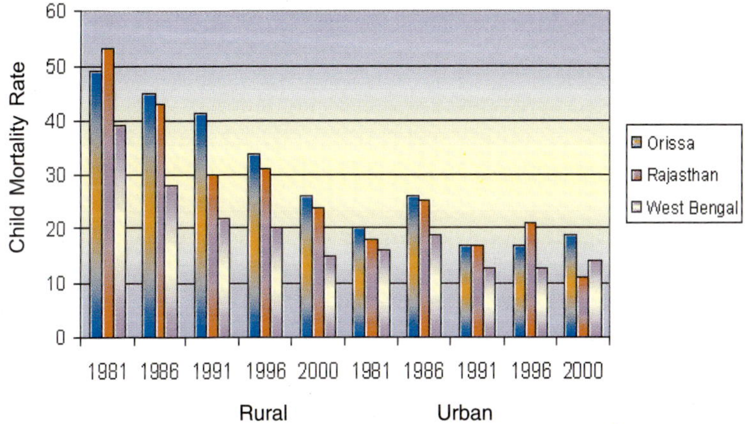

(17), while there was a gap of only point between these two states' urban CMR in 1986 (26 and 25).

The Figure 6.6 presents the difference between rural and urban female child mortality. The death is quite high as compared to Orissa and West Bengal. However, Orissa is not

FIG. 6.6
Child Mortality Rate (Female) of Three States by Residence, 1981-2000

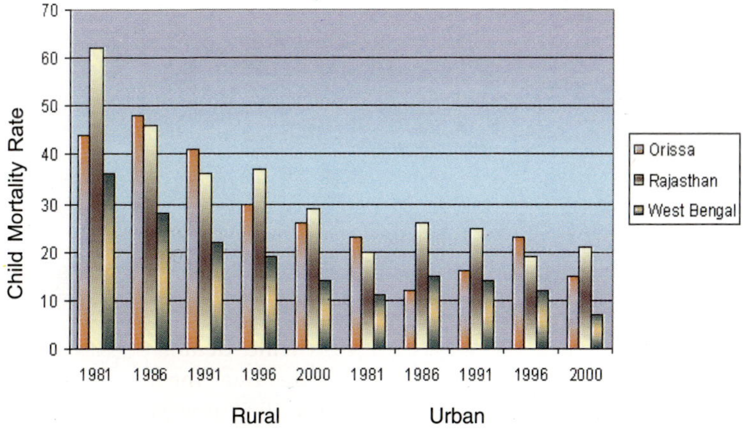

showing significant difference in rural mortality over the years and is highest in 2000. In case of urban mortality Rajasthan has the highest among all the states except in 1981 and 1996. In Table 6.17, results of logistic regression shows that a number of variables have influence on infant mortality like, age of mother at birth, ethnicity, assistance during delivery place of delivery, birth order and birth interval and living standard are important determinants of infant mortality in Orissa and Rajasthan. Among all those places of delivery is highly significant both in Orissa and Rajasthan. However the variable like the sex of children and place of residence play important role in infant mortality neither in Orissa nor in Rajasthan.

In Table 6.17, results of logistic regression shows that a number of variables have influence on infant mortality like, age of mother at birth, ethnicity, assistance during delivery, place of delivery, birth order and birth interval and living standard are important determinants of infant mortality in Orissa and Rajasthan. Among all those, the place of delivery is significant both in Orissa and Rajasthan. However the variables like sex of children and place of residence play important role in infant mortality neither in Orissa nor in Rajasthan.

From Table 6.18, it can be inferred that the variables, which have significant influence on early childhood mortality, are level of education of mothers, delivery assistance, place of delivery, standard of living and mother's occupation. Mother's education was found highly significant with childhood mortality in Rajasthan. Literate mothers have 81% less chance of deaths of their children as compared to illiterate mothers. However, mother's age at birth, ethnicity, sex of child, birth order and birth interval have not shown any effect in case of early childhood mortality.

The decline in IMR started from early eighties and declined upto 63 in 2002. The late eighties show a better trend in infant and child survival and reduction in infant as well as child mortality. It indicates that it is possible for India to reach a low level of IMR in recent years. Progress in reducing IMR has slowed down in recent years. For example, between 1980-90, IMR went down from 114 to 80 by 30 percent. However, between 1990-99, reduction in IMR has been much less from 80

TABLE 6.17

Logistic Regression Coefficients of the Effect of Selected Independent Variables on Infant Mortality

	Orissa		*Rajasthan*		*West Bengal*	
	B	*Exp (B)*	*B*	*Exp (B)*	*B*	*Exp (B)*
Background Characteristics						
Age of mother at birth						
Less than 20 years@						
More than 20 years	-0.428	0.652*	-0.375	0.687*	-0.467	0.627
Ethnicity						
Others@						
SC/ST	0.634	1.884***	0.097	1.102	0.349	1.418
Place of residence						
Urban@						
Rural	0.460	1.583	0.048	1.050	0.094	1.098*
Assistance during delivery						
No@						
Yes	-0.781	0.458*	-0.600	0.549***	-0.657	0.518
Place of delivery						
Institutional@						
Non-institutional	1.103	3.014**	1.103	2.754***		
Sex of child						
Male@						
Female	0.167	1.181	0.070	1.073	0.321	1.379
Birth order and Birth Interval						
First birth order@						
2-3 and <24 months	0.248	1.281	0.108	1.115	0.075	1.078
2-3 and > 24 months	-0.302	0.739	-0.398	0.672*	-0.419	0.658
3+ and <24 months	0.112	1.118	0.456	1.578*	0.229	1.257
3+ and > 24 months	0.508	1.662	0.373	1.452	0.083	1.087
Living Standard						
Low@						
Medium and high	-0.477	0.620**	-0.115	0.891	-0.113	0.8937
Mother's literacy						
Illiterate@						
Literate	-0.599	.549*	-0.974	0.378***	-0.446	0.640

*P<. 10, **p<. 05, ***p<. 01.

TABLE 6.18
Logistic Regression Coefficients of the Effect of Selected Independent Variables on Child Mortality

	Orissa		*Rajasthan*	
	B	*Exp(B)*	*B*	*Exp(B)*
Background Characteristics				
Age of mother at birth				
Less than 20 years@				
More than 20 years	-0.481	0.618	0.031	1.031
Ethnicity				
Others@				
SC/ST	-0.092	0.912	-0.153	0.858
Place of residence				
Urban@				
Rural	0.535	1.707	0.641	1.898
Assistance during delivery				
No@				
Yes	-1.627	0.196*	-0.249	0.779
Place of delivery				
Institutional@				
Non-institutional	1.848	6.348*	0.252	1.287
Sex of child				
Male@				
Female	0.138	1.148	0.216	1.241
Birth order and Birth Interval				
First birth order@				
2-3 and <24 months	0.452	1.571	0.240	1.271
2-3 and > 24 months	0.139	1.150	-0.264	0.768
3+ and <24 months	0.552	1.737	0.282	1.325
3+ and > 24 months	0.233	1.262	0.031	1.031
Living Standard				
Low@				
Medium and high	-0.900	0.407*	-0.287	0.751
Mother's literacy				
Illiterate@				
Literate	-0.387	0.679	-1.614	0.199***
Mother's occupation				
Not working@				
Working	0.468	1.597*	0.327	1.387*

*p<.10, **p<.05,***p<.01

to 70 only 12.5%. There is decline in infant mortality by 23% and child mortality 34% during the period 1981-90.

Child mortality has been declining throughout the less developing region of the world since the 1950's. The early childhood mortality in India have shown substantial decline from 1991 onwards. Although the death rate of rural areas is higher, still the decline in early childhood mortality is faster by 64% in rural areas as compared to urban areas. Despite improvement in the general mortality situation and thereby in infant and child mortality, the latter remain markedly high. Though such a reduction appears to quite encouraging, there are large differentials in the risks of infant and child deaths among different regions and also within the same regions. The variations in infant and child mortality rates differ among different socio-economies and demographic strata. Logistic regression analysis demonstrates that components of early childhood mortality are education, assistance during delivery, place of delivery, place of residence. However, urban-rural differentials in mortality are more in Rajasthan as compared to Orissa. But illiteracy of mother is significantly associated with child death in Rajasthan. But the age of birth, ethnicity, sex of child, birth order and birth interval did not show any effect in case of child mortality.

V. BURDEN OF DISEASES IN RURAL INDIA

Over the years, India has experienced epidemiological transition due to change in disease patterns, improvements in the nutritional and health infrastructure, eradication and control of major killer diseases and socio-economic development. Even after more than five decades of self-governance, these health achievements are not withstanding. The burden of disease is still high due to large-scale poverty, developmental disparities between states, gender discrimination, growing aged population and failure of government policies. Mortality and disability in this country is twice that of China and nearly three times higher than in developed countries. Looking at the diseases adjusted life years (DALY), losses (268953000) of burden second only to that observed in Africa (325198000), a sizeable proportion of this burden is due to communicable diseases (50%) followed by

Non-communicable diseases (33%) and injuries. Health inequalities were observed widely across the country at the same time increasingly being viewed as a major public health concern to meet the planned targets with noticeable inter-state differences in average per-capita spending on health.

Unfortunately, in rural India adequate attention has not been focused at studying disease pattern, trend and its consequences along with the epidemiological transition. To test such hypotheses, paucity of adequate, accurate and appropriate statistical data on one hand and complex pathogenesis of some important diseases (like heart disease, caner, diabetes mellitus) on other hand makes the analysis of disease pattern more complex. In this country of more than one billion population, health indicators are often led to over estimate in some instances and under-estimate in others. Lack of uniformity in assessments has always posed further difficulty for national and international comparisons. Major registration sources are neither reliable nor complete; good percent of cases will go unregistered out of which only 10% of deaths are medically certified. But some sources like Survey of Causes of Death do reveal some interesting pattern that may very well be true.

Keeping above points, here we discuss about the trends of major causes of death groups and change in the ranking of different diseases over a period of time and to assess the intensity of diseases through disease ranking coefficient values for major states. It also provides, for the first time, the estimates of the distribution of age standardized mortality rate (ASMR) of major killer diseases in India. The analyses only confine to the data prior to 1994. More recent data on mortality requires a separate review because the tuberculosis incidence has changed due to the impact of HIV/AIDS after 1995. In addition, subsequent to 1995 some major Indian state boundaries were reclassified due to the proclamation of new states, which may have complicated comparisons.

Methods and Source

Data was mainly extracted from the "Survey of Causes of Death (rural)" annual reports of Registrar General of India (RGI) from 1966 to 1994. Despite of a few limitations like improper medical certification, high proportion of recorded cause of death as 'selinity' and reclassification of disease groups over time, SCD (Survey of Causes of Death) is by far the most reliable source of mortality statistics in rural areas of India. Earlier it was used to analyze accident and violence-related mortality in 1970's and 1980's for international comparisons.

In this section, an attempt is made to bring out the health status of rural India (in its 14 major states) as reflected in the causes of death statistics, which has been either neglected or ignored by researchers. To reveal the trend of major causes of death groups, a five yearly moving average is calculated where the percentage figures show the average of five successive years. Significance test was carried out to test whether average percentage change (APC) significantly differs from null hypotheses 0; this shows change of the rate of increase or decrease.

In order to reckon disease intensity region, disease ranking coefficient values (R) are calculated for fourteen major states and grouped into three classes according to their magnitude. Disease ranking coefficient of a state is the average of disease prevalence ranks of that particular state. Higher the value of ranking coefficient lesser is the disease burden. Disease intensity zone can be defined as the area having similar disease burden in type as well as in magnitude. Coefficient R1 is calculated separately considering equal weight to the ranks of three communicable disease groups ('coughs', 'fever', 'digestive disorder') that can be controlled with proper knowledge of health and hygiene along with health care facilities. High Disease Intensity Zone (R5) shows worst performance in controlling diseases preceded by Moderate Disease Intensity Zone (R 5-10) and Low Disease Intensity Zone (R>10).

Selinity adjusted causes of death in 1991 is calculated where percent deaths in 60+ age group are converted to absolute figures for seven cause groups (excluding 'causes peculiar to infancy', 'maternal death', 'selinity') in 11 states and summed up to get total deaths at 60+ age. For Assam, Haryana and Kerala age-wise death distribution are not available and thereby these states have been excluded from the analyses. The deaths in 'selinity' are distributed among seven cause groups based on their share of 60+ deaths in respective causes. For

TABLE 6.19
Percentage Distribution of 'Causes of Death' Status (Five Yearly Moving Averages), Rural India, 1964-94

Year	*A&I++*	*Cbp*	*Fever++*	*Dgd*	*Coughs++*	*Dcns*	*Ocs*	*Cpi*	*Dcs++*	*Senility*
(1)	*(2)*	*(3)*	*(4)*	*(5)*	*(6)*	*(7)*	*(8)*	*(9)*	*(10)*	*(11)*
1968	3.9	1.3	20.1	9.6	24.7	NA	5.2	10.9	7.9	16.4
1969	4.0	1.3	19.3	9.0	23.9	NA	5.4	11.1	8.1	17.9
1970	4.0	1.2	18.0	9.9	23.8	NA	5.5	11.2	8.5	17.8
1971	3.9	1.2	17.0	9.9	23.3	0.5	6.1	11.4	8.0	18.6
1972	4.1	1.2	15.4	10.1	22.5	1.1	6.7	11.6	7.8	19.4
1973	4.2	1.2	14.7	10.3	21.9	1.7	7.1	11.8	7.5	19.6
1974	4.4	1.2	13.6	10.5	21.6	2.4	7.5	12.2	7.4	19.2
1975	4.5	1.1	12.6	9.8	21.0	3.2	7.9	12.5	7.3	20.1
1976	4.6	1.1	11.6	9.7	20.7	3.4	7.8	12.7	7.9	20.3
1977	4.7	1.1	10.8	9.7	20.7	3.5	7.8	13.0	8.4	20.2
1978	4.8	1.1	9.9	9.6	20.5	3.6	7.9	13.2	8.7	20.7
1979	4.8	1.1	9.2	9.4	20.4	3.6	7.9	13.1	8.8	21.8
1980	5.1	1.1	8.9	8.7	20.3	3.6	7.9	12.8	8.9	22.6
1981	5.2	1.1	9.1	8.3	20.2	3.8	7.9	12.4	8.9	23.1
1982	5.5	1.1	9.3	7.9	20.2	3.9	7.8	11.9	9.0	23.5
1983	5.8	1.1	9.5	7.5	20.3	3.9	8.0	11.2	9.3	23.3

1984	6.1	1.1	9.9	7.5	20.1	4.0	8.1	10.9	9.3	22.9
1985	6.3	1.1	9.9	7.5	20.2	4.0	8.4	10.6	9.4	22.6
1986	6.5	1.0	9.5	7.3	20.2	4.0	8.7	10.4	9.6	22.9
1987	6.7	1.0	8.9	7.1	20.2	4.2	8.7	10.1	9.9	23.1
1988	7.2	1.0	8.5	6.9	19.8	4.3	8.7	10.0	10.1	23.7
1989	7.5	1.0	7.9	6.6	19.6	4.4	8.6	10.0	10.5	23.9
1990	7.9	1.0	7.5	6.4	19.6	4.5	8.4	9.8	10.8	24.0
1991	8.3	1.1	7.3	6.5	19.4	4.4	8.5	10.0	10.9	23.7
1992	8.6	1.1	7.3	6.4	19.2	4.5	8.9	10.0	11.0	23.2

Abbreviations : A&I = Accident and injury, Cbp = Childbirth and Pregnancy, Dgd = Digestive disorders, Dcns = Diseases of central nervous system, Ocs = Other clear symptom, Cpi = Causes peculiar to infancy, Dcs = Diseases of circulatory system.

++Average Percentage Change Significantly differs from 0 at 95% confidence interval.

Source : Survey of Causes of Death, Rural, 1966-94 (RGI).

prevalence calculations, state-wise population and their age distributions are borrowed from Census and Sample Registration Systems (SRS) respectively. Age Standard Mortality Rates (ASMR) was calculated using India's population as a standard.

The trend of major 'cause of death' is reflected in Table 6.19. The combined share of 'coughs', 'digestive disorders' and 'fevers' was more than half in 1960's, but it had diminished to one-third by 1994. The share of 'fever' alone dropped from 20% to 7% for the same period. Within India, death with 'fever' was quite high in Punjab, Madhya Pradesh and it was almost negligible in Karnataka and Maharashtra. However, the decline of deaths in other two groups namely coughs and digestive disorders were not so distinct. Among the deaths 'digestive disorders' accounted for 11% in the eastern states.

Trend shows 'coughs' was major cause of death in almost all the states in general; especially in UP and Rajasthan accounting one-third of deaths with no change over a period of time. Bronchitis and asthma maintained top rank over the two decades accounting more than 8% of total rural deaths in India (Table 6.20) followed by TB of the lungs accounting 6.1% deaths, its rank been dropped slightly in the following decades.

Over the last two decades, deaths due to 'accidents-injuries' have raised from 4% to 9%. Within the cause group of 'accidents and injuries', subgroup death due to drowning was going up (0.8% in 1971 to 1.05% in 1991), but its rank was descending after 1981 partly due to the rapid increase in vehicular accidents (0.6% in 1971 to 2.15% in 1991). Suicide was a new addition in 1991 among the first three fatal diseases under this group. 'Accidents and injuries' accounted a good share of death in Punjab, Uttar Pradesh and Maharashtra. Deaths associated with 'disorders of circulatory system' had increased by 3.1% over the study period and the fatality of this cause was high in Tamilnadu and Orissa followed by Punjab, Karnataka, Andhra Pradesh and Bihar. However, the reasons might have differed among the states as this group incorporated both heart attack and anemia. The most remarkable increase in this cause of death was exhibited by heart attack. Heart attack was not

TABLE 6.20
Percentage Distribution of Deaths by Major Cause of Sub-groups and Rank of Major Killer Diseases

1971	*%*	*Rank*	*1981*	*%*	*Rank*	*1991*	*%*	*Rank*
(1)	*(2)*	*(3)*	*(4)*	*(5)*	*(6)*	*(7)*	*(8)*	*(9)*
1. **Violence and injury**			1. **accident and injury**			1. **Accident and injury**		
A. Drowning	0.8	8	A. Drawning	1.1		A. Vehicular accident	2.15	9
B. Accident from vehicles	0.6		B. Vehicular accident	0.9		B. Suicide	1.87	
C. Fall	04		C. Burns	0.5		C. Drowning	1.05	
2. **Childbirth and complicated pregnancy**			2. **Childbirth and pregnancy**			2. **Childbirth and pregnancy**		
A. Anaemia of pregnancy	02		A. Anaemia	0.2		A. Bleeding of pregnancy	0.25	
B. Post-partum hemorrhage	0.2		B. Puerperal sepsis	0.1		B. Anaemia	02	
C. Aclampsia	01		C. Abortion	0.1		C. Toxemia	0.14	
3. **Digestive disorders**			3. **Digestive disorders**			3. **Digestive disorders**		
A. Dysentery	5	3	A. Gastro ententus	2.8	8	A. Gastro ententus	2.19	10
B. Food poisoning	0.3		B. Debility malnutrition	1.8	10	B. Acute abdomen	1.65	
C. Cholera	0.3		C. Acute abdomen	1.4		C. Dysentery	1.03	
4. **Coughs**			4. **Coughs**			4. **Coughs**		
A. Bronco pneumonia	11	1	A. Asthma and bronchitis	9	1	A. Asthma and bronchitis	8.75	1
B. TB of respiratory system	6.1	2	B. Pneumonia	5.9	2	B . TB of lungs	5.37	3
C. Pneumonia	2	4	C. TB of lungs	5.5	3	C. Pneumonia	4.5	5

(*Contd.*)

Table 6.20 (Contd.)

(1)	(2)	(3)	(4)	(5)	(6)	(7)	(8)	(9)
5. Circulatory diseases			**5. Disorders of circulatory system**			**5. Disorders of circulatory system**		
A. Plague	0.5		A. Heart attack	5.6	4	A. Heart attack	8.23	2
B. Cirrhosis of liver	0.4		B. Anaemia	3.2	6	B. Anaemia	2.96	8
C. Congestive heart disease	0.4							
6. Fevers			**6. Fevers**			**6. Fevers**		
A. Tuberculosis	1.2	5	A. Typhoid	3.2	7	A. Malaria	1.87	
B. Septicemia	1.2	6	B. Influenza	1.8		B. Typhoid	1.84	
C. Diphtheria	1.1	7	C. Malaria	1.1.4				
7. Infant deaths			**7. Causes peculiar to infancy**			**7. Causes peculiar to infancy**		
A. Prematurity	0.8	8	A. Prematurity	4.4		A. Prematurity	4.85	
B. Infections to new born	0.8	8	B. Respiratory infections	1.9		B. Respiratory infections	1.57	
C. Cyanosis	08	8	C. Malnutrition	1.4				
8. Other clear symptoms			**8. Other clear symptoms**			**8. Other clear symptoms**		
A. Diseases of urinary tract	0.5		A. Cancer	2.5	9	A. Cancer	3.89	6
B. Hypertension	0.5		B. Tetanus	1.8		B. Jaundice	1.29	
C. Cerebral Hemorrhage	0.4		C. Cirrhosis	0.9				
9. Not available			**9. Disorder of central nervous syst.**			**9. Disorder of central nervous syst.**		
			A. Meningitis	2.6		A. Paralysis	3.63	7
			B. Paralysis	0.6		B. Convulsions	0.60	
						C. Meningitis	0.49	

among the top ten fatal diseases in 1971, but moved to the second position in 1991 surpassing tuberculosis. Other important changes were exhibited by resurgence of malaria in 1980's increase in the rank of vehicular accidents and cancers. Cancers accounted (except Bihar where jaundice surpasses cancer) for 15% of total deaths in Karnataka and Gujarat followed by Maharashtra (14%), Orissa and Andhra Pradesh (13%), Tamil Nadu and Bihar (12%). Within the causes of infant deaths, prematurely maintained its dominance with a steady increase in fatality (08% in 1971 to 4.85% in 1991). Another important point worth mentioning was the sharp increase in rank as well as the percentage share of paralysis. Demise in selinity as a cause of death was swelling steadily (from about 16% in 1968 to 23% in 1992).

The disease intensity is shown in Tables 6.21 and Table 6.22. In total, it was difficult to interpret the disease intensity, because of the diversity and complexity of major

Table 6.21

Disease Ranking Coefficient of Major States of India, 1991

States	*R*	*R1*
AP	5.88	8.33
Assam	6.31	3.33
Bihar	6.25	5.66
Gujarat	8.25	8.83
Haryana	10.5	9.67
Karnataka	8.25	11.0
Kerala	9.88	13.33
MP	4.56	1.33
Maharashtra	10.38	11.33
Orissa	4.5	5 0
Punjab	8.38	8.67
Rajasthan	1.05	5.67
Tamilnadu	7.13	9.17
UP	6.25	3.67

Note : R—Coefficient considering disease ranking values of ten causes.
R1–Values of fevers coughs + digestive disorders.

disease groups. Good performance of some states in reducing communicable disease burdenwise overshadowed by prevalence of other cause groups. So one set of coefficient value R1 (only ranking values of fever + cough + digestive disorders) combining communicable and infectious disease groups and clubbed into three categories.

TABLE 6.22

Communicable Disease Intencity Zone (I)

HDIZ	*MDIZ*	*LDIZ*
Assam	Bihar, Orissa, Rajasthan	Kerala
Madhya Pradesh	Andhra Pradesh, Gujarat	Karnataka
Uttar Pradesh	Haryana, Punjab, Tamilnadu	Maharashtra

Abbreviations : HDIZ—High Disease Intensity Zone; MDIZ—Medium Disease Intensity Zone; LDIZ—Low Disease Intensity Zone.

Source : 'Survey of causes of death', 1991.

High disease intensity zone (HDIZ) indicates poor performance in dealing with communicable diseases. Madhya Pradesh, Uttar Pradesh and Assam belong to this group with poorest coefficient value (1.33) of the first state, followed by Assam (R1 3.33) and Uttar Pradesh (R1 3.67). Moderate disease intensity zone (MDIZ) embraces eight states with variations of disease intensity. For example, Bihar, Orissa, Rajasthan have R1 value less than 6, hence their disease burden is slightly less than the HDIZ. While Haryana and Tamil Nadu manifest fair performance in this High disease intensity zone (HDIZ) indicates poor performance in dealing with communicable diseases. Madhya Pradesh, Uttar Pradesh and Assam belong to this group with poorest coefficient value (1.33) of the first state, followed by Assam (R1 3.33) and Uttar Pradesh (R1 3.67). Moderate disease intensity zone (MDIZ) embraces eight states with variations of disease intensity. For example, Bihar, Orissa Rajasthan has R1 value less than 6, hence their disease burden is slightly less than the HDIZ. While Haryana and Tamilnadu manifest fair performance in this respect as their coefficient value is near to 10, Kerala, Maharashtra and Karnataka fit into the best group, which is low disease intensity zone with R-values of 13.33, 11.33 and 11 respectively.

The top ten fatal diseases in 1994 had accounted for 57.2% of the total reported deaths excluding 'senility'. It can be observed that Table 6.23 prevalence of bronchitis and asthma is remarkably high among 60+ population, especially in the states of Karnataka, Gujarat, Haryana, Madhya Pradesh, Maharashtra and Rajasthan having prevalence more than the national average. TB of the lung affected mainly the older segment of the population, especially in Haryana, followed by Madhya Pradesh and Andhra Pradesh. In age groups 15-59, dominance of TB was more than the national average in the states of Bihar, Gujarat, Madhya Pradesh, Rajasthan and Uttar Pradesh. Cancer and Paralysis burden is also high among the elderly and it showed highest prevalence in Kerala. Pneumonia however affects children and aged populations.

TABLE 6.23

Age Distribution of Prevalence Rate of Major Killer Diseases in India, 1994 (per 100000)

	0 to 4	*5 to 14*	*15 to 44*	*45-59*	*60+*
(1)	*(2)*	*(3)*	*(4)*	*(5)*	*(6)*
A: Bronchitis and Asthma					
India	33	4	13	87	763
AP	8	3	6	42	510
Bihar	0	12	28	86	523
Gujarat	16	0	21	115	1018
Haryana	17	0	12	96	1077
Karnataka	32	3	9	81	1522
Kerala	0	0	6	54	1061
MP	18	3	12	124	816
Maharashtra	6	0	6	60	795
Punjab	0	9	7	71	381
Rajasthan	43	4	18	63	772
Tamilnadu	17	0	18	36	558
UP	131	3	16	202	687

(*Contd.*)

TABLE 6.23 (Contd.)

(1)	(2)	(3)	(4)	(5)	(6)
B: Heart attack	0 to 4	5 to 14	15 to 44	45-59	60+
India	1	2	27	81	432
AP	0	1	31	71	493
Bihar	0	0	0	0	0
Gujarat	0	0	43	98	650
Haryana	0	3	33	78	260
Karnataka	0	7	38	87	487
Kerala	20	5	35	163	1074
Maharashtra	0	0	23	75	305
Punjab	0	2	51	117	642
Rajasthan	9	5	18	66	183
Tamilnadu	4	0	51	93	967
C: Tuberculosis of the lung	0 to 4	5 to 14	15 to 44	45-59	60+
India	2	6	43	85	192
AP	2	1	27	80	245
Bihar	0	12	46	124	178
Gujarat	0	0	83	128	203
Haryana	6	3	26	72	306
Karnataka	16	26	29	61	197
MP	0	0	94	116	311
Maharashtra	5	4	31	40	74
Rajasthan	0	12	50	117	212
Tamilnadu	0	0	13	40	216
D: Pneumonia	0 to 4	5 to 14	15 to 44	45-59	60+
India	245	12	18	7	48
Bihar	339	11	2	0	13
Haryana	410	6	3	0	45
MP	360	21	7	6	27
Maharashtra	118	6	2	2	9
UP	483	37	10	21	132

In the early sixties, fevers, coughs and diarrhea together contributed more than 50 percent of life losses. Droughts, famines coupled with epidemics like influenza accounted for higher number of deaths. After independence, the fatality of infectious and communicable diseases has started declining with several intervention projects; the remarkable reduction of 'fevers' is mainly due to the implementation of malaria control programmes (1953, 1958, 1977) and filarial control programmes (1955) and also due to imported medical technology from the developed world and widespread of DDT as a control measure of vector. However, diseases related to poverty, poor hygiene and unhealthy environment conditions were declining but still predominant in rural India.

Communicable diseases were still taking a high toll in demographically backward states, the flattening trend of three major communicable cause definitely emphasizes the fact that nation-wide health programmes can reduce the fatality of a disease up to a certain level. Further reduction was depending on the improvement in health infrastructure, micro-level planning for improvements. in sanitation, availability of self drinking water and healthy living conditions. According to the 1991 census, only 9.48% rural households were covered under the rural sanitation programme despite of many schemes introduced by the national government, which means still these basic amenities were dreams of several Indians.

Asthma-bronchitis, TB of the lung and pneumonia were accounting heavy toll among the communicable diseases. About one-third of rural population use wood as fuel for cooking (Census of India, 1991) and coupled with poor ventilation and bad housing conditions might be the causes for prevalence of asthma-bronchitis. TB prevalence was 130.8 per 100,000 in India as one of the major killers in Rural India, while the world average was only 59.7. This may be attributed mainly to lack of early detection, awareness, stigma about disease to pursue the treatment and lack of sincere efforts by the state governments. Reduction in TB has a negative relation with poverty. It was estimated that 52.2% population in rural India were below international poverty line of below $1 per day during the study period in 1992, which caused ignorance, poor sanitation, malnutrition, and irregular treatment, faced with high cost of drugs. A large scale analysis from National Family & Health Surveys in 1992-93 clearly shows that more than half of the women of age group 30 years and older, suffer with risk of active tuberculosis. This may be attributable to bad cooking sources and household smokes and suggests that the use of biomass fuels for cooking substantially increases the risk of tuberculosis in India. Similarly, deaths due digestive disorders are found to be reducing but diarrhoea remains one of the major killers of infants and young children and a formidable challenge to the health system as the suggestive measures of preventing diarrhoea is greeted with skepticism and a certain disinterest in India. The main causes of diarrhoea and other digestive diseases as identified are stale, drifty food, soiled drinking water and climatic conditions. Respiratory infection and fever as well as dirty drinking water, all of which accompany monsoons, is believed to be conductive to digestive disorders in rural areas.

Affluence, progressive aging of population (more older people), upward socio-economic conditions and changed life styles caused increase in chronic and non-communicable diseases, which was showing an overall upward trend a typical characteristic of the second phase of epidemiological transition. While the infectious diseases declined from 56% in 1999 to 25% by 2020, on the other hand, non-communicable diseases projected to increase from 29% in 1990 to 57% in 2020. The most remarkable increases among the non-communicable diseases are observed in heart attacks, cancer and paralysis. The possible reasons for the rising trend of cancer may be increase in life expectancy, more accurate medical diagnosis, rise in tobacco use, pan masala, alcohol consumption, air and water pollution and excessive use of pesticides. India is one among the first few countries in tobacco consumption. Smoking cigarette consumption per adult is one of the highest in India, that is, 236 per adult in 1990-92, much higher than the world average.

High prevalence of respiratory and non-communicable diseases is not only because of the increase in the proportion aged but also for higher death rates in these diseases among population. In a few years, health issues of aged people are definitely going to put our country in trouble, if necessary steps are not taken at the infantile stage. Heart attack is prevalent among the aged people especially in Kerala. The total number of aged (65+ years) has increased from 20 million in 1951 to 57 million in 1991 and in 2001 the figure touched 76 million. It is also likely to be due to changing cultural factors, like diet and stress. Increase in proportion death in vehicular accident and suicide is a point to ponder. The rate of increase of two-wheeler is much steeper than other vehicles and two-wheelers are more prone to accidents than other motorized vehicles. Suicide death in the early reproductive period among women is a matter of concern. Of the various causes, victims commit suicide according to National Crime Records are illness, family problems together accounting 40% of total suicidal deaths. Rest of the factors is love affairs, poverty, and failure in exams, and dowry disputes. Hanging, consumption of insecticides and poisons are very frequent means of suicide in India. Many of the women choose to die by successful termination of life are self-immolation, followed by drowning, by consuming sleeping pills and poisons. More gender-related issues are emerging in the polity recently empowerment of women and mobilization men to change their attitudes towards females of the family are the urgent need in the context of rising trend of suicide.

The above analysis indicates the fragile nature of health redressal system in rural and urban India, where the incidence of poverty, malnutrition and low living conditions are having their adverse effects on longevity and morbidity of different sections of the Indian population, particularly women and children. The health care system would experience further slideback when the contribution and support by the central and state governments would be slashed owing to the compulsions of globalization and internationalization of health care industry thanks to opening up of health services of the country to international competition. A comprehensive health policy should address the tension between 'living longer' on the one hand and health-related 'quality of life' on the other to achieve the health targets. Whether the objective of *faster and inclusive growth* as envisaged in the XI five year plan would be feasible with such high incidence of diseases and morbidity among the country's future workforce, remains a puzzle, as there is no indication in the plan document to reverse the trend by pro-active role of the state in the health sector. WTO's compulsions as delineated in the GATS treaty therefore poses a serious challenge to India's health sector as the analysis above clearly indicates.

7

Concluding Observations

Given the diversity of health outcomes, low levels of human development, high burden of diseases and poor health infrastructure in different states of India, alleviating the health related deprivations warrants massive investment by the central and state governments in the health sector. But the effect of globalisation of health services due to the dictates of WTO under the GATS, and the general change in the economic environment in favour of greater liberalization, have resulted in shrinkage of state support to this sector. As a result, the ills of ill-health, morbidity and deprivations are unlikely to be turned around in the coming years, the rhetoric of inclusive growth notwithstanding. Expenditure on health by the government as a proportion of GDP has been declining over the years for major states, and with the rise in cost of medicines, the plight of poor rural households in mitigating health-related disadvantages are likely to worsen. With the drug price control virtually on its way out and with India having signed the WTO treaty on IPR, we are moving closer to international prices of drugs. The combined effect of both the above facts makes a deadly mixture that results in reduced access for the poor to health care.

Privatisation of health care system has received accelerated emphasis in the new policy era of globalisation, and instead of solving the problems created by shrinkage of state's patronage and participation, it has aggravated 'poor health at high cost', which has made the poor absolutely vulnerable to face the risk of illness and related morbidity, and put a brake on supply of healthy labour force in the coming years to cope with the requirements of accelerated growth syndrome in the coming years. Table 7.1 below summarises the snapshot view of how India is placed *vis-à-vis* some other countries in the world in respect of public sector spending on health.

TABLE 7.1

Public Health Spending in Selected Countries

Indicator	*% Population with income of < $ 1 day*	*Infant Mortality Rate/1000*	*% Health Expenditure to GDP*	*% Public Expenditure on Health to Total Health Expenditure*
India	44.2	70	5.2	17.3
China	18.5	31	2.7	24.9
Sri Lanka	6.6	16	3	45.4
UK	—	6	5.8	96.9
USA	—	7	13.7	44.1

Source : National Health Policy, 2002.

Education and health generate positive externalities which arise in the context of gender-specific poverty alleviation policies. Better education for women, for example, is often associated with better education, nutrition and health of children, particularly daughters. Different studies show that in the recent expansion of the social pension programme in South Africa, pensions received by maternal grandmothers had a large impact in improving their granddaughters' health. In Bangladesh and elsewhere, better opportunities of outside work for young women, particularly in the globalized garment industry, have led to socially more beneficial fertility behavior, through, say, raising the age of marriage. Such externalities make gender equity and productive efficiency go hand-in-hand. There are important dynamic externalities that can arise from community- or neighborhood-specific characteristics, like physical infrastructure (like roads, communication, irrigation and power systems), improving the productivity of private investment or, in the neighborhood case, adult human-capital endowments of neighbors influence the educational investment decisions of the young. Efficiency of government expenditure in alleviating illness and morbidity in rural areas also hinges on the extent of such externality, in which neighborhood effects are important.

Globalisation of health services are being unleashed in the Indian economy thanks to the policy reforms at the international level, namely GATS Agreement. This is a sequel to the launching of Structural Adjustment Policies in India since 1991 thanks to the Washington Consensus. The implication of the new economic policy regime is to enhance the role of the private sector to fill-up the space created due to the gradual withdrawal of the state from a number of economic activities. In case of health sector, the importance of private medical care expenses have been crucial even before the liberalisation regime, and this has gone up after the period, but the provision of health infrastructure did not grow at that rate, and wherever, these facilities have developed they have been so costly that most of the poor unhealthy people of India cannot afford to avail of such facilities. With globalisation of health services being permissible under the GATS, India could take the advantage of Telehealth services and export the services of medical personnels like doctors and nurses and Indian market would expand for medical tourism, because the relative cost of treatment of advanced and critical diseases are cheaper in India compared to many countries in the world, but the benefits of such international exposure are likely to remain confined to only 5% of our population, and would not be inclusive in nature.

In recent years, interest has been expressed by national health services overseas for Indian nurses, to meet domestic shortages. And there are the growing numbers of joint ventures and tie-ups, such as Apollo Gleneagles, Max India and Fortis Healthcare. India is also emerging as a source of foreign direct investment (FDI) in health services, as shown by the regional expansion plans of major players, such as the Apollo group. However, India has barely tapped its true potential in the global healthcare market. Only 5% of all patients treated at reputed hospitals like Escorts are foreign, compared to 25% at equivalent Thai hospitals. Inadequacies in supporting infrastructure, equipment, supplies and domestic regulation, lack of recognition of Indian medical qualifications and disparity in standards of training and quality remain major constraints.

Globalization of our healthcare system can yield many benefits, including improved quality and standards and more money for investment in the sector. Cross-border exchange of practices, know-how, and technologies, resulting from the flow of capital, consumers, health personnel and information, can help in raising standards and the quality of domestic health care. Realizing these benefits depends on how well integrated the domestic system is and how it is managed. It is thus not surprising, that the globalization of health services has not been welcomed unequivocally, stirring debate on the grounds that it "commercializes" a social good. Concerns have been voiced about the possible two-tiering and cream-skimming effects of medical tourism and FDI on the domestic healthcare system, with possible adverse effects on costs, resource allocation and equity within the system. An objective analysis suggests the need is to link the public and private (domestic and foreign) segments, through the sharing of technology, physical and human resources, and information. And to transfer part of the revenues generated through globalisation of this sector towards development of the healthcare system as a whole. This requires a much more coherent and synergistic approach to developing the heath services sector overall than has been the case so far in India.

The globalization and health services is reflected in the increasing cross-border trade and delivery of health services, through movement of personnel and consumers (both by electronic and other means), and in growing number of partnerships, joint ventures and collaborative arrangements. However, the lack of standardized polices and practices has resulted in impartial sharing of benefits and decline in growth opportunities. Non-standardized polices and practices of various countries impose cross-border restrictions, leading to a non-conducive environment for exchange of services, thereby resulting in in-optimal level of capacity to deliver and grow. Using the General Agreement on Trade in Services (GATS) definitions, trade in health services occurs via four modes of supply, and each supply mode has associated benefits and problems.

GATS is proposed to bring in benefits to its participating regions in terms of costs, service availability, quality of health care service, investment opportunities, liberalization of governing regulations, easing of barriers to trade at regional and national levels, balancing public and private healthcare sector, etc. GATS provides the countries the flexibility to manage trade in health services in ways that are consistent with national health policy objectives. The countries can choose to make commitments only in some sectors and can set the limits as required to deal with various policy concerns. But both the novelty of the concept and the concerns about appropriate regulatory enforcement have caused member not to undertake commitments with ease. Such specific commitments by countries on medical, health-related, and social and health-related services including medical and dental services, veterinary services, services of nurses and mid-wives, hospitals services, other human health services and health insurance, have been sluggish, as these require the domestic reforms of the health sector by these countries, which are difficult to accomplish. Globalization of health services is reflected in the emergence of new kinds of healthcare organizations over the past decade and in the emergence of cross-border delivery of health services through movements of consumers, personnel and services. Globalization or liberalization of international trade within the context of multilateral international trade agreements such as GATS (General Agreement on Trade and Services) and TRIPs (Trade Related Aspects of Intellectual Property Rights), have in general impeded efforts towards improving equity in access to health care. Making the free movement of health personnel to and from other countries possible through GATS, are likely to accentuate the present imbalance of human resources for health, especially those needed for rural areas in our country, thereby definitely affecting the access to health care by the poor. With TRIPs becoming effective in many developing countries, the prices of pharmaceuticals will increase considerably, straining the already scarce health resources available to the poorer segments of our population.

Our study of health care system in India during the period of globalisation clearly brings out the appalling nature of health and nutritional deprivation for the country's poor and the vulnerable, including women and children, which are reflected in low human development indices of Indian states. With declining trend of public expenditure in most states as a proportion of net state domestic product in real terms, and rise in private expenditure on health care and disease prevention, but poor public and private health infrastructures, particularly in rural areas, fiscal contraction in the states as a result of economic reforms, has worsened the scenario and actuated the trend for morbidity of the population. The emphasis on pro-poor inclusive growth in the XIth five year plan notwithstanding, the health status of the population and the associated deprivations are likely to be aggravated in the face of globalisation of health services as per the dictates of the GATS agreement because the government has not been able to formulate a comprehensive health policy and reform the health care organization and infrastructure. As a result, we do not expect a turn-around in the country's health conditions in the near future and the benefits of globalisation in the form of better treatment options and better technology being available through trade channels are unlikely to be reaped in India, because bulk of our ailing population would be unable to afford them and the medicines are likely to be costlier than before. The integration of trade policy and health policy reforms in our country are therefore necessary to face the challenges thrown open by the new open regime.

Bibliography

Aggarwal, S.N. (1977), *India's Population Problem,* Tata McGraw-Hill Publishing Co. Ltd., New Delhi.

Allen, L.H. (1993), "The Nutrition CSRP: What is Marginal Malnutrition and Does it Affect Human Function?", *Nutrition Review,* 51, 255-67 and S.R. Gillespie (2001), "What Works? A Review of the Efficacy and Effectiveness of Nutrition Interventions", United Nations Administrative Committee on Coordination/Sub-Committee (ACC/SCN), in collaboration with the Asian Development Bank, Geneva and Manila.

Allison, R.A. and J.E. Forter (2004), "Measuring Health Inequality Using Qualitative Data", *Journal of Health Economics,* 23, 505-24.

Anand, P. (2003), "The Integration of Claims to Health-Care: A Programming Approach", *Journal of Health Economics,* 22, 731-45.

Anne, Darren and Christina (2002), "Economics Status and Health in Childhood: The Origins of the Gradient", *The American Economic Review,* 92(5), 1308-1335.

Ansari, H. (2000): 'Regulatory Aspects in Health Insurance. Report on Conference of Health Insurance', IIM, Ahmedabad.

Asada, Y. and Ohkvsa (2004), "Analysis of Health Related Quality of Life (HRQL), its Distribution and its distribution income in Japan, 1989-98", *Social Science and Medicine,* 59, 1423-1433.

Astha (1998): *Voices from the Roots of the Grass: Impact of SAP and the New Economic Policy on the Poor in Rajasthan* (A Study: First Phase), Rajasthan.

Baldacci, Emanuele, Maria Teresa Guin-Sui and Luiz de Mello (2003), "More on the Effectiveness of Public Spending on Health-Care and Education: A Covariance Structure Model", *Journal of International Development*, 15, 709-725.

Banerjee, A., A. Deaton and E. Duflo (2004), "Health Care Delivery in Rural Rajasthan", *Economic and Political Weekly*, February 24, 944-949.

Banker, R.A. Charnes and W.W. Cooper (1984): "Some Models for Estimating Technical and Scale Efficiency", Management Science , Volume 30, pp. 1078-92.

Bang, R.A., A.T. Bang, M Baitule, Y. Choudhary, S. Sarmukkadam and O. Tale (1989): 'High Prevalence of Gynaecological Diseases in Rural Indian Women', *Lancet*, 1(8629): 85-88.

Barro, R.J. (1996a), "Determinants of Economic Growth: A Cross-Country Empirical Study", National Bureau of Economic Research Working Paper No. 5698, Massachusetts.

———, (1996b), "Health, Human Capital and Economic Growth", Paper for the Programme on Public Policy and Health, Pan American Health Organization and World Health Organization, Washington D.C.

———, and J. Lee (1994), "Source of Economic Growth", Carnegie-Rochester Conference Series on Public Policy, 40, 1-46.

———, (2003), "International Data on Educational Attainment: Updates and Implications", Center for International Development, Working Paper No. 42, Harvard University, Massachusetts

Barro, R.J. and X. Sala-I-Martin (1992), "Convergence", *Journal of Political Economy*, 100(2), 223-51.

Baru, R. (2000): 'Privatisation and Corporatisation', *Seminar*, No. 489, May: 29-33.

Barun, K. (2001), "The World Nutrition Situation", *Journal of Health Management*, 3(1), 135-42.

Baru, V. Rana, Q. Imrana and P. Ritu (2000), "Medical Industry: Illusion of Quality at What Cost", *Economic and Political Weekly*, June 15, 2509-2511.

Berlarge and Terweduwe (1998), "The Classification of Countries by cluster and by Factor Analysis", *World Development*, 16(12), 1527-1545.

Bennett, S. and V.R. Muraleedharan (2000): 'New Public Management and Health Care in Third World', *Economic and Political Weekly*, January 8-14: 59-68.

Berman, Peter (1998): 'Rethinking Health Care Systems: Private Health Care Provision in India', *World Development*, 26(8):1463-79.

Bhargava, A., D.A.P. Bundy, M. Jukes and J.D. Sachas (2001), "Modeling the Effects of Health Status and the Educational Infrastructure on the Cognitive Development of Tanzanian School Children, Commission on Microeconomics and Health", Working paper Series, WGI No. 2, World Health Organization, Geneva.

Bhat, R. (2000): *Management Issues in the Implementation of User Fees Policy in Public Facilities* (First Revised Draft), Report prepared for Health Sector Group, DFID, New Delhi, August.

Bhatia, J.C. and J. Cleland (1995): 'Self-Reported Symptoms of Gynaecological Morbidity and their Treatment in South India', *Studies in Family Planning*, 26(4): 203-16.

Bhatia, M. and A. Mills (1997): 'Contracting Out of Dietary Services by Public Hospitals in Bombay' in S. Bennett, B. McPake and A. Mills (eds.), *Private Health Providers in Developing Countries: Serving in Public Interest?* Zed Press, London.

Bidani, B. and Martin Ravallion (1997), "Decomposing social indicators using distributional data", *Journal of Econometrics*, 77(1), 125-39.

Bidwai, P. (1995): 'One Step Forward, Many Steps Back: Dismemberment of India's National Drug Policy', *Development Dialogue*, No. 1, 193-222.

Bloom, D.E. (2005), "Public Health in Transition", *Scientific American*, 92-99, and Bloom, D.E., David Canning and Jaypee Sevilla (2001), "The Effect of Health on Economic Growth: Theory and Evidence", National Bureau of Economic Research, Working paper No. 8587, Massachusetts.

Bloom, D.E., David Canning and Jaypee Sevilla, (2001a), "Economic Growth and the Demographic Transition", National Bureau of Economic Research, Working Paper No. 8685, Massachusetts.

———, (2002), "Technological Diffusion, Conditional Convergence and Economic Growth", National Bureàu of Economic and Social Research, Working Paper No. 8713, Massachusetts.

———, (2002a), The Demographic Dividend: A New Perspective on the Economic Consequences of Population Change, RAND, Santa Monica, CA.

———, (2004), 'The Effect of Health on Economic Growth : A Production Function Approach", *World Development*, 32(1), 1-13.

Bloom, D.E., and Jaypee Sevilla (2004), "The Effect of Health on Economic Growth : A Production Function Approach", *World Development*, 32(1), 1013.

Bommier, A. and G. Stecklov (2002), Defining Health Inequality: Why Rawls Succeeds where Social Welfare Theory Fails", *Journal of Health Economics*, 21, 497-513.

Castro-Leal, F., J. Dayton and K. Mehra (2000): 'Public Spending on Health Care in Africa: Do the Poor Benefit?', *Bulletin of the World Health Organisation*, 78(1): 66-74.

Canning, David (2001), "The Health and Wealth of Nations", *Science*, 287, 1207-1209. (2003),

———, "The Health and Poverty of nations from theory to practice", *Journal of Human Development*, 4(1), 47-71.

CBHI (Central Bureau of Health Intelligence) (various years), *Health Information of India*, Government of India, New Delhi.

Centre for Monitoring Indian Economy (2000): *Monthly Review of the Indian Economy*, January.

Chakrabarti, Anindita and D.N. Rao (2005) : Variation in Health Expenditures: Is it Just Income or Other Factors? Empirical Investigation Using a Panel of Indian States, *Journal of Quantitative Economics*, July 2005.

Charnes, A., W.W. Cooper and E. Rhodes (1978): Measuring Efficiency of Decision Making Unit, *European Journal of Operational Research*, pp 429-44.

Chatterjee, Mirai, Anil Gumber and Veena Kulkarni (2000): 'Health Insurance for Workers in the Informal Sector', Report on Conference of Health Insurance, IIM, Ahmedabad, April.

Chatterjee, M. (1988): *Access to Health,* Manohar Publications, New Delhi.

Chen, S. and Martin Ravallion (2004), "How Have The World's Poorest Fared Since the Early 1980s", *The World Bank Research Observer,* 19(2), 141-169.

Coulombe, Serge, J.F. Trembly and Marchand (2004), "Literacy Score, Human Capital and Growth Across Fourteen OECD Countries", *International Adult Literacy Survey,* Monograph Series, Statistics, Canada.

Das, D., J. Dhanoa and B. Cowan (1982): 'Letting Them Live', *Future,* III Quarter.

Das Gupta, M. (1987): 'Selective Discrimination against Female Children in Rural Punjab, India', *Population and Development Review,* 13: 77-100.

Das Gupta, R. (1989), "Nutritional Planning in India: Studies in Economic Development and Planning, Mimeo, Institute of Economic Growth, Delhi.

Debreu, G. (1951): The Coefficient of Resource Utilization, Econometrica, Vol. 19, No. 3, pp. 273-92.

Dolan, P. and J.A. Osley, I.A. (2001), "Equity in Health: The Importance of different Health Stream", *Journal of Health Economics,* 20(4).

Dreze, J. and A. Sen (1989), "Economic Growth and Public Support", In *Hunger and Public Action,* Clarendon Press, Oxford.

Dror, David M., (2006), Health Insurance for the Poor:Myths and Realities, *Economic and Political Weekly,* November 4, 2006.

Duggal, R. with S. Amin (1989): 'Cost of Health Care: A Household Survey in an Indian District', Foundation for Research in Community Health, Mumbai.

Duggal, R., S. Nandraj and A Vadair (1995a): 'Health Expenditure Across States: Part I', *Economic and Political Weekly,* April 15, 834-44.

———, (1995b): 'Health Expenditure Across States: Part II', *Economic and Political Weekly,* April 22, 901-08.

Ellis, Randall P, Moneer Alam and Indrani Gupta (2000): 'Health Insurance in India: Prognosis and Prospectus', *Economic and Political Weekly*, Vol. XXXV, No. 4, January.

Fare, R., S. Grosskopf and C.A.K. Lovell (1994): Production Frontiers, Cambridge University Press.

Farrell M.J. (1957). "The Measurement of Productive Efficiency", *Journal of The Royal Statistical Society*, Series A, General, 120 (3) : 253-81.

Filmer, D. (1999), "The Structure of Social Disadvantage in Education: Gender and Wealth", Policy Research Report on Gender and Development, Working Paper Series No. 5, World Bank, Washington, D.C.

———, and L. Pritchett (1999a), "The Impact of Public Spending on Health: Does Money Matter?", *Social Science and Medicine*, 49(10), 1309-1323.

Fogal, R.W. (1991), "New Finding on Secular Trends in Nutrition and Mortality: Some Implication for Population Theory", Workshop, Stanford University.

Gandhi, I.C. (2002), "Public Health in India: Future Challenges", *Indian Journal of Public Health*, 46(4), 134-144.

George, A., I. Shah and S. Nandraj (1997): 'Morbidity, Health Care Utilisation and Expenditure; Madhya Pradesh 1990-91' in A. George (ed.), *Household Health Expenditurein Two States. A Comparative Study of Districts in Maharashtra and Madhya Pradesh*, Foundation for Research in Community Health, Pune/Mumbai.

Ghosh, M. (2006), "Economic Growth and Human Development in Indian States", *Economic and Political Weekly*, July 29, 3321-3329.

Gill, S., A. Iyer and M. Uplekar (1997): 'Models of Coordination and Cooperation between NGOs, Private and Public Health Care Services in the Reproductive and Child Health Programme: A Paper to Aid Discussion', produced for In Develop, Uppsala, A.B., Sweden (unpublished document).

Gill, S.S. (1996): 'Punjab: Privatising Health Care', *Economic and Political Weekly*, January 6:18-19.

GOI (Government of India) (1975): *Report of the Committee on Drugs and Pharmaceuticals* (Hathi Committee), Government of India, New Delhi.

Gupte, M., S. Bandewar and H. Pisal (1999): 'Women's Perspectives on the Quality of Health and Reproductive Health Care: Evidence from Rural Maharashtra' in M Koenig and M.E. Khan (eds), *Improving Quality of Care in India's Family Welfare Programme*, Population Council, New York.

Gragnolati, C. (1990), "Children's Growth and Poverty in Rural Guatemala", Policy Research, Working Paper No. 2193, World Bank, Washington, D.C.

Grand, J.L. (1987), "Inequality in Health: Some International Comparison", *European Economic Review*, 31, 182-199.

Griffen, C. Charles (1992), *Health Care in Asia: A Comparative Study of Cost and Financing*, World Bank, Washington, D.C.

Gumber, Anil and Veena Kulkarni (2000): 'Health Insurance for Informal Sector: Case Study of Gujarat', *Economic and Political Weekly*, September 30.

Gupta, Indrani and Purnamita Dasgupta (2000): 'Health Seeking Behaviour in Urban India: A Case Study of Delhi', Institute of Economic Growth, Discussion Paper No. 16/2000.

Gymiah-Brempong, K. and Mark Wilson (2004), "Health Human Capital and Economic Growth in Sub-Saharan African and OECD Countries", *The Quarterly Review of Economics and Finance*, 44(2), 296-320.

Horton, S. (2002), *The Economics of Nutrition Interventions*, N.J. Human Press, Totowa.

ICMR (Indian Council of Medical Research) (1988): *Utilisation of Health and Family Planning Services in Bihar, Gujarat andKerala: A Task Force Study*, ICMR, New Delhi.

———, (1991): *Evaluation of Quality of Family Welfare Services at Primary Health Centre Level. A Task Force Study*, ICMR, New Delhi.

Iyer, A. and A. Jesani (1999): 'Barriers to the Quality of Care: The Experience of Auxiliary Nurse-Midwives in Rural Maharashtra' in M. Koenig and M.E. Khan (eds.), *Improving Quality of Care in India's Family Welfare Programme. The Challenge Ahead*, Population Council, New York.

Iyer, A. and G. Sen (2000): 'Health Sector Changes and Health Equity in the 1990s' in S. Raghuram (ed.), *Health and Equity: Effecting Change*, Humanist Institute for Cooperation with Developing Countries (HIVOS) Technical Report Series, 1.8, National Printing Press, Bangalore.

Jamison, D.T., J.G. Bremen, A.R. Meashan, G.A. Iieyne, M. Claeson, D.B. Evans, P. Jha, A. Mill and P. Musgrove (2006), *Priorities in Health,* World bank, Washington, D.C.

Jesani, A. with S. Ananthraman (1993): *PrivateSector and Privatisation in the Health Care Services: A Review Paper for the CSSRICMR Joint Panel on Health: August 1990,* Foundation for Research in Community Health, Mumbai.

Kawachi, I., Wilkimon, Richard and Kennedy (1999), "The Society and Population Health Reader", *Income Inequality and Health,* Vol. 1, *New Press,* New York.

Khan, M.E., S. Ghosh Dastidar and R. Singh (1982): 'Nutrition and Health Practices among Rural Women: A Case Study of Uttar Pradesh, India', Paper presented at the International Symposium on Problems of Development of Underprivileged Communities in the Third World, New Delhi, October.

Koenig, M.A. and M.E. Khan (eds) (2000): *Improving Quality of Care in India's Family Welfare Programme: The Challenge Ahead,* Population Council, New York.

Krishnan, T.N. (1995): 'Access to Health and Burden of Treatment in India: An Inter-State Comparison', Paper presented at International Workshop on Health Insurance in India, Bangalore, September 20-22.

Levine, R. and D. Renelt (1992), "A Sensitive analysis of cross country growth regression", American Economic Review, 82(4), 942-963.

Koopmans, T.C. (1951): "An Analysis of Production as an Efficient Combination of Activities" in T.C. Koopmans (ed.), *Activity Analysis of Production and Allocation,* New York Cowles Commission for Research in Economics, Monograph No. 13, John Wiley and Sons.

Liv, Y., W.C. Heuso and K. Eggleston (1999), "Equity in Health and Healthcare: Chinese Experience", *Social Science and Medicine,* 49, 1349-56.

Lucas, E.J. (1998), "In the Mechanic of Economic Development", *Journal of Monetary Economics,* 22, 3-42.

Madhiwalla, N., S. Nandraj and R. Sinha (2000): *Health, Households and Women's Lives: A Study of Illness and Childbearing among Women in Nashik District, Maharashtra,* Centre for Enquiry into Health and Allied Themes, Mumbai.

Mankiw, N.G., D. Romer and D.N. Weil (1992), "A Contribution to the Empirics of Economic Growth", *Quarterly Journal of Economics*, 107, 407-37.

Martens, P. and M. Hyunen (2003), "A Future Without Health? Health Dimension in Global Scenario Studies", *Bulletin of the World Health Organization*, 81, 896-901.

Mason, J.J. Hunt, D. Parker and U. Jonsson (1999), "Investing in Child Nutrition in Asia", *Asian Development Review*, 17(1, 2), 1-32.

Mathiyazhagan, K. (1998): 'Willingness to Pay for Rural Health Insurance through Community Participation in India', *International Journal of Health Planning and Management*, Vol. 13, pp. 47-67.

Maunko, S. and Starfield (2004), "Wages Inequality, the Health System, and Infant Mortality in Wealth Industrialized Countries, 1970-1996", *Social Science and Medicine*, 58, 279-292.

Measham, Anthony, R. Krishna, D. Rao, Dean, T. Jamison Jia Wang, Alaka Singh (1999) : Reducing Infant Mortality and Fertility, 1975-1990—Performance at All-India and State Levels, *Economic and Political Weekly*, May 29, 1999.

Meer, J.L.M. Douglas and S.R. Harvey (2003), "Exploring the Health-Wealth Nexus", *Journal of Health Economics*, 22, 713-730.

Muraleedharan, V.R. (1999): *Characteristics and Structure of the Private Hospital Sector in Urban India: A Study of Madras City*, Small Applied Research Paper 5. Partnerships for Health Reform Project. Bethesda: Abt Associates Inc.

Musgrove, P. (1983), "Family Health Care Spending in Latin America', *Journal of Health Economics*, 2.

———, (1996), "Public and Private Roles in Health", Technical Report 339, World Bank, Washington, D.C.

———, (2004), "Health Economics in Development", Health, Nutrition and Population Series, World Bank, Washington, D.C. .

Naylor, David C., Prabhat Jha, John Woods and Abusaleh Shariff (1999): 'A Fine Balance: Some Options for Private and Public Health Care in Urban India', *Human Development Network*, World Bank.

Nandraj, S. and R. Duggal (1997): *Physical Standards in the Private Health Sector : A Case Study of Rural Maharashtra,* Centre for Enquiry into Health and Allied Themes, Mumbai.

NSSO (National Sample Survey Organisation) (1992): 'Morbidity and Utilisation of Medical Services' (NSS 42nd Round 1986-87), *Sarvekshana,* No. 52, Vol. XV, No. 4, April-June.

———, (1998): *Morbidity and Treatment of Ailments* (Report No. 441), NSS Fifty-Second Round, July 1995-June 1996, Department of Statistics, Government of India, New Delhi.

Osmani, S.R. and A. Bhargava (1998), "Health and Nutrition in Emerging Asia", *Asian Development Review,* 16(1), 31-71.

Pelletier, D.L. and E.A. Frongillo (2003), "Changes in Child Survival are Strongly Associated with changes in Malnutrition in Developing Countries", *Journal of Nutrition,* 133, 107-119.

Peter, F. (2001), "Health Equity and Social Justice", *Journal of Applied Philoso*phy, 18, 2.

Phadke, A, A Fernandes, L Sharda and A Jesani (1995): *A Study of Drug Supply and Use of Pharmaceuticals in Satara District,* The Foundation for Research in Community Health, Mumbai.

Prabhu, S., M.W. Uplekar and N.H. Antia (1995): *Health Care Financing in India: A Status Paper Prepared for the ICMR-ICSSR Joint Panel for Health,* Foundation for Research in Community Health, Mumbai.

Pradhan, D., E. Shan and D.S. Younger (2003), "Decomposing World Health in Equality", *Journal of Health Economics,* 22, 271-293.

Prescott, E.C. (1998), "Needed: A Theory of Total Factor Productivity", *International Economic Review,* 39, 525-551.

Psacharopoulos, G. (1984), The Contribution of Education to Economic Growth: International Comparisons, Ballinger Publishing Co., Cambridge, and Massachusetts

Purohit, B.C. and R. Mohan (1996): 'New Directions for Public Health Financing', *Economic and Political Weekly,* February 24: 450-53.

Purohit, B.J. and T.A. Siddiqui (1995): 'Cost Recovery in Diagnostic Facilities', *Economic and Political Weekly,* July 8: 1700-04.

Rajeshwari (1996): 'Gender Bias in Utilisation of Health Care Facilities in Rural Haryana', *Economic and Political Weekly,* February 24: 489-94.

Randall, A. and Gupta (2000), "Health Insurance in India: Prognosis and Prospects", *Economic and Political Weekly,* 35, January 22, 207-217.

Rane, W. (1996): 'Analysis of Drug Prices, 1980-1995', *Economic and Political Weekly,* August 24-31: 2331-2980.

———, (1998): 'Price Control on Drugs is Essential', *Economic and Political Weekly,* October 17-24: 2697-98.

Rao, K.N. (2004), "Trends in Health Status I Andhra Pradesh: An Empirical Study", *Indian Economic Journal,* 5(1), 81-88.

Rao, V. (1998), "Diet and Life Expectancy: Across National Analysis", *Journal of Population Economics,* 1, 225-33

Ravallion, M. (1997), "Good and Bad Growth: The Human Development Reports", *Journal of Econometrics,* 77, 141-158

Reddy, S. and J. Vandemoortele (1996): *User Financing of Basic Social Services: A Review of Theoretical Arguments and EmpiricalEvidence,* UNICEF Staff Working Papers, Evaluation, Policy and Planning Series, Number EVL-97-001, UNICEF, New York.

Reutlinger, S. and M. Selowsky (1976), *Malnutrition and Poverty: Magnitude and Policy Options,* Johns Hopkins University Press, New York

Robinson, W.D. (1965), "Nutrition in Medical Education", In *Proceeding of Western Hemisphere Nutrition Congress*

Ruger, J.P., J. Dean and D.E. Bloom (2001), *Health and Development,* Aspen Publishers, Gaithersburg, MD.

Sala-I-Martin, X. (1996), "The Classical Approach to Convergence Analysis", *The Economic Journal,* 106 (437), 1019-1036.

Sankar, D. and V. Kathuria (2004), "Health System Performance in Rural India", *Economic and Political Weekly,* 27, 1427-1433.

Shatrugna, V., P. Vidyasagar, T. Sujata and G. Vasanthi (1993): *Women's Work and Its Impact on Child Health and Nutrition,* National Institute of Nutrition, Hyderabad.

Savedoff, W. (2003), "How much should Countries spend on Health", Discussion Paper, World Health Organization, Geneva.

Schroeder, D.D. (2001), *Malnutrition*, N.J. Humana Press, Totowa.

Schultz, T.P. (1993), "Mortality Decline in the Low-Income World: Causes and Consequences", Discussion Paper No. 681, Yale University, New Haven.

Seguino, S. (2000), "Gender Inequality and Economic Growth: A Cross-Country Analysis", *Journal of World Development*, 28(7), 121-1280.

Selvaraju, V. (2000): 'Role of ESIs in the Emerging Health Insurance Market', Report on Conference of Health Insurance, IIM, Ahmedabad, April.

Sen Gita, Aditi Iyer, Asha George (2002): Structural Reforms and Health Equity: A Comparison of NSS Surveys, 1986-87 and 1995-96, *Economic and Political Weekly*, April 6, 2002.

Sen, G., A. Iyer and A. George (2002): 'Class, Gender and Health Equity: Lessons from Liberalisation in India' in G. Sen, A. George and P. Östlin (eds.), *Engendering International Health: The Challenge of Equity*, The MIT Press, Cambridge.

Smith, L. and L. Haddad (2000), "Explaining Child Malnutrition in Developing Countries: A Cross-Country Analysis", IFPRI Research Report No. 111, International Food Policy Research Institute, Washington, D.C.

Sparton, M.J. (1976), "A Health Policy for Developed Countries", Oxford University Press, New York.

Squire, L. (1993), "Fighting Poverty", *Economic Review*, 83(2), 377-382.

Strauss, J. and Thomas, D. (1998), "Health, Nutrition and Economic Development", *Journal of Economic Literature*, 36, 766-817.

Sule, M. (1999): 'Health Manpower in the District' in S. Kavadi (ed), *Health Resources, Investment and Expenditure: A Study of Health Providers in a District in India*, Foundation for Research in Community Health, Pune.

Sundar, R. (1995): 'Household Survey of Health Care Utilisation and Expenditure', NCAER Working Paper No. 53, National Council of Applied Economic Research, New Delhi.

Teresa, J. (1982), "Measuring Health as a Component of Living Standard", World Bank, Washington, D.C.

Thomas, D. and J. Strauss (1997), "Health and Wages: Evidence on Men and Women in Urban Brazil", *Journal of Econometrics*, 77, 159-85.

Thorbecke, E. and C. Charumilind (2002), "Economic Inequality and its Socio-Economic Impact", *World Development*, 30(9), 1477-195.

UNDP (1990), *Human Development Report*, Oxford University Press, New York.

U.S. Census Bureau (1999), *Poverty in the United States*, U.S. Department of Commerce, Washington, D.C.

Vella, V. (1997), *Health and Nutritional Aspects of Well-Being*, World Bank, Washington, D.C.

Vijayaraghavan, Brahman, Balakrishan, Arlappa and Kumar (2000), *Diet and Nutritional Status of Rural Elderly*, National Institute of Nutrition, Hyderabad, India.

Wagstaff, A. (2002), "Inequality Aversion, Health Inequalities and Health Achievement", *Journal of Health Economics*, 21, 627-641.

Wildman, J. (2003), "Modelling Health, Income and Income Inequality: The Impact of Income Inequality on Health and Health Inequality", *Journal of Health Economics*, 22, 521-538.

Wilson, D., Eva, M. Fisher and Fuqua (1971), *Principles of Nutrition*, Wiley Easter Private Limited, Delhi.

World Bank (1993), *World Development Report, 1993: Investing in Health*, Oxford University Press, London.

———, (1998), *Reducing Poverty in India: Options for more effective Public Services*, Report No. 17881-IN, Washington, D.C.

———, (2000), *East Asia: Recovery and Beyond*, Washington, D.C.

———, (2000), *The Quality of Growth*, Oxford University Press, New York.

———, (2005), *World Development Report, 2005*, Oxford University Press, New York.

World Development Report (2006), *Equity and Development*, Washington, D.C.

World Bank (2000): *World Development Report, 2000/2001*, The World Bank, Washington, DC.

World Health Organization (1981), "Global Strategy for Health for all by the Year 2000", Switzerland.

———, (1987), *Evaluation of the Strategy for Health for all by the Year 2000*, Geneva.

World Health Organization (2001), *Macroeconomics and Health: Investing in Health for Economic Development*, Report of the Commission on Macroeconomics and Health, Geneva.

Yudkin, J. (1964), "Disagreement", In *Nutrition Today*.

Zon, A.V., and Joan Muysken (2001), "Health and Endogenous Growth", *Journal of Health Economics*, 20, 169-185.

Index

Adolescent Girls and Children :
  Undernourishment, 219
AIDS :
  Knowledge, 101
Anaemia among :
  Women, 142
  Children, 150
  Pregnant, 144
ANC (Antenatal Care), 98
Ansari, A.R., 113
ASR (Adult Survival Rates), 67

Bhore Committee, 113
Birth Attendant, 229
Birth Control Methods, 137
Birth Interval, 227
Birth Order of the Child, 227
BOD (Burden of Disease), 9, 18, 135

CED (Chronic Energy Deficiency), 84
Chakrabarti Anindita, 92
Child Health, 99
Child Malnutrition, 218
Child Morbidity :
  Indicators, 207
Child Poverty Risk :
  Indicator, 211
Children's Anaemia :
  Trends, 151
Children's Nutritional Status, 201
Child Survival, 99
CHSI (Communication Health Status Index), 86
Commercial Presence, 30, 38
Consumption Abroad, 37
Contraceptives :
  Social Marketing, 137
Coronary Attack, 161
CPR (Contraceptive Prevalance Rates), 66
Cross-border Delivery, 24, 37
Cultural Globalization, 12

DAC (Development Assistance Committee), 54
DALYs Lost in India :
  Cause, 123
Data Development Approach, 184
Death in India :
  Specific Causes, 121
Debreu-Farrell Approach, 182
Doorslaer, 61
Dror, David M., 101

Early Childhood Mortality Rates, 147
Efficiency :
  Concept, 181
Efficiency Measurement :
  Methodology, 182

Family Planning Acceptors, 141

Family Welfare Programme, 137
Fertility and Family Planning, 97
Financial Globalisation, 12

GATS, 5, 266
GATT (General Agreement on Tariff and Trade), 20
  Modes of Supply under, 24
Gaur, Kamal K., 102
GEC (Genetic Engineering Council), 27
Globalisation, GATS and Health Sector, 11
Government Interventions and Undernourishment, 219
Grifin, 61
Growth of Public Healthcare Expenditure, 171

HCE (Health Care Expenditure), 93
HDIZ (High Disease Intensity Zone), 256
Health Among SCs and STs, 131
Health and Development, 45
Health Expenditure, 3
Health :
  Expenditure of Central and State Governments, 170
Health Indicators, 115
  among SC/ST, 131
Health in Post-Independence Era, 114
Health Outcomes :
  Efficiency, 180
Health Personnel:
  Movement, 35
Health Services Abroad :
  Consumption, 27
Health Services and GATS, 23
Health Status, 118, 129
  Disparities, 132
  Indicators, 129
Heart Attack, 258
Heart Diseases, 101
HIV in India, 151
HMOs (Health Maintenance Organizations), 32
HRQL (Health Related Quality of Life), 77
Huynenm 76

ICDS (Integrated Child Development Services), 218
Immunization of Children, 136
Imrana, 85
IMR Trends in India, 145
India :
  Health Sector, 112
  Effect of Cancer, 156
  Prevention and Treatment Strategies, 157
  Private Health Care Sector Dominates, 167
  Health Status, 175
  Poverty, 192
  Under-nutrition, 192
  Morbidity, 192
  Infant and Child Mortality, 222
Indian States :
  Human Deprivation, 194
Industrial Globalization, 12
Informational Globalization, 12
Infant and Child Mortality :
  Rural Urban Differentials, 228
Infant Mortality Differentials, 230

Jaisoorya, N.M., 113
Jonsson, 65

Khan, Hakim Ajmal, 113

Life Expectancy, 133

Maternal Health, 98, 138
MDGs (Millennium Development Goals), 9 135
Measham, A.R., 109
Medical Termination of Pregnancy, 138
Mehta, Jeevraj, 113
MIMC (Multiple Indicators, Multiple Causes), 86
Most Favoured Nations, 39
  National Treatment, 39
Mother's Education, 228
Musgrove, 60, 80
Muysken, 70

National AIDS Control Pogramme, 154
National Health Policy, 178

National Human Development Report, 179
Natural Persons :
Presence, 34
NCAER (National Council of Applied Economic Research), 131
NCHS (National Center for Health Statistics), 203
NHIS (National Health Interview Survey), 77
NICs (Newly Industrialized Countries), 60
NPAG (Nutrition Programme for Adolescent Girls), 220
NPC (National Planning Commission), 113
Nutrition and Anaemia, 99

OECD (Organization for Economic Cooperation and Development), 54
Ohkusa, 77
Olsey, 69
Osmani, 64

Pareto-Koopmans Approach, 182
Pathak, Prashanta, 102
PEM (Protein Energy Malnutrition), 56
Pneumonia, 258
Political Gloablisation, 12
PPI (Pulse Polio Immunization), 118
Prenatal Care, 229
Pre-natal Sex Determination :
Prevention, 139
Primary Prevention, 158
PSID (Panel Study of Income Dynamic), 75
Public Health Care Expenditure:
Centre and State's Roles, 166

Rao, D.N., 92
Roy, B.C., 113
Rural India :
Burden of Diseases, 247
Efficiency of Health Outcomes, 174

Saheb, Khan, 112
SAP (Structural Adjustment Programme), 14
Second Oil Crisis, 15
Sex of the Child, 227
Sokhey Committee, 113
SRHS (Self-Reported Health Status), 76
SRS (Sample Registration System), 109

TFP (Total Factor Productivity), 65
Total Fertility Rate, 139
Trade in Health Services :
Implications, 3
Treatment Facilities, 159
Trend of Public Health-care Expenditure, 170
TRIPs (Trade Related Aspects of Intellectual Property Rights), 42
Tuberculosis of the Lung, 258

Under-nutrition :
Indicators, 204
Under-nutrition Morbidity and Poverty :
Linkages, 212
Cumulative Risks, 215
UNICEF (United Nations Children's Fund), 4, 55

Vijayaraghavan, 84

Wagstaff, 72
Water and Sanitation :
Trade, 39
WHO Conference, 46
Wildman, 74
World and India :
Distribution of Deaths, 120
World Development Report, 81
World's Health Problems :
India's Share, 119
WTO (World Trade Organization), 20